RITA MARKER

Deadly Compassion

The Death of Ann Humphry and the Case Against Euthanasia

HarperCollins*Publishers*

HarperCollins*Publishers*
77–85 Fulham Palace Road,
Hammersmith, London W6 8JB

A Paperback Original 1994
1 3 5 7 9 8 6 4 2

A catalogue record for this book
is available from the British Library

ISBN 0 00 638073 5

Set in Baskerville

Printed in Great Britain by
HarperCollinsManufacturing Glasgow

For Paul, Tom, Jennifer, Cheryl, and Little M and M—with the hope that the world they inherit will be one in which those who are sick, old, or dependent are cared for, not killed

PREFACE

∎ ∎ ∎

Although euthanasia has become one of today's most volatile and hotly debated topics, many people have no idea what it is. The typical discussion of euthanasia, couched in the language of choice and individual rights, gives the impression that a person's right to be free of painful and unwanted medical intervention is at issue. This perception, coupled with euphemisms like the "right to die," "death with dignity," and, more recently, "aid-in-dying," has led to a mistaken belief that euthanasia allows the natural process of dying to take its course.

Nothing could be further from reality. Euthanasia is *making* people die, rather than letting them die. It is giving a cancer patient a lethal injection, for example, actually to cause death, as opposed to stopping chemotherapy and allowing that patient to die. Put bluntly, euthanasia means killing in the name of compassion.

Neither law nor medical ethics requires that "everything

be done" to "keep a person alive." To force someone to use every means technologically available to postpone death is not only against current law and practice but also cruel and inhumane. The current debate over euthanasia centers on whether the law and medical ethics will permit—and eventually promote—giving that lethal injection or using some other means to bring about death. The right being considered is not the right to die; it is the right to kill.

In the fall of 1984 I attended a right-to-die conference for the first time. At that conference I discovered that the mental image I had of euthanasia advocates was totally erroneous. Previously I'd assumed that anyone working for euthanasia would be crass and unfeeling. But in the years during which I have become deeply involved in writing about and debating euthanasia, I've met very few people who are unpleasant or disagreeable. Even now, when I go to right-to-die conferences and am known as an opponent, I seldom experience overt hostility. Euthanasia activists are—with rare exception—warm, committed, sincere, well-meaning, and courteous people.

But their sincerity and good intentions do not automatically make what they are promoting beneficial or good.

When we examine a topic as important as the ending of a human being's life, it is critical—indeed, it is a matter of life and death—to look beyond the pleasantries and ask, "What is this really about? Where did it come from? Where is it headed? Is there more to the story?"

I do not pretend to be a dispassionate observer. I fully acknowledge my strong personal opposition to euthanasia.

My own father was in poor health for all the time I can

remember. When he died at an early age, he had diabetes, heart trouble, and Parkinson's disease, and the struggle to pay for medical care had led to my parents' losing their home. If euthanasia had been legal, I believe he would have felt intense societal pressure to "choose" an even earlier death.

In addition, years of involvement in human rights activities have made me aware of the bias that exists against people with disabilities. I have seen how easily they come to be viewed as dispensable because they are perceived by some people as somehow less than human.

And I believe we today have reached a crossroad where, as individuals and as a society, we will soon be determining the direction we will take for years to come. One road will lead to death on demand. The other, appearing steeper and more difficult, will take us to the realization that when we cannot cure, we must continue to care for and never kill.

I've written this book to share information and insights about euthanasia that I've obtained over the years and to carry out the wish of my friend Ann Humphry. The cofounder of the Hemlock Society, perhaps the best-known euthanasia advocacy group in the country, Ann blazed a trail, fulfilling the words she had chosen for her high school yearbook in 1959. At the time of her death in October 1991, the trail she had blazed was precariously close to crossing a line she had come to believe should not be crossed. The book *Final Exit*, which had been published by Hemlock, had been a best seller for weeks. And the Hemlock Society seemed to be within a month of realizing its goal to legalize aid-in-dying in Washington State, making it lawful for the first time in the modern world for doctors directly and intentionally to kill their patients.

As you read the story of my friendship with Ann, it will be for you to judge the meaning of the "right" to die.

ACKNOWLEDGMENTS

■ ■ ■

There are many people who have helped to make this book possible and here I recognize but a few.

I wish to give a huge thank you to Andy Ambraziejus for his long hours of wonderful help with the text and his assistance in the preparation of the manuscript. Thanks also to Will Schwalbe of William Morrow and Company for his patience and guidance, and to Phyllis Heller for her enthusiasm.

My thanks to Rick Urbanski, Julie Horvath, and Pam Wilson for their insights and reminiscences. Others who were willing to share their memories of Ann did not wish to be publicly acknowledged. I am no less grateful to them.

Thanks also to Kathi Hamlon, Dr. Joseph Stanton, and Anne Beaudry for their help in critiquing early drafts of the manuscript. Their wisdom and frankness, as well as their encouragement, have been invaluable. Robert Hiltner's research to document the tiniest details regarding historical events was much appreciated.

My family has been a constant source of strength and joy during this time of writing: My adult children—Michael and his wife, Marcie, Tim, Pat, Sue, and Dan—have helped me maintain a sense of direction. My youngest children, Paul and Tom, and my grandchildren, Jennifer, Cheryl, and Little M and M, have helped me keep sight of what really matters. It is to them that I have dedicated this work.

And, saving the best until last, I give my thanks and love to Mike, my husband and best friend for more than thirty-two years.

I will not follow where the path may lead,
but I will go where there is no path, and I
will leave a trail.

—Words under Ann's senior class
portrait, St. Mary's High
School yearbook, 1959

CHAPTER 1

■ ■ ■

I knew December 6, 1989, would be a very important day for me. I had spent the morning at the Supreme Court in Washington, D.C., to hear the oral arguments in the case of Nancy Beth Cruzan. The Cruzan case was the first right-to-die case ever to reach the nation's highest court. Nancy Beth Cruzan had been injured in a car accident in 1983. Severe brain damage left her totally disabled, though she was not on any life support equipment. Three and a half years after her accident her parents, who were her coguardians, began court proceedings to force the Missouri Rehabilitation Center, where Nancy was being cared for, to remove her foods and fluids. A court decision authorizing the removal was handed down, then reversed, and the case had now reached the U.S. Supreme Court.

After leaving the court building, I rushed back to my hotel to contact the International Anti-Euthanasia Task Force public information office. A resource center for individuals and groups seeking information about the rights of the terminally and chronically ill, the elderly, and persons with disabilities, the task force was issuing a press statement about the case. As director of the task force I needed to approve the statement.

I also knew that I'd be called upon to comment on the morning's arguments at the Court. The task force had filed a brief in the Cruzan case, pointing out discrepancies in the testimony and citing reasons why Nancy Beth Cruzan, a profoundly disabled young woman, should receive the same protection afforded to any other person. After answering some calls from newspaper reporters and returning messages from radio stations, I called our main office in Steubenville, Ohio.

"Mark has a message for you. It doesn't have anything to do with Cruzan, but I think you'd better take it," the office manager told me. She transferred me to Mark's phone.

If there is one word to describe Mark Recznik, director of research for the task force, it's "calm." The tall, scholarly father of two is unflappable. When Mark gave me the message, however, he was anything but calm.

"You're not going to believe this," he said.

"What do you mean?"

"You won't believe who called you."

"Who?"

"Ann Humphry."

"Are you sure?" I asked.

"That's what she said."

"Are you kidding?" I should have known better. Mark doesn't joke around a lot, particularly about something like this.

"No, I'm serious."

"But why would Ann Humphry be calling me?"

"She said she has cancer and Derek has abandoned her. She needs to talk to you. She's at her home in Oregon and asked that you call her. If she doesn't answer, she wants you to leave a message on her answering device, and she'll get right back to you." Mark gave me the phone number.

After hanging up, I sat staring at the phone, wondering what to do. Although I had met her on a number of occasions at conferences and symposia, I didn't know Ann Humphry well. At most we were courteous adversaries. The second wife of Derek Humphry, she and Derek had cofounded the Hemlock Society. Ann had written many articles favoring euthanasia, as well as coauthored the books *Jean's Way* and *The Right to Die* with Derek. I had listened to her speak and had heard her icy rebuttals to anti-euthanasia arguments. To me, this woman seemed sophisticated, intelligent, and very self-sufficient, a person able to handle anything. Why would she be calling me?

Then I wondered whether the call was someone's idea of a joke. If so, it was in very bad taste. I had heard about Ann's cancer soon after the diagnosis less than three months before. Ann had breast cancer, the same illness that Derek's first wife, Jean, had battled. I hoped that the irony of it all had not brought out someone's twisted sense of humor.

Stalling, still not sure what to do, I called directory assistance in Monroe, Oregon, and asked for the number of Derek Humphry. The number the operator gave me was the same as on the message from Mark. Yet verification of the number didn't mean that Ann Humphry had made the call. It only meant that I'd reach the Humphry home if I called that number.

I finally told myself that I couldn't put off the call any longer. If whoever answered didn't know what I was talking about, I'd apologize and merely say that someone must be playing a trick on both of us. In no way would I explain the message that had been left. As I dialed, I said a quick prayer.

The phone rang. Once. Twice. Three times. I felt silly for being nervous, but I was afraid that I was playing a part in some terrible joke that could upset a seriously ill woman and her husband.

"Hello."

"Mrs. Humphry?"

"Yes."

"This is Rita Marker. I'm returning your call."

"Oh, Mrs. Marker. Thank you for calling back," she said. She really had called!

"How can I help you? What can I do?"

She didn't answer directly. Instead, in what seemed like a need to talk, coupled with a reluctance to do so, she recited the devastating events of the last three months.

"I have cancer. Derek has left, and he isn't coming back," she said in a matter-of-fact way. "I'm alone. I don't have any family here. There's no one. Here I am on a fifty-acre farm. I have animals to feed and take care of . . ." She paused.

"And here I am alone," she repeated, "with cancer and no resources. The one part-time farmhand is going back to Mexico next week." Her words weren't fitting the picture

I had of Ann Humphry: sophisticated, sure of herself, and coolly elegant.

"Derek has abandoned me. . . . I'm going through cancer treatment, driving myself back and forth for treatments. . . . No one from Hemlock has offered to help." She spoke slowly and carefully, as if searching for words and struggling to keep her voice under control.

"It's like I'm already dead. Derek and I started Hemlock. We've spent the last ten years talking about helping people with life-threatening illnesses. Yet when I got cancer, he left. . . ."

I continued to listen, trying to absorb everything Ann was telling me. She seemed to be trying to make sense of what had happened to her and—despite the deep hurt, which was so apparent—excuse her husband's behavior.

"I know he just couldn't face this again. I saw the terror in his eyes when he heard 'cancer.' He's running away because he can't deal with another wife with cancer."

In addition to the abandonment, Ann told me she had more to contend with—the possible loss of her medical insurance—at the very time she was still undergoing radiation and chemotherapy. "I was given three months' medical leave from Hemlock," she informed me. "Now that's almost up, and I'll lose my medical insurance because I'm not ready to go back to work." (Whether or not, in fact, her coverage would have lapsed, Ann was under the impression that she would be without medical care at this critical time.)

She went on to describe the stark reality of life without the support systems she thought she had developed over the years. Within the span of a few weeks she had lost her health, her husband, and her job.

I didn't know what to think about what I was hearing. Could Derek Humphry and the Hemlock Society really do the things that Ann was describing to me? I found it hard to believe. If Ann had been a courteous but distant adversary during the past few years, Derek had been an amiable one, once signing a book for me, "For Rita, a real and friendly opponent." Even though Derek's mood seemed to change in 1988 following our joint appearance at a public forum on aid-in-dying at the University of San Francisco, when I heard that Ann had been diagnosed with cancer in the fall of 1989, I thought of sending a note to Derek because I felt bad *for him*.

At that point in our phone conversation the only thing I could say to Ann Humphry was "I'm so sorry." But as she talked about driving herself back and forth for the cancer treatment, about returning sick and alone to an empty house, about how it felt to have no one who was there for her, I could only imagine the horrible isolation that must have led her to call me, a relative stranger. I told her that I didn't know anyone near Monroe, Oregon, who could lend a helping hand with the farm chores. But I did ask her if I could make some calls to friends in the area without using her name. Maybe there would be a way of working something out.

Ann seemed relieved just to hear the offer. "No," she said. "I think I'll be okay for right now." It was as though she felt a little better just talking about her feelings right then.

She also told me she was being portrayed by her husband

as emotionally unstable and as someone not to be taken seriously by the Hemlock Society any longer. However, in order to keep her insurance, she had to work, even though no one wanted to have anything to do with her. A board meeting was scheduled for the following month, and Ann wanted to prepare for it to clear her name and fight for her medical insurance. "Everyone on the Hemlock board believes Derek right now. I want them to know what's really happened," she told me.

Before we hung up, we had dropped the formal "Mrs. Humphry" and "Mrs. Marker" language. Although I still had to sort out everything that I had heard, I was moved by what Ann told me and believed it to be true—at least at some level. I told her I was planning to be on the West Coast in January and asked if I could drive down from Seattle to Monroe to see her. She seemed to like the idea, and we agreed to keep in touch by phone until then.

Hanging up, I felt puzzled, surprised, and taken aback. Why had Ann Humphry called me? I kept asking myself. And what was behind it all?

Later in our friendship Ann wrote to me: "I've admired you for years; known you had a large family and were determined to still have a voice and not be submerged in the overwhelming responsibilities of family life." Was that need to be surrounded by the love of a family and still maintain her own identity an indication of what Ann viewed as her own struggle? Was I an ally to her? She felt she was being vilified by Derek and had been totally cut off from those with whom she'd worked for years. She'd gone through surgery, was in cancer treatment, and had just been released from the hospital, where she had admitted herself after suffering emotional exhaustion. Perhaps more than anything, she was trying to affirm her own credibility, even with the opposition.

I also wondered whether Ann had called me because I was an "opponent." Did she sense I would be open—perhaps even anxious—to hear the bad things that had been done to her? She could have been testing. Was she hoping that even though, in her view, Hemlock had dealt horribly with her, maybe it would be pleasant in comparison with the way the "other side" would respond to her?

It also may have simply been a case of having had nowhere else to turn. While her cousin, whom I met after Ann's death, was always close to her, I later learned that her cousin had been going through some difficulties of her own at the time and that Ann had not wanted to lean on her for support because of that. In addition, Ann had a close friend, Julie Horvath, but Julie lived in California, was going to school, and working as well. Ann was the type of person who didn't want to "be a burden."

On the plane flying back home to Ohio, I thought of other possibilities and again wondered whether all this was some kind of trick. Perhaps it was a ploy to see if I would make some kind of statement about Ann or Derek? Could it all be as Ann had described it? I still found it hard to believe that Derek Humphry and the Hemlock Society could be so unfeeling.

Getting back to the office, I focused my energies back on Nancy Cruzan and other euthanasia-related cases. A few weeks later I received a note from Ann thanking me for my encouragement and warning, "It goes without saying that our conversations should be kept between ourselves, for your sake as well as mine."

I agreed. It seemed prudent not to publicize our conversations. Not knowing Ann well, I thought that if she were to reconcile with the Hemlock Society and with Derek—it still seemed possible—it would be embarrassing for both of us if I were publicly to discuss our talks. But in the back of my mind, even though I told myself I was being melodramatic, I had the feeling that the whole situation was somewhat ominous.

In retrospect, the situation was indeed ominous, but before the final, tragic outcome there was much to cherish. During the next two years Ann and I became trusting friends. Over the course of many, many phone conversations and several visits Ann related her life to me. As I discovered, it was full of many ups and downs and a lot of pain, and I could see how all that could be used mistakenly to paint a picture of Ann as emotionally unstable. However, alongside all the pain, or perhaps because of it, I also discovered a vibrant, articulate, loving human being who was a survivor. The tragedy of it all is that as Ann became more caught up in the euthanasia movement, it served to wear down her instinct for survival, instead of bolstering it. As Cal McCrystal, a journalist who had known both Ann and Derek Humphry for years, wrote in the London *Independent*, "Death was stalking the Humphrys as determinedly as the Humphrys were selling death."

CHAPTER 2

■ ■ ■

Ann Ayers Kooman, later to become Ann Wickett Humphry, was born on June 16, 1942. She was the second daughter of Arthur Kooman, a Boston banker, and Ruth Ayers, a minister's daughter who worked as a secretary after finishing college during the Depression. A nursemaid, Mrs. Fitzgerald, was hired to take care of Ann immediately after she was born. Ann was sent to camp every summer during her early childhood. Her sister went away to boarding school at a young age, and in 1956, when Ann was fourteen, her parents sent her to St. Mary's Academy, a strict exclusive girls' school in Sewanee, Tennessee, run by Episcopal nuns.

Those are the bare facts of Ann's early life, in many ways typical of any young woman brought up in a respectable, well-to-do family at that time. Ann remembered a darker side to her early life, however. The Kooman house in Belmont, Massachusetts, was a place where one worried about appearances, where being "proper," as befitted the house

and children of a Boston banker, was valued; where frivol-
ity was out of place, and where warmth and love were
noticeably absent. The relationship between Ann's parents
was cold. Her father was the strong, take-charge type,
while her mother, prim and upright, withdrew when something displeased her, avoiding confrontation when she
could.

What Ann found especially difficult to accept was her
mother's distance from her. Ann had learned that her birth
was not welcomed by her mother, who had not wanted to
have another child, and Mrs. Fitzgerald was hired to take
Ann off her hands. This remained a source of bewilder-
ment to Ann throughout her entire life; she always spoke
warmly of Mrs. Fitzgerald as the first person really to care
about her. Later on Ann described herself as someone who
had missed being cared for and loved by her mother, and
those close to her during her youth agree with this assessment.

Ann's relationship to her father was problematic also.
She remembered him as someone who was very lonely,
who took her on trips and did things that even at a young
age she felt were "inappropriate."

Ann described this behavior in fictional form in *Double
Exit*, the book she wrote as she was trying to work through
her feelings about her participation in the deaths of her
parents. Published by the Hemlock Society in 1989, the
book tells of a fictional couple, Claudia and Hank, who
help Claudia's parents commit suicide. Ann and Derek
always acknowledged, however, that the book was about
her own parents, with certain things altered to prevent
legal repercussions.

In discussing her relationship with her father, Claudia says that she became aware of vague sexual overtures while she was still a small child. None of the sexual overtures were overt; she remembers that her father slept in her bedroom for a time and enjoyed holding her in his arms. She also remembers becoming more and more uncomfortable about his behavior, sensing his need for closeness yet being embarrassed by it, too.

These themes of love and loss seemed to recur again and again in Ann's life. Yet she always retained a sense of determination that was accompanied by a fun-loving, inquisitive side. At St. Mary's Academy Ann participated in all the misadventures of her classmates, finding a sense of community for the first time. St. Mary's was a teenage girl's dream. Located in the green rolling mountains of Tennessee, it was delightfully close to not one but three schools for young men. The boarding school was small— there were only sixteen young women in Ann's graduating class—and it was here that her quick wit and mischievous humor began to emerge. By this time Ann had also become an accomplished musician, playing the piano extremely well.

After St. Mary's Ann went on to college. She dropped out twice, finally graduating cum laude from Boston University, followed by graduate school at the University of Toronto. She spent a year in Spain, learning to speak fluent Spanish, and in 1966 she left for Nigeria, where she was to have spent two years teaching in a secondary school under the auspices of the Canadian University Service Overseas, a program similar to the Peace Corps. But the war in Biafra halted her Nigerian sojourn after only a couple of months.

Through all these years Ann's parents paid her expenses, and whenever she talked about them, she always made it clear that, while they didn't provide emotional support, they always saw to it that she had whatever she needed financially—with one very important exception.

In early 1968, when Ann was living in Toronto, she became pregnant. This was her second pregnancy. She never gave me the details of her first, except to say that she'd had an abortion and developed such severe complications that she was told she would never be able to have another child.

With this second pregnancy Ann made up her mind that she would not have an abortion. She went home to Massachusetts and appealed for help from her family. It seemed a reasonable expectation because her parents were aware of Ann's relationship with the baby's father and, in fact, approved of him. However, they were horrified that she was pregnant again and incredulous that she could even consider having the baby. It was made abundantly clear that no one was to find out about the situation. To have a pregnant unmarried daughter was more than the family could possibly bear. Ann's sister looked on as Ann's parents told her to leave, to consider herself disowned. Ann was informed that, if she had the baby, she would have to provide for all of her own and her baby's needs.

Pregnant and abandoned by her parents, Ann returned to Toronto, where she got a job as a domestic to support herself while she waited for the birth of her baby.

On October 22, 1968, Ann's son was born. She named him Ian Matthew. For two and a half months she loved him and nurtured him, but try as she did, she realized that she was being unfair to her baby. "He deserved so much more," she told me.

Tentatively she contacted an agency to see what needed to be done to relinquish her son for adoption. "I thought it would take awhile," she said, "but in just a few days they called and told me to come in. They said I was to bring him with me." She dressed him quickly, wrapped him in a little blanket she'd made for him before he was born, and brought him to the agency.

She left a letter with him to be given to his adoptive parents. "In giving him up, it doesn't mean I want him less, but that I love him enough to know he deserves much more than what I can give him. Please give my little monkey the biggest hug and kiss for me. And perhaps in his own little way, he might know I'm always with him," she had written.

He was almost twenty-three years old before she saw him again.

The days after she had relinquished Ian were very difficult. She was no longer seeing Ian's father, and she received no counseling to help her deal with the grief of separation from her baby. In those days, once the child had been given up, the mother was on her own. No counseling was given to deal with the sense of loss that was very real and painfully present.

Within months Ann had married Tom Wickett, a Toronto attorney. "I thought marriage would bring stability to my life," she said. And she thought it would fill the gap left by her being disowned by her parents and giving up her son. It didn't. Wickett, described to me by Ann and others as no-nonsense, perhaps even cold, was not the type on whom Ann felt she could lean. He and Ann separated after only a couple of years. The failing marriage precipitated another crisis. Ann attempted suicide, swallowing a massive dose of pills in combination with liquor. When she was brought to the hospital, she was thought to be dead. After the suicide attempt Ann spent several months in the hospital.

While I don't know what was going on in Ann's mind at that time, I do know that—as she made clear in our conversations later—she felt a deep sense of failure throughout her life. She felt like a failure for having broken relationships with her family, for being unable to raise a child on her own, for having broken marriages. Not being able to walk away from things and just forget, though at every turn she was told that that was exactly what she should do, Ann often felt overwhelmed and very much alone.

By 1973 she had gone back to school and completed work on a master's degree at the University of Toronto. Good grades helped her earn a scholarship. Money from the sale of the house she and Tom Wickett had bought before their separation provided her just enough to see her through. And now, with no baby in the picture, her parents were once again willing to provide generous checks whenever necessary. She headed to England for further study in Shakespearean literature. Life was starting over again.

Ann read. And wrote. And studied hard. She was well on her way to getting a Ph.D. in English literature at Birmingham University, proud of her accomplishment. But there was one thing missing. She was lonely. In August

1975 she put an ad in the personal column of the *New Statesman*. It read: "Attractive, blonde, piquant, 33, about-to-be-divorced, PhD student (but not all that heavy into academia), seeks compatible male, 35 or older, interesting, keen mind, good sense of humor, type to put his feet up on the furniture. Objective? Friendship, camaraderie, or more if chemistry so encourages."

That ad was answered by Derek Humphry, then forty-five years old and a widower for five months. (Jean had died in March.) Ann and Derek arranged a first meeting at a London pub. They talked and talked. They walked around Covent Garden. Each confided a background of loveless childhood. Derek had been the second son of an Englishman and an Irish model. His mother left when Derek was very young. When his parents divorced, his father gained custody of Derek and his brother. His mother left for Australia, giving no forwarding address. Subsequently Derek lived in the home of first one relative, then another.

Soon after meeting, Ann and Derek decided to marry, but they put off the actual date until spring since, as Ann said, "It would have looked bad for us to marry too soon after Jean's death." The marriage took place on February 16, 1976, in London's Marylebone Registry Office. Ann wore a long Elizabethan type of dress. Her long blond hair was pulled into Nordic-style twists over each ear. Photos taken that day show Ann looking adoringly at Derek.

Following the ceremony, the couple toasted each other over lunch at Rule's, the same restaurant where, only a few months earlier, Derek had taken a Harley Street doctor for a "slap-up dinner" after Jean Humphry's death. The doctor had been the one who provided Derek with a lethal dose of pills for Jean.

The newlyweds settled into married life, acquiring a small Victorian house in London. Soon Ann began to urge Derek to write about Jean's death. She regarded the events he had described to her, when they first met, as a love story. She wanted him to share it with others.

After Ann's death a member of her family said, "If *Jean's Way* hadn't been written, there wouldn't have been a Hemlock Society. And if there hadn't been a Hemlock Society, Ann would still be alive. With that book, Ann started a runaway train. . . ." When Ann tried to stop the train, she was thrown off; some might say it ran over her.

Together Ann and Derek Humphry set about writing *Jean's Way*, the book that became both the foundation and the centerpiece of the Hemlock Society. The story—as it was told—turned Derek into a symbol of the caring husband who would speak with authority on the romantic and bittersweet realities of standing by a spouse through a devastating illness.

According to the account in *Jean's Way*, during one of her hospitalizations for treatment of breast cancer, Jean and Derek made a pact. Derek promised Jean that if she ever asked him if it was time for her to kill herself, he would give her an "honest" answer. Furthermore, if he told her it was the time, he would provide her with the means to carry it out and she would do so immediately. Derek later wrote that after exchanging these promises, they never talked about it again.

Nine months passed. On the morning of March 29, the

day before Easter, Jean Humphry sat up in the couple's bed, nibbling toast and sipping tea. She gazed at her beloved roses growing outside the window of their little country cottage. Then she turned to Derek and asked him the question: "Is this the day?" Knowing what she meant, he told her that it was.

After he had mixed the lethal dose of drugs he'd already obtained into a mug of coffee, he handed her the brew and watched her drink it. Then he sat by her bedside with two pillows nearby, intending to use them to smother her if the pills didn't work. However, in *Jean's Way* he stated clearly that he did not need the pillows since the drugs took effect less than an hour after she'd taken them. According to Derek, Jean died peacefully at 1:50 P.M. on March 29, 1975, as he sat by her side.

Even before Ann and I became friends and I found out more about events that had transpired, I found the book incredibly sad and troubling—not the "tender and rare love story" that some reviewers have claimed it to be.

Most important, Jean *asked* Derek if it was the day for her death. He *told* her that it was. Even if the argument is made that Jean was the one who chose the time to ask the question, the fact remains that it was a question. It was not a direct statement.

Jean does make a direct request in the book—over and over. According to the account, Jean urged Derek on a number of occasions to seek sexual release elsewhere since she was so ill. Finally he did so. The next time she brought this up, telling Derek that he should have no compunctions about having another woman as a lover, Derek replied that, in fact, he had done just that.

Derek described himself as unprepared for Jean's reaction. By the expression on her face, he could see right away that he had made a terrible mistake in admitting what he had done. He also added that knowing that he had made love to another woman was a real "blow" to Jean. She seemed "stunned," and they both were overwhelmed with dismay.

I've often wondered if it was possible that Jean Humphry had the same mixed feelings about her famous question as she had in urging her husband, over and over, to take another woman as a lover. Could she, as well, have been hoping against hope that when she asked, "Is this the day?" her husband would say, "No"?

Derek has since changed the story a bit, playing down his part in what happened. As he tells it in interviews today, it was Jean's wish, and hers alone, that she end her life. He further declares that this decision cannot be made for someone by anybody else. At the same time he now states adamantly that during the nine months preceding Jean's death, many discussions took place about her plans.

It was after I had listened to this new variation that I asked Ann about it. "Was that really the way it happened?"

According to Ann, the story as they wrote it in *Jean's Way* was, indeed, far different from what Derek had told her when they were writing the book. The family was in great turmoil, and there were shouting arguments and many tensions, all of which was very different from the tranquil country scene pictured with the solicitous husband/grieving widower.

But the reality did not make it the type of book they wanted it to be. They used "A Love Story" as the subtitle, and in order to have the book conform to that premise, Ann claimed much was either omitted or altered.

According to Ann, an example of the way she and Derek played with the facts is the mention of the two pillows by Jean's bed. In the book Derek says he didn't have to use them. But in my conversations with her Ann implied that Derek had used the pillows to smother Jean. In the suicide note I received from her in October 1991, she was very definite, writing: "Jean actually died of suffocation. I could never say it until now; who would believe me?" Derek has consistently denied this version of events.

Because she truly believed that Derek had acted out of love, Ann had no problem with romanticizing or omitting facts. She emphasized that it was her decision as much as Derek's to "sanitize" the story, as she often put it. She did know, however, that leaving out every unpleasant aspect would have made the story appear unrealistic. Although they argued about it, Ann insisted that some of these points, such as the mention of the pillows, be left in.

She also said that the famous question "Is this the day?" was asked only once and that "they didn't discuss and discuss it," as Derek now says. Since she thought then that Jean really wanted to kill herself, Ann felt it was important to portray Jean as the decision maker. Later, as she dealt with her own cancer, Ann said: "Now, though, after what I've been through, I see her so differently. And I will always find myself wondering what Jean would say if she could speak. I suspect it would be rather chilling."

But at the time they wrote *Jean's Way* Ann was not questioning Derek. Talking about those early years, as well as about all their time together, Ann never tried to blame

Derek for what she saw as her own responsibility and choices. She never attempted, in any of the long discussions we had, to paint herself as a misguided innocent "led astray" by Derek. She maintained that Derek would have been more or less content to have written the book and left it at that. Believing in the cause, however, Ann was the one who was most anxious for the book to turn into something more.

She went to meetings of EXIT, the British euthanasia society, founded in the 1930s, and talked about Derek to Nicholas Reed, then EXIT's general secretary. Reed didn't pay much attention to Ann when she handed him a copy of the book, but when she told him Derek was a journalist, he became interested. A friendship was struck between the Humphrys and Reed.

(Three years later Reed was sentenced to thirty months in prison—eventually reduced to eighteen months—for aiding and abetting the suicides of elderly and disabled people. As he was led from the court, Reed shouted that his sentencing showed the "idiocy of the present law." Though at his trial his lawyers argued that Reed and a codefendant had acted out of compassion for desperate people who wanted to die, a bedridden woman brought into the courtroom on a stretcher told a different story. Saying that Reed's codefendant had become furious with her when she decided not to use the do-it-yourself suicide kit—a kit containing liquor, drugs, and plastic bags—he'd given her, she testified that the codefendant had angrily told her, "You are the only person to disobey me.")

It was not only EXIT that began to show an interest in Derek Humphry and *Jean's Way*. A British tabloid printed an excerpt, paying Humphry three thousand pounds. A television documentary came soon after. A police inquiry also began, generating publicity that boosted book sales. If Derek had been convicted of assisting a suicide, he could have faced up to fourteen years in prison.

Before the investigation was completed, Derek and Ann had left Britain to move to the United States. While some have implied that Derek fled the country to avoid prosecution, Ann told me this was not the case at all. "He had asked for and received permission to leave," she said. The decision to move to the United States had nothing to do with the investigation.

"At the time," Ann explained, "I really wanted to go back to the States. And Derek was looking for something else as well. Everyone was certain that the *Times* was going to fold. We knew that would mean he'd be out of work."

Derek had worked at the *Times* of London for eleven years. Though the paper never did fold, by then Derek was forty-eight years old and prospects of getting a position on any other British paper seemed dim. Not being a "great" journalist—Ann thought of him as someone competent who had plodded on for years—and not having a lot of friends or contacts, Derek and Ann both believed it was time for him to move on.

Derek landed a one-year contract with the Los Angeles *Times*, and he and Ann moved to California in 1978. While they were en route, British officials announced that Derek's case would not be prosecuted. Lack of evidence was cited as the reason.

The additional publicity brought about by the inquiry led to invitations for Derek to speak. He was invited to do a one-month tour as a guest of New Zealand's Humanist Association and two Australian euthanasia groups. The Euthanasia Educational Council, which had recently changed its name to Concern for Dying and which was one of two euthanasia societies in existence in the United States at that time, reported favorably on *Jean's Way* and invited Derek to be a speaker at a San Francisco conference. A planned U.S. edition of the book added to the warm welcome that the Humphrys received on their arrival in California. According to Ann, it was at that time that Derek realized he had a special ability to mesmerize an audience. And he thrived on it, becoming very much aware that he had a certain quality that made people want to listen.

When Derek's contract with the Los Angeles *Times* was not renewed, the Humphrys set out to make death their life's work. No more would Derek try to earn a living as a full-time journalist, reporting on what others were doing. Together he and Ann would start an organization that would make a difference. As Derek said some years later, "I don't mean to change the world. I mean to change little parts of it."

Those "little parts" were the laws that had, throughout the history of the modern world, prohibited any kind of direct and intentional killing of the sick, the old, and the disabled. His movement, according to a recent Humphry boast, "represents one of the last great social reforms in modern society."

Derek Humphry's efforts to alter existing euthanasia laws in this country were by no means the first attempts to do so. On January 17, 1938, *The New York Times* announced the formation of a national euthanasia organization, which became known as the Euthanasia Society of America. Although acknowledging that there would be strong opposition from physicians, lawyers, and the clergy, one of its founders told reporters that opposition to euthanasia was based on emotion and fear of possible abuse. His organization, he claimed, would draft a law that would prevent any such possibility of abuse.

Within a year the Euthanasia Society of America was ready to offer a proposal that would legalize "the termination of human life by painless means for the purpose of avoiding unnecessary suffering." While the measure was limited to "voluntary" euthanasia, the society "hoped eventually to legalize the putting to death of nonvolunteers beyond the help of medical science."

The goal of involuntary euthanasia—in which people who have *not* requested it are put to death—was echoed in 1939 by the group's new president, Dr. Foster Kennedy, who urged the "legalizing of euthanasia primarily in cases of born defectives who are doomed to remain defective, rather than for normal persons who have become miserable through incurable illness." (In a 1941 poll of twenty-five thousand New York State doctors by the Euthanasia Society, 80 percent of respondents favored euthanasia for adults, while 27 percent approved of killing severely disabled children. However, as one euthanasia activist stated, the wording of the poll was unfortunate since the question about children "did not differentiate between newborn versus older defectives.")

By 1942 Dr. Kennedy had come up with a plan for child euthanasia. In an *American Journal of Psychiatry* article, he wrote: "I believe when the defective child shall have reached the age of five years—and on the application of his guardians—that the case should be considered under law by a competent medical board. . . ." If careful board examination determined that the child was considered to have "no future or hope of one," he continued, "then I believe it is a merciful and kindly thing to relieve that defective—often tortured and convulsed, grotesque and absurd, useless and foolish, and entirely undesirable—of the agony of living."

While Kennedy boldly stated the goal of the Euthanasia Society, the organization's public stance generally revolved around the more acceptable concept of voluntary euthanasia. Even at this early stage the importance of politically correct terminology seemed to be recognized.

The Euthanasia Society continued its efforts to advance its cause, but it made little headway in the years following World War II. As the horrors of the German euthanasia program and the Holocaust became known, the mere mention of the word "euthanasia" caused people to recoil. In this country it was not until the mid-sixties that the euthanasia movement took a real step forward. The year was 1967, and two crucial events took place. The first was the establishment of the Euthanasia Educational Fund as a branch of the Euthanasia Society of America. (The fund soon became known as the Euthanasia Educational Council.) Its purpose was to distribute information about euthanasia and to garner large donations for this new tax-exempt arm of the movement. From 1967 to 1974 contributions increased significantly with one bequest alone amounting to more than one million dollars.

Even more important was the second event, which, more than any other single factor in the history of the American euthanasia movement, has influenced and channeled attitudes of the public in general. At a meeting in Chicago Luis Kutner, a member of the advisory board of the Euthanasia Educational Council, proposed a new document that helped "promote discussion of euthanasia." The document was the Living Will.

A signed and witnessed directive, a Living Will usually contained standard language expressing a person's right to refuse certain types of medical treatment. Many people who were concerned about the very real issue of overtreatment and denial of a patient's rights saw the Living Will as the way to prevent their being subjected to procedures and equipment they found abhorrent, frightening, cruel, or unnecessary.

Immediately the previously unknown document began to be mentioned in magazines and newspapers, on television and radio, and in professional journals. But according to the *Euthanasia News*, the official newsletter of the Euthanasia Educational Council, the greatest stimulus for acceptance was the publicity given the document in "Dear Abby" columns. "Abby," Abigail Van Buren, was listed by the Euthanasia Educational Council as being a member of their advisory committee for a number of years, a position that I have never seen noted in her columns.

The Euthanasia Society of America concentrated on promoting the Living Will. Efforts began to focus on passing laws so that people could sign Living Wills. Few people seemed to recognize that anyone could sign anything, that a new law wasn't needed to allow someone to sign the document. Nevertheless, in keeping with the goal to gain public acceptance of euthanasia and to pass laws that could become the foundation of legally approved euthanasia, a campaign to pass Living Will laws was initiated.

Thus began a controversy that has often left the public puzzled over why anyone would oppose Living Will laws. Contrary to what some have assumed, opposition to such laws does not stem from any disagreement about a person's right to make wishes known regarding medical matters. The concept of informed consent to medical treatment is extremely valuable, as is the practice of informing others about how one feels about particular medical interventions. Opposition to Living Will *laws*, however, is rooted in both the purposeful way they are foisted on the public and into the legislatures as a beachhead for the euthanasia movement and in the way such laws have generated confusion about the difference between euthanasia and allowing nature to take its course.

In campaigns to pass Living Will laws it was stated over and over that doctors needed such laws to protect them from lawsuits if they removed useless treatment. Yet to this day there has been only one criminal case in the country in which physicians were charged for removing care—and that case was thrown out of court.

In promoting the Living Will, the Euthanasia Society studiously avoided the inflammatory rhetoric used in its early days. Any references to future goals were limited to conferences and publications directed at those who already agreed with the concept of euthanasia. At one such conference, held by the Euthanasia Educational Council in 1972, members were told of the need to "walk before we can run." The problems of "who shall speak for those who are incompetent or incapable of speaking for themselves" were to "wait until the general public accepts the fact that man has an inalienable right to die."

While the Euthanasia Educational Council was carrying out the advance work with the public, the Euthanasia Society of America worked in the legislative arena. Sensitivity to the word "euthanasia" led to a major name change for both organizations: In 1975 the Euthanasia Society of America changed its name to the Society for the Right to Die. In 1978 the Euthanasia Educational Council became Concern for Dying. Meanwhile, in 1976 the first Living Will law, called the Natural Death Act, had passed in California.

By the early 1980s the euthanasia organizations had succeeded in gaining the moral high ground. Using the language of "rights" and "choice," they gained great support for what came to be called the right to die. For Derek and Ann, it was a good time to start a new euthanasia organization for another reason. Infighting between the Society for the Right to Die and its sister group, Concern for Dying, had resulted in the severing of their close relationship in 1979. (The two groups recombined in 1991 under the name Choice in Dying.) Concern for Dying charged that it had been carrying the entire financial burden for both groups. Anger that the society had "chosen to circulate material implying that it has been the focus of the euthanasia movement, failing to credit the development of the Living Will" to Concern for Dying, made for hard feelings and bitter rivalries. According to Ann, a hefty sum of cash claimed by each group as its own also led to the bitter organizational split.

Ann and Derek thought a new group could provide the impetus to propel efforts forward. An organization with headquarters on the West Coast—the other two groups were based in New York—could also be new and appeal to the less stodgy. Derek was being asked more and more to talk about *Jean's Way*, and he'd already been asked to be present at an international meeting of euthanasia groups in Oxford, England.

Hemlock's "birthday"—the name was Ann's idea—is referred to as August 21, 1980, although official status was not obtained until March 10, 1981, when the group's articles of incorporation were filed with the Office of the Secretary of State in California. In addition to Ann and Derek, the initial directors of Hemlock were Gerald Larue, Barbara Waddell, and Emily Perkins. Its registered agent was Richard Scott, who served as Hemlock's first legal counsel and later became the attorney in an important California right-to-die case—that of Elizabeth Bouvia. (Scott committed suicide in August 1992.)

The organization was no more than a handful of people at first. But with resolve and an abundance of chutzpah, Ann and Derek forged ahead. The couple answered the often asked question "How big is your group?" with the reply "Small but growing."

The growing enterprise continued to attract attention, as the Humphrys threw themselves into building Hemlock's reputation. Some embroidering of credentials took place, with Ann describing herself as having a Ph.D., in part to offset Derek's anemic academic credentials. Ann had a master's degree but had not completed doctoral studies; Derek was a secondary school dropout. Derek also intensified his speaking efforts. "I remember him getting up at three in the morning to get ready for a two-hundred-mile drive just to speak for a high school class," Ann said. "He really, really was dedicated."

For Ann those were happy times. Death was a topic of discussion, not a reality. Euthanasia was a debatable issue, and it made for lively debate. It was a time when principles were proclaimed, manifestos were written, and the whole world seemed as bright as the California sunshine. Although Ann and Derek constantly worried about money, the financial struggle just made everything more exciting, more challenging.

In October 1980 the *Hemlock Quarterly* was started with Ann as its editor. The lead article in its first issue was written by Gerald Larue, who made no attempt to hide the fact that Hemlock was committed to making death more accessible. He wrote that already Hemlock organizers "have been strengthened in our belief that we must soon make available to our members the best information we can gather on self-deliverance." He called for counselors to address helping people who had chosen to die and explained that he was working with other professionals (trained therapists and psychologists) "to discuss the training of counselors prepared to help those who are considering self-deliverance. . . . I am prepared to do whatever I can to help now, whenever possible," he wrote.

By the time that Hemlock was formed, neither suicide—"self-deliverance," as Larue called it—nor attempted suicide was illegal. What was unprecedented in Larue's remarks was the open espousal of making it easier for people to commit suicide by helping them do so. Hemlock's aims were not limited to assisted suicide (providing a person with the means or encouragement to commit suicide). Rather, the principal objective of the organization from its inception was the legalization of euthanasia (intentional ending of one person's life by another). Once achieved, that objective would bestow equal status on the options of caring for or killing certain individuals.

Ann's first editorial, which appeared in the *Quarterly*'s initial issue, reflected the concept that euthanasia was to be considered an acceptable means of dealing with life-threatening conditions. ". . . we would like to strive towards an objectivity which considers any tenet of voluntary euthanasia a valid one—even if it's in opposition," she wrote. "We hope our articles reflect a tolerance towards the various alternatives which people opt for when confronted with a terminal illness. . . . Surely the base of the pyramid is broad enough to absorb us all."

What really put the Hemlock Society on solid monetary ground was the publication of *Let Me Die Before I Wake*. First published in 1981 and sold only to members of Hemlock, the book was later revised and made available to the general public. In relating the stories of how various people coped with the terminal illnesses of loved ones, *Let Me Die Before I Wake* in effect became Hemlock's first suicide manual. In late 1982 Hemlock began utilizing the services of a professional Hollywood publicist to bring attention to the book. The book's sales brought in income; publicity about the book brought in new members and donations.

Ann remembered that much of the early publicity was negative, and at first it bothered Derek and her. "But we learned fast," she added. "Some of the articles made Derek seem like Caligula, but it didn't hurt. It was the bad publicity that got people roused. It got them off their backsides. It got people angry—galvanized.

"Even when the things that were said were absolutely soul-destroying, we learned we could profit from it. . . . The bottom line was that we ended up with more money in the bank than we had before."

By the beginning of 1984 Hemlock had published its edition of *Jean's Way* and was preparing to market it at the annual American Booksellers Association convention. It was offering guidance on how suicide support groups could avoid legal problems, and it was attracting attention in the national media. Psychologist B. F. Skinner, a Hemlock member, made highly supportive comments about the group on the nationally televised *Merv Griffin Show*. And Hemlock officials were preparing to send a first delegation to a conference of the World Federation of Right to Die Societies that was to be held in France later that year.

CHAPTER 3

■ ■ ■

By 1984 the United States had three national euthanasia groups (the Society for the Right to Die, Concern for Dying, and the Hemlock Society) while the international euthanasia movement numbered twenty-six organizations, claiming a total of 415,000 members throughout the world. The biennial conference of the World Federation of Right to Die Societies, the umbrella organization of all euthanasia societies worldwide, was held in Nice on the French Riviera that year. It was being billed as the biggest conference yet. Unlike previous conferences (Tokyo in 1976, San Francisco in 1978, Oxford in 1980, and Melbourne in 1982), this one was to be open to the public. It was also the first right-to-die conference that I attended.

The actual meetings took place in the posh Palais des Congrès. The official hostesses, their short peach and turquoise costumes blending perfectly with the soothing plums, magentas, and blues of the thickly upholstered chairs in the outer hall, stood ready to answer questions, take orders for cool drinks, or deliver messages to people across the hall.

The press was waiting as well, spurred on by the release of a "manifesto" and the report of a physicians' survey that had become big news. Only the day before, leading French newspapers had carried front-page stories about an unprecedented document signed by five French physicians who had declared that they had administered euthanasia by giving lethal doses to sick patients with the intention of making them die. Furthermore, the doctors had said that they hoped a majority of their medical colleagues would join with them in approving the practice of euthanasia. Several of the signers were expected to address the convention.

During the same week *Tonus*, a French medical publication, had carried results of a survey of general practitioners in which 81 percent of the respondents indicated their support of active euthanasia. The right-to-die conference had been promoted in conjunction with the survey's release. Security was also out in full force.

I was informed by a fellow conventioneer that security was so tight because Dr. Christiaan Barnard, the famed South African heart surgeon, would speak at the conference. His keynote address was to be the high point of the three-day event. Hearing rumors of an antiapartheid protest, the authorities were afraid of an attack on him. The threatened disruption, however, never took place.

Barnard had been the subject of promotional features in right-to-die publications for months. The *Hemlock Quarterly* had devoted a large article to his participation in the conference. It was right across the page from an article quoting

B. F. Skinner's statement that "we dispose of an old dog in a way that is called humane. . . . Many old people, living in pain or as a burden to others, would be glad to be put to death caninely."

"This surgeon and humanist who has left his mark on the frontiers of medical science is one of our most distinguished members" was the way the conference program described him. While Barnard was world-renowned for performing the first successful heart transplant operation, his advocacy of euthanasia was little known publicly prior to the Nice conference. However, he had spoken out and written in favor of it: In the late seventies Barnard and his brother, Marius, also a physician, had announced a pact in which each had promised to help the other die, and in 1980 Barnard had written the book *Good Life, Good Death*, in which he called for legalization of euthanasia. His euthanasia advocacy was well known to right-to-die supporters and made him a potential star in their ranks.

When the sixty-two-year-old Barnard and his twenty-year-old girl friend put in an appearance on opening day, middle-aged professionals and white-haired ladies flocked around them like fans at a rock concert. Impeccably dressed in a cream-colored suit, Barnard held his arm around his blond friend, striking in tight white slacks, fringed blouse, and gold bracelets. The couple patiently posed for pictures.

When Barnard appeared at the podium on the third day of the conference, the crowd was equally in awe, all edging forward in their seats to ensure that not a word that fell from his mouth was lost. Slowly he began. Discussing the role religion initially played in his life, he described his childhood days as the son of a missionary. Then he related how, as a small boy, he sat beside his mother on the organ bench, his little legs dangling over the side, his feet not touching the ground. Sometimes he played a note or two while his mother played hymns during services conducted by his father. Religion was very important in the life of the young Christiaan Barnard. "You don't have to be an atheist to be a humanitarian," he said.

"My father was a very religious man, and he taught me a lot about stories in the Bible. The one I remember extremely well was the story about the crucifixion of Christ. . . . He told me that they took this man called Christ and nailed Him to a cross . . . and then He was left there to die.

"Even in those early days, I wondered why Christ had to suffer. Why could it not have been an easy and quick death?" Barnard said he was certain his father would have told him it was God's will that Christ suffer. "But that's not the right answer," Barnard continued. "The sufferings of Christ were meaningless. It was His life that had meaning. His life was full. There was purpose in His life. And there was purpose in His death. But not to the suffering that preceded it."

As if to drive home the point, he repeated each word. "There . . . was . . . no . . . purpose . . . to . . . the . . . suffering.

"If we wish confirmation of this, we need only look at the words of Christ himself when He cried out, 'My God, My God, why have Thou forsaken me?' " Barnard looked out over the audience. Heads were bobbing in agreement.

"And," Barnard went on, "during my career as a doctor,

which is now nearly forty years, I have often wondered what really is the purpose of suffering. I have found that there is none. Suffering never ennobles. People who suffer never become better people as a result of it." Quoting a friend, he said, "If God is good, then there is no God. And if God is bad, then He is not God."

He went on to ask, "Is it playing God to interfere with the natural process in a terminally ill patient?" He answered his own question: "If it's playing God to stop suffering, I don't think God would mind very much." Life, he explained, is not really present when the patient is in the terminal stage of a disease. "I honestly don't believe we take a life under those circumstances. I think life is already ended. There is just existence that's left."

The audience was by now completely captivated as Barnard shifted to a personal confession.

"I admit I have not had the courage of my convictions," he said. Even though he had seen the "need" for euthanasia, he had allowed patients to live when he "should have terminated their lives." The reason, he explained, was that South African law treats euthanasia as premeditated murder, punishable by hanging.

Only once, he said, did he get close to actually administering euthanasia. It was a long time ago. He was a very young physician, working late at night. A young woman whose name was Maria was suffering from cervical cancer. The cancer had infiltrated the nerves on the back of her pelvis, causing constant, severe pain. She was crying out in agony.

No longer able to tolerate seeing her suffer, he stole ten grains of morphine from the hospital supply. "With shaking hands and fingers, I diluted the morphine and drew it up in a syringe." He walked down the hallway to her room with the idea of giving her the overdose to end her suffering. "When I came to her, she was quiet. There was this peaceful look in her eyes. And I decided I couldn't kill her under those circumstances. So I walked back to the office and squirted out the injection of morphine," he said. "Three weeks later Maria was met with great pleasure by her two little children as she walked out of the hospital."

He went on to explain that some would say this illustrates how easy it would be to make mistakes in administering euthanasia. He disagreed. It only showed how he, as a very young doctor, should not have made the decision on his own. He should have asked for the opinions of other doctors in the hospital.

He then turned to the question of who should decide if a person is a "candidate" for euthanasia. "There is only one person who can make that decision. There is only one group of people who can make that decision. And that is the medical profession. I don't think you can allow the priest or the lawyer or the family to make that decision. The quality of life is a medical decision," he repeated.

Heads turned as people looked at one another in surprise. This was not expected.

Barnard continued, asking, "How wise is it to get the family and patient involved? This involvement may sound very nice when we're sitting here, but in hospital practice you will find that this is totally different."

He asked another question: "Would you want to know when it's going to happen? I doubt whether I'd want to know that the doctor is going to kill me at this particular moment."

To prevent the patient and family from becoming too involved in what he described as a medical decision, Barnard suggested that there be laws passed that would make it necessary for hospitals to provide an additional form for patients to sign. Then, at the time of hospital admission, the patient could, if he or she wished, give the doctor permission to practice euthanasia if the doctor determined it was appropriate.

That way, he said, "When the time comes, you don't have to ask the patient. You don't have to consult the relatives. The patient can be quietly put to sleep without having the feeling that he knows this is going to happen now."

Heads were shaking. Disapproval was now very clear. But Barnard went on. "The doctor must be the one to carry out the decision. I'm not in favor of giving the patient something by mouth or giving him something and saying, 'Take this. If you drink it, you will kill yourself.' I don't believe this is really humane," he said.

He went on to explain the way in which euthanasia should be performed. "This is to give the patient an intravenous injection of barbiturate and a relaxant so death will occur quietly without pain in a few minutes. I believe it is our duty to take these steps," he said, concluding his presentation. "Otherwise, I think our patients will call out in a loud voice saying, 'My doctor, my doctor, why have thou forsaken me?' "

There was a race to the microphones as angry delegates

rushed to challenge him, asking how he could determine when it was time for someone else to die.

"It's a medical determination," he said.

"But how do you know when it's best for me to die? What if I feel there's no quality to my life and I decide it's time to leave? What if you think it's not time yet?" asked one participant.

Barnard held firm to his view that it was the doctor's right to decide the time. "When the patient's quality of life has totally gone, it's a medical question," he repeated.

Stepping into the fray, Dr. Pieter Admiraal of Holland (the previous day he had received a standing ovation for his description of euthanasia practices in Holland) attempted to strike a conciliatory note.

"It's the patient who decides," he said, but it is the doctor who sets forth the options. "If there is no medical solution for his problems, I tell the patient I can't go on any longer with him. I then offer him euthanasia. If he wants it, we do it. And that is one of the most decent moments in our hospital."

Unlike Barnard, Admiraal said the family should be involved. "Most of the time the family is there, and one of our priests. The patient knows the exact moment. It is his life, and he wants to terminate it at that moment."

But even Admiraal did not succeed in calming the ire that had been raised. An eighty-year-old founding member of the French organization sponsoring the event took to the microphone.

Glaring at both men, she shook her finger. "Don't you see? You're only talking about sick people. Nobody has said anything about healthy old people. Don't you understand what it's like to be an old person?

"They haven't got cancer. They're not seriously ill. But they have false teeth. They've lost their hair; their hearing's going; they can't see the headings on television, the subtitles, anymore. It's progressive, slow decay.

"They can't go in their garden. They stay in their rooms. Life is nothing. . . . Don't you realize that when a person thinks he or she has lived enough, a doctor should help them end their life before it's too late," she scolded.

Barnard stammered, "It's difficult for me to reply to this. But I do say that there are patients in old-age homes who would fit my ideas of what is meant by no quality of life. In those circumstances I believe that those old people should have the right to die with dignity."

Barnard did his best to explain his position as the session wore down, but his words had created a sour ending for the conference. Those who had awaited his speech so anxiously left disappointed, and the emotions expressed were very strong: hurt, betrayal, disbelief.

In the succeeding years Dr. Barnard has lost status in the euthanasia movement. However, this may be due more to his becoming a promoter for a line of cosmetics than for what he said in Nice.

The controversy that he created at the 1984 conference regarding the physician's role in euthanasia has now crystallized into a general consensus within the movement. The overwhelming majority of euthanasia proponents espouse the notion that the doctor should carry out—not make— the death decision. Derek Humphry has described this as a situation in which physicians are the "servants of society" who have a duty to "obey the wishes of society" by administering euthanasia on request.

Although this view expresses best the goal of self-determination, I believe it neglects the reality that it is the doctor who controls the information and options available to a patient, and it is the doctor who, by spoken or unspoken means, can demean a patient's life or convey a sense of hopelessness to the point at which the patient would "choose" euthanasia.

Overlooked, as well, in all the discussion about self-determination is the harsh reality that millions of people have no doctor or medical care. In the current economic climate, in which any guarantee of even minimal medical attention is unavailable to so many, legalization of euthanasia could make it an option for the rich and the only medical "treatment" the poor could afford.

While Dr. Barnard created a discordant note at the conference, there was agreement on other issues. Participants were urged to promote the Living Will as a way of changing the law and winning public support for the right to choose death.

Special tribute was given to some in attendance, such as Tenrei Ota of Japan, for organizing the very first world conference on the right to die in 1976. The Japanese euthanasia movement had taken the lead in the mid-seventies but has since "fallen behind" other countries on the world stage. Adrienne van Till of the Netherlands was invited to give an impromptu overview of the progress of the Dutch euthanasia movement, viewed by many in right-to-die circles as a model for the rest of the world to follow. Van Till's message concluded with a cautionary note that "euthanasia tourism" was not yet available to those who wished to come to Holland to end their lives.

It was clear to the delegates that changes in policies and practices in every country needed to be sought if all were to have ready access to euthanasia. And, as a means of bringing this about, public opinion would be gradually shaped to favor ending life by appointment.

The power of the well-told story as a crucial element in gaining this support was apparent in the presentation of Dr. Léon Schwartzenberg, a French cancer specialist and an outspoken advocate of euthanasia, who received the best reception at the conference. With every prematurely gray, wavy hair on his head in perfect place, the debonair Parisian talked about case after case from his oncology practice.

The most poignant story described the predicament of a woman in her mid-fifties who had come to Schwartzenberg several years earlier with ovarian cancer. Before agreeing to any treatment, she asked him to promise that, if she could not be cured, he would help her die. He agreed.

Undergoing difficult treatment, she fought to overcome her cancer, but it became apparent after many months that this was not to be. He then recounted what took place.

She asked, "Will you still help me?"

"Of course I will."

"But not just yet. You see, my daughter's expecting a baby—my first grandchild. May I wait until after the baby is born?" Schwartzenberg had assured her that this was all right. It was her decision to make, not his.

Several weeks later the woman called. "The baby is here. She's so beautiful," she told Schwartzenberg. Again she asked him, "Will you still help me?"

And again he replied, "Of course."

"Not at once, though. I'd like to be there for the christening. . . ."

"All right."

Days later she phoned again. "I'm ready now," she said.

"Would you wish this at the hospital or at home?"

"Oh, at home. It would be better at home." She lived on the outskirts of Paris, not far from the hospital where Schwartzenberg made his rounds. The appointment was set for the following Monday night at eight o'clock.

Shortly before it was time to go, Schwartzenberg put all that was needed in his medical bag. "I had this terrible taste, this bitter taste which I always have for this task ahead of me," he said. Then, with a map in hand, he set out.

"I can tell you, no matter how well you know Paris, it is easy to get lost," Schwartzenberg reminded the audience. "So many one-way roads or streets that aren't even marked on the map. I got hopelessly lost."

Already half an hour late he tried to find a telephone. The first telephone booth had been vandalized. In the second, his money came back. He continued to drive around, looking for a telephone in working order. Third and fourth phones were also not working. Finally, at ten o'clock, he found a phone that he could use.

"I was apprehensive, and a bit cowardly, while I waited for it to ring. I thought to myself that we'd need to postpone [the matter]." As he was telling himself, "I won't need to do it tonight," someone answered the phone. It was the woman's daughter.

Schwartzenberg apologized and explained what had happened. "It's a bit late now," he said.

"Yes, but it doesn't matter. She's waiting."

"Can't we delay for a couple of days?"

"No, no, no. She's expecting you." Directions were given.

He got back in his car and drove to a store on a corner a short distance away. There was no elevator. He climbed the steps to the apartment above the market and knocked on the door.

Five people were there, waiting. The woman was sitting in an armchair. Her husband, the daughter with her new baby in her arms, and another daughter sat close by. They all chatted for a few minutes. Just small talk.

Finally the woman said, "Don't worry. I'm very well. I know I could have lasted a few months. I've settled everything. Seen the priest. My conscience is at rest. When you want, I'm ready."

Her husband stood up and walked over to her chair to help her. "No, let me go alone," she said, pulling herself up from the chair. She walked into the bedroom, slipped off her shoes, and lay down on the bed.

The daughter who had the baby reached over and stopped the doctor as he was at the bedroom door. "May I go in?" she asked.

"If your mother will allow this. Then, yes, of course." Her mother nodded approval.

The husband, who had been standing just outside the

bedroom, said, "I would rather not be here." He went into the room, bent over to kiss his wife, and went back to the other room.

"Now it was time," Schwartzenberg said. As he prepared the syringe, the woman said, "You don't know how happy I am."

Schwartzenberg described the final moments: "As I finished injecting her, she closed her eyes. I looked on as she went peacefully to sleep. As I raised my head, I noticed that her daughter, sitting so close beside her, was breast-feeding her baby.

"What better example? As the mother peacefully left this life, the daughter was nurturing new life. It was the most beautiful experience in my medical career."

Schwartzenberg stopped speaking. There was complete silence in the auditorium. Then thunderous applause erupted as six hundred people rose to their feet.

Following his presentation, people lined up behind the microphones placed in each aisle. Adulation poured out as, one after another, participants paid tribute to Schwartzenberg's "magnificent portrayal of what medicine should really be . . . how wonderful is the right to choose . . . in a world where self-determination and autonomy must be respected, this is a most beautiful example. . . ."

I can recall sitting in that auditorium, looking over the sea of faces, feeling myself being drawn into the euphoria. It sounded so good and so alluring. Killing, so compassionately described, seemed inviting to me also.

Then the mood was broken. An older gentleman, who had been patiently waiting his turn at the microphone, stepped forward and identified himself as a psychiatrist. "I could not help wondering," he said, "as I heard you tell how [the woman] kept waiting, putting it off, if she might not have been depressed. I wonder if—" The man was stopped in mid-sentence as the audience turned toward him en masse and began first to shout, "Sit down, sit down, sit down," and then to hiss. The man bowed his head, turned, walked back to his place, and sat down.

Schwartzenberg had so captivated his listeners that they seemed unwilling to allow anyone to raise potentially troublesome questions. A year after the conference Schwartzenberg wrote a book, *Requiem pour la vie*, which chronicled his "agonizing search of his own values." He described his quest as one that ultimately led him to make euthanasia house calls. First he had given a lethal injection to a close personal friend, next to patients he'd known for a long time. Then he expanded the practice to those with whom he'd had little contact.

From that time on Schwartzenberg's name became well known throughout France, and he became a recognized media guest. In 1988 he was appointed to the Ministry of Health but was asked to resign only nine days later because of his controversial statements on euthanasia and other issues. In 1990 his advocacy of euthanasia earned him a one-year suspension from the French Medical Association.

Named as a minister to the European Parliament, in 1991 Schwartzenberg was appointed to the position of rapporteur (an official advocate for a particular measure under consideration) for a resolution that would endorse the practice of euthanasia throughout Europe. The resolution is wending its way slowly through the various stages of consideration. If Schwartzenberg is successful in persuading the European Parliament to adopt it, the next step could be an attempt to elevate the resolution to "directive" status. Directive status would create a "right to euthanasia," which each of the European Economic Community (EEC) member countries would be compelled to accept, and would achieve a goal toward which the worldwide euthanasia movement has labored for many years. If such new guidelines are set in place, it is predicted that physicians would easily adapt to providing euthanasia as just one more medical option.

CHAPTER 4

■ ■ ■

Ann Humphry wasn't at the 1984 conference in France. More comfortable with writing and doing research than speaking, Ann was content to let Derek be the spokesperson for the Hemlock Society.

"Derek is good at being a front man," she explained to me. "It's that British accent and his smile." People reacted positively to both qualities; the voice conveyed authority, and his smile said "nice." Here's this man who's so important, and he's listening to me, people seemed to think. It was a winning combination.

There was another reason why Ann opted to forgo traveling. By the early eighties she had recognized she was suffering from agoraphobia. Afflicting 14.5 million Americans, agoraphobia manifests itself in a dread or terror of any number of things—leaving one's own house, being in open places like shopping centers and streets, or being in enclosed places like subways and airplanes. Though its origins are not completely understood, it is thought to be triggered often by stress.

Determined to overcome this debilitating condition, Ann forced herself to go out, but the struggle became more and more difficult. Finally she sought professional help for the condition. After Derek had abandoned her, he as well as other members of the Hemlock board referred to Ann as being "mentally ill" and "very disturbed," pointing to long periods of counseling in her life. Much of the counseling she received was to deal with her agoraphobia.

A counselor worked patiently with her, helping Ann realize she could control her situation. Reassured by the fact that she could determine when and if she left the secure walls of her home and that she could do it at her own pace, Ann very slowly began to venture out. Gradually she made her way back into social activities.

With Ann preferring to stay in the background, Derek flew from place to place, apparently enjoying his growing role as Hemlock's spokesman. Derek had received little notice at the 1984 conference in Nice; he held a position on the World Federation's board but was not successful in an attempt to be elected vice-president and had not been selected as a speaker for the conference. Hemlock, however, continued to grow.

In 1985 its total revenue stood at $434,000. Together Ann and Derek received a combined income of $69,000 from the organization. Financially and organizationally things were definitely looking up. There was even money to pursue Hemlock's main objective: to change the laws in America.

To obtain tax-exempt status, Hemlock had been formed

as an educational organization rather than as a political group that would engage in legislative activity. The society's articles of incorporation state, "No substantial part of the activities of this corporation shall consist of carrying on propaganda, or otherwise attempting to influence legislation. . . ." However, from its inception Hemlock directed at least significant effort toward changing the laws related to euthanasia. By 1985 this goal was being voiced openly in major publications. For example, a Hemlock advertisement in *The New York Times Book Review* described the society as "supporting voluntary euthanasia for the terminally ill or the seriously incurably physically ill" and invited readers to "join the Hemlock Society, help break taboos, change antique laws."

In December of that year a "Dear Member" appeal letter, asking for tax-deductible donations and signed by Derek, stated, "In 1986, we shall launch legislation to permit physician aid-in-dying. . . ." The letter went on to describe the legislation and noted that "we shall try it first in California. . . . As opportunity occurs we shall introduce this Act in other states with the help of the Chapters we are now forming nationwide."

Yet in IRS reports Hemlock continued to describe itself in a manner that in no way reflected its activities as intended to result, directly or indirectly, in legislative change. In its tax report filed in May 1986, expenditures of more than three hundred thousand dollars were reported for "program services." The explanation of these services stated, "The program of Hemlock supports the [*sic*] active, voluntary euthanasia for the terminally ill, through publication of books, newsletters, and other literature. It aids people to share their feelings in problems of coping with terminal illness."

In 1986 *The Right to Die* was published. It was the first book by Derek Humphry to be released by a major New York publisher. Coauthored by Ann, it was reviewed in *The New York Times Book Review* and added credibility and growing respectability to Hemlock, though it ended up selling relatively few copies. To publicize the book, the publisher sent Derek on a promotional tour.

As someone who had spoken publicly about euthanasia ever since attending the right-to-die conference in France, I had been asked to appear on *Kelly and Company*, a Detroit television talk show, on which Derek was promoting his book. It was the first time I had been on any show with—or, more accurately, in opposition to—Derek. He was not only tremendously articulate and comfortable in front of the cameras but witty and charming during station breaks as well. And I saw for myself that he had a way of winning over the studio audience that was most impressive. As he told the story of Jean, his voice seemed to break just slightly when he described her last moments. Then, as always, he made a plea for legalization of aid-in-dying.

If things were going well for Hemlock, personal life for Derek and Ann was another matter. Derek had been under a great deal of pressure. According to Ann, trouble with two of his sons and the death of his brother had left him in bad shape. "He was just falling to pieces" was the way Ann put it to me.

On top of this, Ann's parents were in failing health. Her father, Arthur, was now ninety-two and had congestive heart failure. Her seventy-eight-year-old mother, Ruth, had had a stroke. While neither was terminally ill, they could no longer care for themselves without some outside assistance.

Ann's parents began to phone to tell her how bad things were. At one point Arthur had fallen down the stairs. Unable to get up, he called for his wife, but she didn't hear him because her bedroom door was closed. (The couple had slept in separate bedrooms for years.) Ann told me that although her sister lived nearby, she wasn't providing the day-to-day support that they now required.

The calls kept coming. Ann was in a quandary. She was in Los Angeles, three thousand miles away from Belmont, Massachusetts, where her parents still lived. To try to resolve matters, she went to see them in April 1986 and suggested a number of possibilities: a retirement home, a nursing home, or home health care. Although cost was not a factor, Arthur rejected all of them. According to Ann, he said there was only one way out: He was going to commit suicide. It was decided that Ruth would do the same, and Ruth, as she had throughout her life, passively acquiesced, letting Arthur make all the decisions.

Although both her parents were members of Hemlock, Ann tried to dissuade them from the decision. When it was clear that her father would not change his mind, she tried to persuade her mother to reconsider. Convinced that her mother, at least, was not ready to die, she still hoped to come up with a viable solution, such as her mother's moving out to California. However, nothing could be worked out, and Ann returned to Los Angeles, to make preparations for what her parents had decided to do.

In the first week of May a call was made to a Zurich

pharmacy. An order for five hundred Vesparax tablets was placed and charged to Derek Humphry's Visa card. Vesparax, which is not available in the United States, is a combination of two barbiturates and a tranquilizer. It has always been one of Derek Humphry's lethal drugs of choice. In his book *Final Exit* he even explains that he stores it in a closet, in a jar with a tight lid.

According to Ann, Derek had found out about this source of Vesparax the previous year. A psychologist-author had given him the name of the Swiss pharmacy along with instructions on how to get the necessary dose: Call the pharmacy, say you are Doctor So-and-so, place an order, charge it to a credit card, and give assurances that you will forward a written prescription. The person's brother had originally discovered this easy source of drugs while on a trip to Switzerland.

The pills—enough to kill Ruth and Arthur Kooman as well as a number of other people—arrived by mail.

Ann explained that after the pills were in hand, Derek wanted nothing more to do with it. "You take care of your stuff. I'll take care of mine" is what she remembered him saying. However, Arthur and Ruth were not going to do it on their own.

To complicate matters, Ann and Derek had planned a holiday in Colorado in an attempt to lessen the increasing tensions in their marriage. According to Ann, there had been a rift in their marriage for quite some time, and in many ways it was their work for Hemlock that was their strongest link.

At the last minute Ann decided that she couldn't go to Colorado. Instead she wanted to go back to Massachusetts once more to see if anything could be worked out. Derek was angry. He had already blocked out time for the vacation following a scheduled trip to Florida to interview Roswell Gilbert, who had recently lost an appeal of his murder conviction.

Two years earlier Roswell Gilbert had fired two bullets into his wife's head as she lay on the sofa in their Sea Ranch Lakes, Florida, condominium. News reports had said that Emily Gilbert, who had Alzheimer's disease, had begged her husband to kill her. However, under cross-examination, Gilbert had testified that he had "never talked with Emily about killing her and had decided to shoot her from behind so she would not see the gun." Derek had previously called Mrs. Gilbert's shooting an act of "premeditated mercy" and had been using coverage of Gilbert's appeal to draw attention to Hemlock's legislative efforts.

According to Ann, Derek did join her in Massachusetts after he had finished in Florida, but it wasn't out of any "noble motivation" on his part to help her deal with her parents. "It was because we had planned this holiday, and Derek never did well on his own," she recounted. "He couldn't cope for himself. He couldn't do his own laundry. . . ."

All of Ann's last-minute attempts to find some kind of acceptable living arrangement for her parents were met with Arthur's rejection. He had decided that he and Ruth would die, and there would be no turning back. The suicide note was written. Its text, appearing in their obituary in the Boston *Globe* on July 23, 1986, reads: "We have led full and fruitful lives, but now that we are in frail health we choose to die in a peaceful and dignified manner."

Derek and Ann prepared the Vesparax, pulverizing it and mixing it with food. Then they helped the elderly couple to their rooms. Derek accompanied Arthur to one room for his death. Ann and her mother went into the other bedroom. According to the plan, Ann fed the lethal mixture to her mother, who took it with the stoicism that had marked her entire married life. But everything did not go as expected.

Ann later described what happened: "My mother started to die, and then something went wrong, and it was awful. Her breathing started to get sort of agitated, and I got really scared. And Derek had always said to me, you know, 'Just use a plastic bag or a pillow.' And I just did it because I was so terrified. There was a plastic laundry bag with her linens, her soiled linen in it, and I took the bag and I just very gently held it over her mouth. And I have never gotten over that. And she died very peacefully.

"But I walked away from that house thinking we're both murderers and I can't live like this anymore."

In the days and weeks after Ann and Derek had returned home from Massachusetts, Ann tried to work through her feelings about what she had done. After all, she told herself, she'd written about "helping" people die for years. In real life, however, it wasn't turning out the way it had on paper. Ann couldn't stop thinking about her parents. She cried. She looked at old family pictures. All she wanted to do was talk about her mother and father.

Some of what Ann was feeling can be seen in *Double Exit*, the book she wrote a year later as a way of trying to come to terms with it all. After we had become friends, Ann made it clear that this book, like *Jean's Way*, was greatly sanitized. But sanitized or not, *Double Exit* is extremely depressing and incredibly sad. The shy, sensitive little girl, trying so hard to do whatever would make her parents love her, was still there.

Describing events in the last hours before her parents died, the narrator Claudia, says, "It's clear now: My mother and father are going to orphan me. For all the terrible rifts that have existed between us, for all the unfinished business that I had hoped would be put to rest and wasn't, they are still my mommy and daddy and I am somewhere back in ankle socks and braids. . . ." Soon after they died, the fictional Claudia, while looking at old family photographs, reflects on how distant her parents always seemed to her and to each other. "In the end, I am the residue of two strangers' lives," she says.

According to Ann, Derek was not interested in sharing any of her grief. He was immersed in plans for the upcoming Hemlock conference scheduled to take place in Washington, D.C., in September. This particular conference was to be a very important step—the first big Hemlock event to be held away from the West Coast. Everything needed to be perfect. In the nation's capital Hemlock would unveil its plans to launch a campaign in California to have euthanasia laws changed. Scheduled to keynote the event was Betty Rollin, whose book *Last Wish*, about her mother's death, was topping the best seller lists.

Just two weeks after they had returned home from Massachusetts, Derek told Ann that she was to give a presentation on mercy killing at the conference. She found the idea appalling so soon after the deaths of her parents.

"I was a basket case," she said, in relating the story to me later. "I hadn't had time to grieve. There'd been no memorial service. . . . There's a very, very hard part of Derek. . . .

"He told me, 'You're giving that speech about mercy killing cases whether you like it or not . . . and if you don't do it, I'm going to be forced to act in such a way that won't be pleasing to you.' "

Ann felt he'd given her an ultimatum. If she didn't give the speech, he'd leave. He told her, "I'm sick and tired of hearing about your parents, and I never want to hear about them again as long as I live."

When he said that, Ann started crying again, repeating that she couldn't give the speech. "I was just a wreck," she told me.

According to Ann, Derek wouldn't take no for an answer. He insisted, saying, "I do it all the time. Why do you think you should be any different, for Christ's sake?"

After that argument, Ann remembered, Derek walked out of the living room and went into the bathroom. She could tell he was angry, and that was very rare. Ann admitted to being the one with the hot temper, but while Derek rarely got angry, when he did, it was time to back off.

This time, however, Ann couldn't. She knocked on the bathroom door and recalled saying, "I want to ask you something."

Derek opened the door. "What?"

"I saw you mourn for Jean for two years, and I held your hand. I saw you through the grieving, and I helped you write a book about it. She's been part of our marriage for all these years, and I've never complained. Yet my parents have been dead for just two weeks, and you've told me I should never speak about them again."

Ann told me Derek just looked at her and said, "Well, that's different. We made a business out of Jean."

The third annual Hemlock conference took place in Washington in September 1986. Ann did as Derek had ordered. She was listed on the program as an authority on mercy killing and, according to her own account, gave the worst speech she'd ever given.

I was in the audience at that conference, and I remember her presentation very well. At the time I thought she was the coldest speaker I had ever heard at a euthanasia meeting. She recited case histories. She listed statistics. She spoke intelligently, but in a voice that was totally devoid of feeling.

It was clear from mealtime discussions afterward that others had been put off by her demeanor as well. "They shouldn't have her speak. She makes it sound so awful," one woman seated across from me said. Others at our luncheon table, all avid Hemlock supporters, nodded in agreement. "Keep her off the stage. She's fine as a writer, but she's terrible as a speaker. No compassion at all," said one. Of course, no one at the time had any idea of what Ann was going through.

Other speakers at the conference did come across with feeling, discussing compassion, caring, and support. After a workshop session on grief, Dr. Admiraal of Holland told how enriching it is for children if they're present when their parents die. "We invite them to be there the moment I give the needle injection," he said.

On the first evening of the conference Derek Humphry introduced the keynote speaker, Betty Rollin, by saying, "Helping another to die is a great act of love."

In her speech Rollin talked about her mother, who, she said, "died coolly. She picked the day. . . . She died in charge. She died herself. . . . My memory of her is a memory of a person I know—not of a disintegrated vegetable." When the book about assisting her mother's suicide came out, Rollin said she "had expected to be, at worst, arrested and, at best vilified." But the negative reaction hadn't materialized. Rollin told us she had received a thousand letters. "Only one was even mildly critical, and a lot of these people are religious people. . . ."

During the question and answer session, Rollin was asked if she had ever tried to talk her mother out of suicide. Had she ever even questioned her mother's decision or her own role in helping her mother commit suicide? She responded that she had not. Her mother, she explained, knew what she wanted, and Rollin at no time felt that her mother had made the wrong decision. "She had such a good life. . . . All I did was listen and not turn away. I didn't try to talk her out of it because what she wanted was clear, and it was the most reasonable thing in the world."

Rollin, who has been a news broadcaster for both ABC and NBC, told the conference audience, "I'm happy you are all here fighting for changes in the law. People who aren't in favor of this don't have much imagination. . . ."

The next day the proposed law change was introduced. Derek explained that Hemlock had given fifty thousand dollars in seed money to create a new, "purely political" organization. Two months earlier the *Hemlock Quarterly* had announced that a Miami man had donated fifty thousand dollars to Hemlock for the purpose of launching the legislative effort.

Called Americans Against Human Suffering (AAHS), the new sister organization of Hemlock—Derek later called it "Hemlock's affinity group"—would target California. "California is a bellwether state," Humphry explained. "It was that state where the first Living Will law was passed. . . . The real action is just about to begin. . . . Once one influential state has accepted the principle and made it law, then others will follow. . . ."

Plans called for AAHS to gather signatures in California to place an initiative measure on that state's 1988 ballot, allowing for euthanasia by such methods as lethal injection or drug overdose. Derek explained that using the ballot box and public opinion would be far more likely to succeed than any attempt to get changes in the law directly through the legislature.

Robert Risley, a Los Angeles attorney, had been tapped to head AAHS. Derek and Ann both were on its board of directors, and Derek was the group's vice-president. Betty Rollin was a member of its advisory committee.

Risley, along with Hemlock officials Alan Johnson and Curt Garbesi, as well as Texas physician William Winslade, who had been present at the very first organizational meetings of Hemlock, told conference participants about the proposal. Called the Humane and Dignified Death Act, it would not be a totally new law but would, instead, amend the existing California Living Will law to allow for aid-in-dying.

"We're involved in a bold venture," Risley said. "We seek

to change sanctions that have existed in Western civilization for four thousand years. How dare we be so bold? Because we seek human dignity, self-determination and the right to privacy." Life that was "devoid of hope . . . is not the type of life we cherish."

The proposal would allow euthanasia "only" for those who were predicted to have life expectancies of six months or less. "It may be too narrow but, again, it's kind of a political thing that we're making it so narrow," Risley went on to say. Then he listed other reasons why California was likely to be the place where the first aid-in-dying amendments would pass, explaining once again that these amendments to the Living Will law would make only minor changes to existing California law.

Risley pointed to a recent court case as support for the concept of physician-induced death. Just five months before the conference, a California appeals court had decided that twenty-eight-year-old Elizabeth Bouvia had a "right to die." Mrs. Bouvia, severely disabled from cerebral palsy and arthritis, had checked herself into a hospital in late 1983, asking that she be given pain medication while she starved herself to death. In his concurring opinion, one judge, Justice Lynn D. Compton, had written:

> Elizabeth apparently has made a conscious and informed choice that she prefers death to continued existence in her helpless and, to her, intolerable condition. . . . The fact that she is forced to suffer the ordeal of self-starvation to achieve her objective is in itself inhumane. The right to die is an integral part of our

right to control our own destinies so long as the rights of others are not affected. That right should, in my opinion, include the ability to enlist assistance from others, including the medical profession, in making death as painless and quick as possible.

The appeals court decision had been but the latest in a series of court proceedings surrounding Mrs. Bouvia. Although news coverage centered almost entirely on her disabilities, little mention was made of other factors in her life that may have prompted her death wish. For example, in the twenty-four months immediately preceding her decision to starve herself, her brother had died, she had dropped out of graduate school, she had suffered a miscarriage, and her marriage had dissolved. Yet the court, in making its decision, chose to ignore those matters, assuming that her disability was the sole reason she found her life unbearable.

For the newly formed AAHS, however, the court decision—especially Justice Compton's words—seemed to bode very well for getting a euthanasia initiative on the California ballot. "A more striking pronouncement from the bench has not occurred before this," Robert Risley said.

Although California was to be the main target for changes in the law, conference participants made it clear that other states would not be neglected. The director of the Hemlock chapter in Illinois explained that his chapter was promoting aid-in-dying with legislators. "We're talking with our state representatives about dovetailing into the Living Will act we have now," he said. One participant also suggested that those in attendance from states where Living Will laws weren't yet on the books might want to concentrate their efforts on passing such measures.

The Hemlock Society, along with AAHS, was off and running toward its goal: passage of aid-in-dying amendments to existing laws. With the formation of AAHS, the first concrete step to change the law had been taken. As Derek had announced, the real action was about to begin.

CHAPTER 5

■ ■ ■

Although in that fall of 1986 Ann's conflicts about the deaths of her parents continued, and her relationship with Derek remained strained, she hoped the writing of *Double Exit* would help her resolve her feelings. If Derek could deal with what had happened, she told herself, she should be able to. All she needed was some sort of catharsis, perhaps something that would come from her work on the book. Writing *Double Exit* took much of her focus for the next two years.

The work for Hemlock was also increasing. The task of garnering support for the California initiative was to go into full gear by the beginning of 1987 and would last for seventeen months. Along with this new activity came the need to protect Hemlock's tax-exempt status. At this point the organization was bringing in more than a half million dollars a year.

According to Ann, a lot of pressure was being put on

Hemlock to pour more and more money into political activity. Money also became a topic of much discussion. Ann remembered that a lot of "juggling" had to be done with mailing lists, goods and services, and the flow of money, so that Hemlock, which wasn't supposed to be engaged in legislative activity, could funnel funds to its sister organization, AAHS, without incurring tax problems.

Ann was careful to acknowledge that much of the juggling on Derek's part was a genuine attempt to stay within the law. It was not so much an effort to be deceptive as it was the unfamiliarity with U.S. law and the newness of dealing with an organization that had so quickly obtained large amounts of cash.

Ann referred to another activity going on during this time, which was not made public and was kept hidden even from other Hemlock officials. She told me that board members had made it clear that Hemlock was not going to become involved with any kind of death-producing drugs, and they had expressly forbidden Derek to do so. According to Ann, however, Derek ignored them, though he kept it very discreet and didn't even tell her about all the cases.

She explained how it was done: "He would receive calls at the office. If he believed they were genuine, he would bundle up Vesparax and send it out in a plain brown envelope with no return address, no means of identification. Sometimes he wouldn't go into great detail with the people who were calling. He'd just say, 'This is the way it's going to be, and this might help.' "

There were many pills left from the five hundred that had been ordered when Ann's parents had decided to kill themselves. Ann and Derek had used some on her parents. Ann kept some for herself, and Derek kept the rest.

The thought that the pills were being given to other people, however, sickened Ann.

Although she wasn't involved in the process, Ann did claim to know that when Derek ran out of Vesparax, he started providing information—the name, address, and phone number of the Swiss pharmacy, as well as instructions on how to place an order. According to Ann, the Swiss pharmacy was an active source of Vesparax for at least three years, but it eventually stopped shipping drugs ordered by phone.

Hemlock focused much of its activity throughout 1987 on the upcoming California initiative. In January 1988 the movement received a huge boost with the now-famous "It's Over, Debbie" article that was published in that month's issue of the *Journal of the American Medical Association*.

The article was written by an anonymous resident physician, who related an incident in which a twenty-year-old cancer patient, known only as Debbie, was intentionally given a lethal dose of morphine. According to the story, Debbie hadn't asked for an overdose. The doctor, after hearing her say, "Let's get this over with," as she sat in her bed, had requested that a nurse prepare a syringe of morphine sulfate—enough "to do the job." Debbie was told she would be given "something that would let her rest." She was dead within minutes.

No one knows if there really was a Debbie. Dr. George Lundberg, *JAMA*'s editor, later admitted that there had been no attempt to authenticate the piece. He said it had been published to serve as a catalyst for the discussion of euthanasia. Whether authentic or not, the article gave new impetus to the debate over mercy killing. It marked the first time the question of euthanasia was given serious consideration by one of the two major medical journals in the country. Euthanasia was no longer seriously discussed just within the confines of right-to-die conferences; it had now entered the realm of respectable debate within the general medical establishment.

This development was reinforced ten months later, when Dr. Marcia Angell, executive editor of the other major U.S. medical journal, the *New England Journal of Medicine*, wrote an editorial in which she stated, "Many of us believe that euthanasia is appropriate under certain conditions and that it should indeed be legalized. . . ."

All the publicity and the spate of articles surrounding the Debbie controversy were very important to Hemlock and AAHS as the May deadline for getting the California initiative on the ballot approached. In April the World Federation of Right to Die Societies was holding its seventh biennial convention in San Francisco, with Hemlock as the host organization. In addition to marking the fiftieth anniversary of the American euthanasia movement, the conference was expected to be a victory celebration for the signature-gathering effort to put aid-in-dying on California's November ballot. The convention was even called "A Humane and Dignified Death," named after the ballot proposal's title.

A formal debate between Hemlock and the International Anti-Euthanasia Task Force was scheduled as the "curtain raiser" for the conference. Since its beginning in 1987, the task force, headquartered in Steubenville, Ohio, had concentrated its efforts on public education about euthanasia. As part of that effort there had, of course, been many occasions during which informal debates between task force and Hemlock representatives had taken place on radio and television programs. These had all been arranged by the media and, due to the time constraints of programming schedules, often left audiences with many unanswered questions. The San Francisco debate was different and allowed adequate opportunity and equal time for exploration of the volatile topic from both points of view.

The task force had extended an invitation to Hemlock two months before the conference, believing it important to raise awareness about some of the consequences that could follow legalization of aid-in-dying. Four of us, two for Hemlock and two for the task force, were scheduled to speak. The agreed-upon title was "Aid-in-Dying: The Right to Die or the Right to Kill?"

The debate took place at the University of San Francisco. Robert Risley, speaking for Hemlock, emphasized that polls over the past decade had indicated growing public approval for the concept of "physician assistance in dying." I was one of the speakers for the task force and pointed out that as written, the California initiative would allow aid-in-dying to be administered by any licensed health professional acting under the direction of a physician, a category that, in California, includes dispensing opticians, podiatrists, and acupuncturists. I was also concerned that it be understood that aid-in-dying was defined in the initiative as "*any* medical procedure which swiftly, painlessly, and humanely terminates the life of a qualified patient."

In his speech Derek emphasized that a brighter, more educated public wants to make decisions about "how they shall die at life's end." He also discussed "the myth which comes up of the Hippocratic Oath" and how the medical profession has altered it whenever needed. Dr. Joseph Stanton, a task force adviser and a former professor of medicine at Tufts University, asked that everyone reflect on what it would be like for the person in the hospital if aid-in-dying became the law of the land. "When the hospital door opens," he said, "the patient could never be sure whether the care giver bears water or the syringe with the fatal dose in the outstretched hand."

We at the task force were pleased by the debate. While Hemlock supporters seemed to outnumber ours in the audience, we thought we had given both sides a good hearing and had made people think more seriously about the headlong rush to death on demand.

I was surprised by one thing at the debate, however, and that could best be described as Derek's change in attitude. Contrary to his usual politeness and good cheer, to me he seemed sullen, almost abrupt and rude. It was as though Derek, feeling seriously challenged for the first time, took it all very personally. It seems we were no longer friendly adversaries—just adversaries.

Later I found out that by this time it was clear to Hemlock members that contrary to their expectations, they would not have enough signatures to put the California initiative on the ballot in November. Their supporters attributed the failure to poor organization and lack of funds, vowing to continue their efforts in other states.

* * *

In his remarks at the debate Robert Risley had briefly
referred to what had become the most heated development
on the euthanasia front, which continues to this day: the
issue of removing food and fluids to bring about death.

Basic care—food, water, a warm bed, and attention to
personal hygiene—had been regarded throughout history
as a right of all patients. By the mid-eighties, however,
the removal of food and fluids from profoundly disabled
individuals had been elevated to a topic of debate by respected ethicists. The controversy was *not* about those who
could not tolerate food and fluids in the final hours or days
of life. Cases that came to public attention had nothing to
do with patients who were dying. Instead they centered on
attempts to *make* people die.

More than anything else, the food and fluids debate has
influenced the course of medical ethics today. Central to
the discussion is the inaccurate implication that tube feeding is a new technology of a rare and exotic nature. However, food and water have been provided by means of what
is called a gastrostomy tube for more than one hundred
years. A gastrostomy tube is inserted through the abdomi-
nal wall directly into the stomach by a simple surgical procedure that can be performed under local anesthesia. Once
the tube has been inserted, the small incision heals and
causes little or no discomfort to the majority of patients.

It soon became obvious that the classification of tube
feeding as extraordinary medical treatment depended
greatly on the social or economic status of a patient as well
as on the desires of the patient's family. A prime illustration

was the case of Mary Hier, a resident at a Beverly, Massachusetts, care facility.

Ninety-two years old, Mary Hier had lived in mental
institutions for more than half of her life. She was not
terminally ill; in fact, she was not physically ill at all. She
was severely demented, however, convinced that she was
the queen of England.

Because she had a benign condition that made it almost
impossible for adequate food and fluids to pass down her
esophagus into her stomach, she had received food
through a gastrostomy tube for years. Somehow, in an
unexplained incident, the tube became dislodged. When
the care facility where she was a resident sought permission
to replace the tube, physicians testified that this would not
be in her best interests. A Massachusetts court ruled that
Mary Hier would have refused the procedure if she were
competent and called its replacement a "highly intrusive
and risky procedure." The decision was reported in a Boston paper.

Another story in the same newspaper concerned a
ninety-four-year-old woman, who was described as doing
well following "minor surgery to correct a nutritional problem." The surgery had taken place on an outpatient basis
under local anesthesia. The procedure, which had been
described as "minor surgery," was the insertion of a gastrostomy tube. But this woman's name was Rose Fitzgerald
Kennedy.

For Mary Hier, demented and poor, insertion of a gastrostomy tube was described as highly invasive and highly
risky. For Rose Kennedy, mother of a former President

and matriarch of a rich and powerful family, it was termed a minor medical procedure.

Fortunately for Mary Hier, others intervened on her behalf, and the judge allowed reinsertion of her gastrostomy tube. For years Hier continued to live comfortably and happily—still signing her name, "Mary Hier, Queen of England." The court's decision, however, remains unchanged on the books.

Other stories have not had such happy endings, especially in cases of severely brain-damaged individuals. Throughout the time when board-certified neurologists have been called as expert witnesses to testify about the medical condition of various patients, conflicting diagnoses have been given and a dehumanizing process has occurred. Often the most demeaning language has been used to describe such individuals, as happened in the case of Nancy Ellen Jobes.

While driving to her job as a lab technician in Dover, New Jersey, on the morning of March 11, 1980, twenty-five-year-old Nancy Ellen Jobes was in a car accident. She was four months pregnant at the time. While her injuries were not severe, a follow-up ultrasound determined that the baby had died.

During surgery to remove her dead child, an anesthesia accident occurred, leaving Nancy Ellen Jobes with brain damage. Three months later she was transferred from the hospital to Lincoln Park Nursing Home. She was on no "medical equipment" but was totally dependent on others for her care. Food and water were provided to her through a feeding tube. She was in such good health that she did not receive a single dose of antibiotic medicine during her years as a resident at Lincoln Park Nursing Home. Her ability to live with only the same level of care as that provided to thirty-one other patients in the same facility was not questioned. And because her injuries were related to a car accident, all medical expenses, including all nursing home costs, were covered by her car insurance.

Her husband, John Jobes, filed a malpractice suit against the doctors and nurses who had participated in his wife's surgery. Four years after that the case was settled for nine hundred thousand dollars, and, a short time later, Nancy Ellen's husband requested that her food and fluids be stopped. The question was not, *Could* she live? Instead it was, *Should* she live?

At the court hearings experts were called to testify. Dr. Fred Plum, the director of neurology at Cornell University Medical College, testified, "Mrs. Jobes is generally in excellent medical condition, almost without complications," but he said he would stop her feeding.

Another neurologist described her as a "monstrosity." "She is not functioning," he said in his testimony. "She is receiving the same kind of care that we would lavish on an experimental project in our laboratory to maintain something as in an animal we are working on. . . ."

Other expert witnesses disagreed with these positions. Dr. Maurice Victor, a board-certified neurologist, professor of neurology at Case Western Reserve, and coauthor of a leading neurology textbook, stated that Mrs. Jobes was aware and responsive. "I gave her a number of verbal requests, and it became apparent the patient could hear and understand what I was saying. . . . I said, 'Pick up your head,' . . . and within no more than one or two seconds she picked up her head. . . . I said, 'Nancy, wiggle your toes,' . . . she made a distinct recognizable movement of the toes."

Dr. Allan Ropper, an associate professor of neurology at Harvard Medical School who maintains an active practice treating patients with severe brain injury, testified that Nancy Ellen could see and hear, respond to commands, make purposeful and volitional movements, could fatigue and feel pain. Ropper also explained that tests performed by physicians who concluded that Mrs. Jobes was in a vegetative state may have been invalid because of the high level of medication given to her prior to testing.

News accounts continued to label her as "comatose," and the Reverend George Vorsheim, pastor of the Presbyterian Church of Morris Plains and religious adviser to the Jobes family, said that "prolonging the shell is the essence of futility."

Dr. Daniel Carlin, a neurologist at Morristown Memorial Hospital, said, "Nancy died and she should have a funeral." Her husband told the Associated Press, "I'd really like to get on with my life," but said he couldn't do so until he had spread Nancy Ellen's ashes over Lake Tahoe.

Following an appeal of a lower court ruling, the New Jersey Supreme Court, in a six to one decision on June 24, 1987, granted John Jobes the right to order that his wife be starved and dehydrated to death. According to the nursing home, he had gone for a year without visiting her.

When Lincoln Park Nursing Home's administration and staff continued to voice strong opposition to carrying out the order, Nancy Ellen was transferred to a nearby hospital. Not giving up, Jeryl Turco, Lincoln Park's administrator, took out an ad in the local newspaper, begging that Nancy Ellen's life be spared. She went on to describe the horrifying process of what would happen to Nancy Ellen if she were dehydrated to death:

1. Her mouth would dry out and become cracked or coated with thick material.
2. Her lips would become parched and cracked or fissured.
3. Her tongue would become swollen and might crack.
4. Her eyelids would sink back into their orbits.
5. Her cheeks would become hollow.
6. The mucous lining of her nose might crack and cause her nose to bleed.
7. Her skin would hang loose on her body and become dry and scaly.
8. Her urine would become highly concentrated causing burning of the bladder.
9. The lining of her stomach would dry out causing dry heaves and vomiting.
10. She would develop a very high body temperature.
11. Her brain cells would begin drying out causing convulsions.
12. Her respiratory tract would dry out giving rise to very thick secretions which would plug her lungs and cause death.
13. Eventually her major organs would fail including her lungs, heart, and brain.

Obviously doses of medication can be given so that the distress of the patient is masked, making it appear to observers that death by dehydration is not a horrible fate. Additionally, some who advocate the removal of food and water from severely disabled patients point to cases of people who, when they are within hours or a few days of death, discontinue taking any nourishment or liquid and die without experiencing any of the horrifying symptoms of dehydration. Yet this latter type of case, in which the body is naturally shutting down as death draws near, is far different from that in which a totally dependent, nondying individual still needs food and water. In the nondying person, death is not approaching; it is induced by the removal of a basic necessity.

In commenting on Nancy Ellen Jobes, Turco observed: "There is nothing 'merciful' about this process.... The Nancy Ellen Jobes case has demonstrated that American society is far more interested in the earning potential than the lives of its citizens, but to ask our hospitals and health care institutions to become exterminating grounds is the greatest insult to the medical profession and the gravest injustice to God and to humanity.... We ask the community to speak up against this outrage." The silence was deadly.

Nancy Ellen Jobes died on August 7, 1987, only days after her food and fluids had been stopped. Writing later in the *Hastings Center Report*, Paul Armstrong, the attorney for the Jobes family, and B. D. Colen described patients in Nancy Ellen's condition as "nonmentative organ systems, artificially sustained like valued cell lines in cancer laboratories."

The appalling reality of a death such as that of Nancy Ellen Jobes has been at the core of the euthanasia movement's arguments. In prefacing his remarks at the debate at the University of San Francisco, Robert Risley had stated that the word "kill" was "absolutely an inappropriate concept" in discussions of aid-in-dying. Outlining his argument, he stated that in most states there are Living Will statutes that permit the withholding or withdrawal of food and water. This, he explained, means that "you are going to die either of starvation or dehydration. . . .

"There must be a better way," he went on to say. "There is a better way." The better way he was referring to, of course, was aid-in-dying. When compared with something as horrible as death by dehydration, giving a lethal injection or a fatal overdose does, indeed, appear humane.

This logical progression—from causing death by dehydration to causing death by more humane methods—has been noted by a number of euthanasia advocates, notably Helga Kuhse, a professor of philosophy at Monash University in Melbourne, Australia. Lately at the forefront of advocating ending the lives of handicapped newborns, Kuhse has said that once people see how painful death by starvation and dehydration is, then, "in the patient's best interest," they will accept the lethal injection.

It is, of course, correct that once it has been decided that the patient must die, the lethal injection is quicker, more efficient, and more humane than the long, often gruesome five- to twenty-one-day deathwatch during which a person dies slowly from lack of food and water. The difference is one of method.

As Dr. Stanton reminded the audience at the California

debate, just as "a rose is a rose is a rose," so, too, "killing is killing is killing."

Neither Ann nor Derek was a major player at the 1988 world conference, which took place right after the debate, though each of them did have a part in the proceedings. Derek introduced one session featuring Brian Clark, the author of the hit play *Whose Life Is It Anyway?*, which served as a focal point on the discussion on the effect of literature on the progress of the euthanasia movement. Ann served as the moderator for a panel discussion of modern attitudes toward the beginning and ending of life.

By this time—almost two years after her parents' deaths—she found herself in the paradoxical position of being second-in-command of the country's most outspoken euthanasia group although her own doubts about mercy killing were by no means resolved. Still very much the good trouper, however, Ann dutifully delivered her performance at the conference with the cool efficiency that she had perfected.

The apparent failure to gather enough signatures for putting the aid-in-dying initiative on the California ballot dampened the 1988 conference for Hemlock and its supporters. It was not the victory celebration it had been intended to be, though it did receive a fair amount of publicity.

The focus of the conference was on "rights," as speaker after speaker called for legalization of aid-in-dying. Speaker of the California Assembly Willie Brown keynoted the conference and set the tone when he described the central issue as "whether or not you have a right to control your destiny and seek assistance" in matters related to your life.

Sidney Rosoff, chairman of the Society for the Right to Die (and now president of the Hemlock Society), recounted the fifty-year history of the American euthanasia movement. In acknowledging that advocacy for aid-in-dying went back to 1938, when his organization had started as the Euthanasia Society of America, he made the point that "In a sense, our origins are what Hemlock represents today." It was an indication that although the major euthanasia organizations in the country had different images and methodologies, they all were coming together and supporting what Hemlock was actively promoting: eventual change in the laws of all states to allow the administering of euthanasia. While the goals of the movement had always been the same, it was just the public image that was different. As George Annas, professor of health law and chief of the health law section at the Boston University School of Public Health, observed, "Euthanasia is much more nuanced, more subtle today than when it began in 1938." Annas had served on the board of the Euthanasia Educational Council and later was a legal adviser to the organization.

Remarks made by two conference speakers were neither subtle nor nuanced, reflecting the disdain with which some euthanasia advocates view those in opposition to it.

Colin Brewer, a British psychiatrist, is known for his leadership in England's euthanasia movement as well as for being the premier instructor on the method of achieving "self-deliverance" by means of a plastic bag. (It is Brewer's how-to method that has been widely publicized by the Hemlock Society.)

Currently serving on the Working Party of the Institute of Medical Ethics in England, Brewer has advocated planned death for the incapacitated as well as for the terminally ill. He contends that severely disabled persons should be eligible for death if their condition will distress others. According to Brewer, euthanasia could effectively prevent a person from being remembered "as a slobbering wreck."

At the California conference he expressed outrage at those who would base opposition to euthanasia on religious principles. "In Britain we don't take our religious lunatics seriously," he said.

Stephen K. Yarnell, a California psychiatrist who was active in Hemlock, invoked freedom of religion as the basis for passing aid-in-dying laws. "I am a Humanist," he said, "and I belong to the Unitarian Church." He explained that his religion supports the right to euthanasia, and because of his own weakening condition from AIDS, he should be able to receive aid-in-dying in an atmosphere where his family, friends, minister, and doctor could be present without fear of legal repercussions. He said the help of the doctor is needed both to administer euthanasia and to decide when it's the right time to die.

When he was asked what ramifications euthanasia acceptance might have on nursing home patients, Yarnell replied, "I think it's a horrible travesty to *let* people die. We ought to kill them because it will bring it right out in the open and make it a decision people will have to think about." (Yarnell died of AIDS three months after the conference.)

Canadian delegate and the outgoing president of the World Federation Patrick Nowell-Smith expressed the "need" for legalization of euthanasia in a more novel way. Nowell-Smith, who was at one time a philosophy professor at Toronto's York University, said, "People who want to commit suicide want to do it in a manner that is not horrendous either to themselves or those who have to clean up the mess. That's why we believe it's necessary to have medical aid-in-dying. It's essential if we're to avoid people blowing out their brains or throwing themselves under subway trains."

One of the conference highlights was a special by-invitation-only reception to honor Abigail Van Buren, who received an award from the Society for the Right to Die. It was her second such honor. In 1983 the society had given her an award for her work in promoting the Living Will. This time she received the Helen B. Taussig Medal for "distinguished services to the cause of patients' rights."

At the end of the conference Derek Humphry did find himself in the limelight—literally—when the play *Is This the Day?*, the dramatic adaptation of *Jean's Way*, was performed as a means of obtaining constructive criticism before any attempted public presentation. It was not a great success, however, and it was several years before it was performed briefly in London. Attempts to promote it commercially in the United States have resulted in only one brief run in Eugene, Oregon, in early 1992.

A few months after the world conference, in the summer of 1988, Hemlock moved its national headquarters from Los Angeles to Eugene, Oregon. With the failure of the California initiative, the states of Oregon and Washington were seen as more fertile ground for accomplishing Hemlock's goals. A cozy little white-frame bungalow complete with black shutters and neatly trimmed shrubbery became the new center of activity for the organization. During the following year a number of different fronts—the courtroom, the classroom, and the legislature—kept Hemlock busy in its work of pushing the euthanasia movement forward.

Ongoing support was being provided for Marty James, a thirty-four-year-old man who had said on a March 31, 1988, broadcast of *Nightline* that he had prepared the deadly concoction of barbiturates that killed his lover, ill with AIDS. His statement prompted an investigation by the San Francisco district attorney's office, and Hemlock paid legal fees for him. When it was announced that he would not be prosecuted—his admissions of guilt were considered insufficient evidence—Derek expressed disappointment that the case had not gone forward. "Whilst we are glad to see Mr. James freed of the danger of prosecution and imprisonment, it would have made a significant test case of a person's right to choose when to die, and to get help as well," he said.

The following month James appeared on Seattle television, accompanied by his attorney, Michael White. White had been the coauthor of Hemlock's 1988 California aid-in-dying initiative and James's Hemlock-paid attorney in the *Nightline* investigation. On the Seattle show James claimed he had participated in the induction of at least eight deaths and supplied lethal doses to six other unidentified AIDS patients.

He described how he had helped one man, known as Joey, kill another, whom he called Ronnie. "Very gently Joey and I placed the plastic bag over his head. When we went to secure the bag with a belt very lightly, Joey reached his hand out and said, 'If we're going to murder Ronnie . . . then I want to do it.' " These admissions on the Seattle program did not result in any legal action.

The lack of inquiry into the circumstances surrounding Ronnie's death raises yet more disturbing questions. Would there have been similar uninterest by those sworn to protect *all* citizens if Ronnie had been someone's husband and father or if he had been the heir to a fortune? Or was he, like those who are disabled or poor, considered in a separate category—a category of expendable people? Is admitted murder by means of a plastic bag secured with a belt around the victim's neck somehow acceptable if the victim is gay? Or does the silence following the televised program speak volumes about societal attitudes?

At the same time Hemlock was also involved in another case on the other side of the country—that of Peter Rosier, a physician. It was another instance of compassion being given as the reason for assisting in a death, yet the case showed how much more could lie under the surface than at first appears in so many of these situations.

The story had many bizarre twists and turns. According to published reports, forty-three-year-old Patricia Rosier had been told by her husband that she would die a horrible death from her lung cancer. And so, after an elegant farewell dinner and one last time of lovemaking, she took the barbiturates he had given her. When the pills failed to end her life, Peter Rosier injected her with what he thought was a lethal amount of morphine. Four hours later she was still alive. It was then that her stepfather, who was also at the couple's home, realized he couldn't wait any longer for her to die. He had a plane to meet. While Rosier was out of the room, Patricia Rosier's stepfather put his hands over her face and suffocated her.

Rosier caught the attention of a local prosecutor when he discussed his wife's death on a Florida television show and talked about the book he had written about it. He wanted to have the book published and made into a movie. The TV appearance apparently did not attract a publisher. The local prosecutor, however, brought charges.

Prior to the trial, Patricia Rosier's stepfather obtained immunity in exchange for agreeing to testify on behalf of the prosecution. He admitted to suffocating his stepdaughter. A former friend testified that Rosier had boasted about getting rich by writing the book on his role in his wife's death. Rosier was found not guilty.

Commenting on the verdict, Derek called it a victory but said there were lessons to be learned from it, one of which was "Don't invite the whole family to the deliverance" since that could discourage a doctor from helping.

A few short months after the Rosier verdict Derek made a significant trip to Iowa. At a meeting there—which he attended to comment formally on a newly drafted model aid-in-dying law—he met the person who was one day to replace Ann as Hemlock's deputy director.

The event was a one-day hearing held on April 4, 1989, at the University of Iowa College of Law. The law school, which is noted for drafting laws that subsequently receive serious consideration in legislatures, had drafted a Model Aid-in-Dying Act. Invitations had been extended to various groups, inviting testimony on the proposal. Derek was there to testify in favor of the model law; I was present to oppose it.

The model law, which was later published in the *Iowa Law Review*, went further than even Hemlock had previously ventured. It would, for example, allow parents of children under the age of six to request aid-in-dying for their child. A child, who is six years of age or older, could make a death request, and if the parents disagreed, the child could take his or her request before a special aid-in-dying board, where the final decision would be made. The commentary to the model law explains that "minors have the right to request aid-in-dying whether or not their parents agree."

Aid-in-dying, defined to include "the administration of a qualified drug for the purpose of inducing death," could be administered not only by doctors and nurses but also by one who paid a fee and passed a test (somewhat similar to the procedure for obtaining a driver's license).

Among drafters of the model act was Cheryl Smith, a student in her final year of law school. She was selected to provide transportation for Derek Humphry while he was at the university to testify for the proposal. The day after the meeting Smith sent Derek a letter to follow up on a discussion they'd had about her applying for work with Hemlock after her graduation. Six weeks later she was hired, and Derek sent her a "welcome to the team" memo.

Cheryl Smith, one of the drafters of the model law that would allow second graders to request death for themselves, was now on board at Hemlock. She was to move to Eugene and begin work in September.

CHAPTER 6

■ ■ ■

When Derek and Ann moved Hemlock's headquarters to Eugene, Oregon, in the summer of 1988, they moved their residence to Monroe, less than a half hour drive from Eugene on Oregon's Highway 99. A town of 465 people with a bank, four churches, a volunteer fire department, and a phone company owned by the mayor, this close-knit community was where Ann and Derek bought forty-two acres of land, calling it Windfall Farm.

They both liked the pastoral serenity of the place. A rustic, inviting wooden house is set at the end of a long, narrow drive bordered with split timber fencing. A few hundred feet past the carport, down an incline covered with thick tangles of wild blackberry vines and underbrush, is a clear natural pond where swans—Derek's birds, Ann used to call them—as well as geese and ducks made their home. The pond is hemmed in on three sides by heavy maples nestled among Douglas and Noble firs. From atop a hill, one can look over acres of lush green fields full of wild dogwood flowers. The silence is broken only by the rustling of leaves, the soft whinnying of a horse, or, if the wind is right, the sound of a logging truck down on a distant road.

It was in this setting of peaceful contentment that Ann's world shattered one morning in September 1989. When Ann woke up—it was a typical early-September morning—fog hung gently, like a cozy blanket, over the house and pond. Getting out of bed, she went into the bathroom and turned on a warm shower. She stepped in. First she worked shampoo into her hair and, head bent back, let the rich whipped-cream lather run off her hair down her back. Then she began to rub soap on her arms, her neck, her breasts— She stopped. Just on the underside of her breast she felt something.

Wide-awake now, she touched it again. It hadn't been there before—or at least she hadn't noticed it. But there it was. Later she described it as a clump. A small mass, just the size of an acorn. So tiny but, at the same time, so powerful that with its discovery it took over her life.

Her reaction, Ann later explained, was strange. "It was one of resignation, of knowing *it* was coming."

She told Derek right away. Then she scheduled an appointment with the doctor. That morning Derek did something he'd never done before. He drove off to work without saying good-bye. Ann spent the day numb, waiting, and feeling very much alone.

After dinner that evening she told Derek, "I want you to know if this is cancer, I'm not going to allow it to linger. You won't have to worry, I don't want to end up a skeleton propped in a hospital bed in the living room, needing somebody to help me get to the bathroom, crying out, wasting away. . . . I won't do that to you. And I won't do that to me. . . . You don't have to worry."

Reliving that evening, Ann added, "I'll never forget the look on his face. It was one of such complete relief. . . . He didn't say, 'Good,' but his face said it all.

"And I realized right then I hadn't wanted him to say that. I'd wanted him to say he'd be there for me no matter what. . . ."

The next month passed in a blur. Yes, it was cancer. Surgery was scheduled, but life went on as usual. Family plans, work schedules, and farm chores were still there, just as they had been the month before.

Ann's distant cousin Nita, then seven months pregnant, had been planning to visit and bring her six-year-old daughter, Hilary, along. They arrived on schedule. As Nita described it, Derek was waiting for them when they got off the plane. When Nita didn't see Ann, she asked where she was.

"He told me, 'Ann was diagnosed earlier today with breast cancer. She needs a lot of support,'" Nita recalled. "And then Derek told me, 'I can't believe this can be happening to *me* again.'"

As they drove the winding two-lane highway from Eugene to Monroe, Nita remembers asking whether it would be better for her to leave so that Derek and Ann could be alone. Derek assured her that it would be good for Ann to have company.

Nita also remembers the entire stay as a time of almost unbearable tension. "There was Ann, putting on a brave face. She seemed to be in her own world a lot of the time.

But she took time, too, to play with Hilary. Hilary loved it. Ann had let her help feed the animals.

"Derek, when he was there, would sit around, being cordial, but it seemed like such an effort. He'd talk about himself. His work. Things that interested him.

"There was no warmth. When I'd visited them when they lived in California, there was affection. He'd put his arm around her. They'd do little things together like getting dinner ready," Nita recalled.

"This time they were like strangers. There was a coldness. The house seemed cold. Cold on the outside. Cold on the inside.

"When he picked me up at the airport, Derek had said Ann needed a lot of support. But I didn't hear him offer to help. There wasn't any hugging. There wasn't any touching at all that I saw. They seemed to be avoiding each other. When they did speak, there was arguing.

"It really got a little scary. Ann got so angry a couple of times. Once she took her hand and swept everything off the counter onto the floor."

The arguments—those that Nita couldn't avoid hearing—were over Ann's cancer.

In an interview after Ann's death Derek described Ann during that time as making self-pitying comparisons with Jean, his first wife, telling him that he didn't love her or cry for her as he had for Jean. "I would say, 'Ann, I don't think you're dying,' " he told one journalist. Ann thought she was dying. Derek told her that was nonsense. Neither of them, of course, knew for sure. Though optimistic, Ann's oncologist had said her survival couldn't be guaranteed even after surgery and treatment.

Nita remembers being puzzled by a young woman who showed up at the house. She later learned the woman's name was Gretchen. Gretchen eventually became Derek's third wife.

"She'd come to the door. Derek would say he was going to go clear some land, and then they'd get on the tractor and go riding off. It was really strange.

"Here was his wife in the house. She'd just found out she had cancer, and he'd go riding off for hours at a time with some woman! This was support?"

It was with relief that Nita and her daughter flew back home a week later. "It had been awful," she said.

A few days after Nita left, on Friday, September 22, Ann had the scheduled surgery. Derek told her afterward that she had looked so gray it was as if she were dead. By then, however, she was determined to fight the disease. The initial giving up and giving in to what she was sure was inevitable were gone. She was going to be strong. She was going to get well. She was going to be superwoman.

Months later Ann told me it had taken every ounce of strength she had just to survive those first days after she got out of the hospital.

Only two weeks after her surgery she had driven herself home from a doctor's appointment. It was just getting dark. She was tired, dizzy, and hurting.

More than a year later she described the scene to me. "I opened the front door," she recalled. "Every light in the house was out. There was Derek sitting in the chair, a drink at his side. No dinner. No anything. Just Derek, sitting in a cold house, looking lost, waiting for me to get home and fix things for him. . . . He hadn't even picked up anything at the store. . . . I got really angry. . . .

"I was the one with cancer. Couldn't he at least help a little? . . . I turned around, drove back into Eugene, and picked up groceries. . . . I was so weak I had to lean on the shopping cart. I didn't know if I could get the bags into the car. . . . Right then I wanted so badly for someone just to take care of me. . . . I wanted him to say, 'I love you,' . . . to say, 'I'm here. . . .'

"Didn't he realize I needed to be taken care of? . . . But it wasn't all his fault, either. I'd always done everything . . . picked up his dirty clothes off the floor . . . done all the laundry . . . bought all the groceries. . . . For a woman who considers herself a feminist, that wasn't too smart, was it?" she said with a humorless chuckle.

Then she went on. "It had been hard for him . . . we were both hurting . . . he was under stress, too."

But that still hadn't prepared her for his leaving.

Three weeks after her surgery, on Friday, October 13, 1989—just one day after she had started what was to be a six-month stretch of chemotherapy and radiation—Derek went on what he said was a business trip. He gave no phone number at which he could be reached.

He did leave messages—on the answering device at their home—telling Ann he was not coming back.

The timing of his departure—while Ann was beginning her battle against cancer—prompted questions that continued to plague Derek after Ann's death. At first he acknowledged the poor timing but defended his position. When a Canadian television reporter asked him if a husband should walk out on someone who's got breast cancer, Derek replied, "In these circumstances you do, and I did."

Some months later, on a Boston television interview, he answered a similar question by claiming, "She was cured of cancer when I left her."

Ann listened to the messages Derek had left on her machine. Over and over she played them. They were brutal. Cold. Short. Right to the point. Derek was leaving. He wished her well. His words were clipped, stilted. It sounded to Ann as if there were a touch of distaste in them, as though by even speaking to her, he were somehow contaminated by her illness.

But even though she knew how final it was, Ann was still hoping that he'd change his mind and come home. Four days after he had walked out, she wrote him a letter, pouring out her pain and heartache. And like many who are victims, she blamed herself.

She told him she understood why he'd left. She said she could feel his "utter terror and fear" and knew that was what had motivated him to act the way he did. She'd been wrong not to let him know better how she felt—Derek later complained that she had been uncommunicative—but she had, in her own turmoil, been "an emotional mute." Then she went on to write: "You have been the great love of my life, and I cannot describe in words the feelings of overwhelming love and delight I experienced when we found one another." Again she apologized that *she* hadn't done better.

"I really want to say now how much love and loyalty I

felt for you," the letter went on. "I've always said I'm loyal like a dog and I could never let go of the kindnesses and patience you extended to me over the years. That went a long way, and I'll never forget that. And the sweetness. That went a long way too. For whatever reason, I'll hang on to all that. It helps," she wrote.

Derek, however, would express no kindness, sweetness, or patience after Ann wrote.

During this period Ann felt both physically and emotionally drained. And she became increasingly frightened. With months of treatment still ahead, she would have to battle both cancer and loneliness. She was also facing an ultimatum she had been given by the Hemlock Society: return to work in December or else she would lose her job—and medical benefits.

After her cancer diagnosis Ann had been given a medical leave of absence from her duties at Hemlock for three months. However, upon returning to work, she was to travel around the country, interviewing people whose family members had been euthanized by their doctors. She was then to write a book based on the interviews. It was her understanding that if she didn't cooperate, giving her all to Hemlock, she would lose her job and, along with it, her medical insurance.

Ann found the mere thought of the proposed project distasteful. Finally, she took her case to Hemlock's board, writing in a letter on November 2, 1989, that she found the insistence that she write a book of that sort while she was undergoing treatment for cancer to be "somewhat inhumane." She also assured board members that, although she had been contacted by members of the press who had heard of the Humphrys' separation, she had refused to make any comment.

By then, apparently, Derek had made numerous personal contacts with board members to persuade them of Ann's "emotional instability." Although Derek later said that he only responded to press statements given by Ann, by some reports he began, as early as three days after leaving her, to describe her as "crazy," "mentally ill," "mentally unbalanced," and "insane." Over and over, to Hemlock staff, to board members, and later in an open letter to the press, he described her as irrational and as a woman who had been unstable for years. In addition to battling cancer, Ann now faced emotional assaults.

They came with increasing frequency. The harassment reached the point at which Ann said her doctors believed it was jeopardizing her health. According to Ann, Derek continued to contact her not to express concern for her but only to ask her to return his belongings. She began to feel that he was intentionally trying to sabotage her cancer recovery.

Derek was almost certainly aware that virtually all the heavy work on the farm—getting the feed to the animals, carrying huge bags, and all the other chores that had to be done to maintain a forty-two-acre farm with seventeen head of cattle and other livestock—was being done by Ann with the help of only a part-time farmhand. Yet Ann maintained that in mid-November, when he knew she was in Eugene for cancer treatment, Derek returned to the property and removed a tractor and other farm tools that she needed. Derek later acknowledged taking the equipment, asserting that it was his. Then he put it in storage because he didn't need it.

This proved more than Ann could handle. Suffering from mental exhaustion and anxiety—a normal response, considering the blows she had suffered over the preceding weeks—Ann realized she needed help to deal with all that she had to contend with. On November 22, the day after the equipment was taken, she checked herself into the hospital in Eugene. She was to stay fewer than two weeks, checking herself out the first week of December. It was also at this time, on December 6, that Ann made the first phone call to me.

Derek used Ann's vulnerability at this point to escalate his allegations that she was unstable. In a day when it is—and should be—seen as a sign of character and balance to seek help at times of crisis, he twisted her willingness to recognize her own limitations as an occasion to send out another volley of accusations. In a memo sent to all board members he reported that "Ann was hospitalized in the psychiatric ward. . . ."

In Eugene word travels rapidly. Derek would almost surely have known the date when Ann *checked herself* into the hospital and when she checked herself out. On December 7 he issued a memo directing that all locks at the Hemlock office be changed and that everyone except Ann be given a new key.

In another memo, written on the same day to all staff, Humphry stated that Ann had been giving interviews to newspapers. Ann had given no interviews, however. Nor had she contacted any newspapers. The first newspaper

contact did not take place until the following month—and
that was made on Ann's behalf by a friend.

Humphry also said in his memo: "I must, as Hemlock's
chief, make the following rules in order to protect our
organization: Ann must not come to the office. . . . Any
requests by telephone for information [from her] must be
politely but firmly refused. . . ."

Ann was counting on the Hemlock board of directors.
At this time she was still technically the deputy director
and a board member of the national Hemlock Society, the
organization she had cofounded, as well as a board member of Hemlock of Oregon. Ann hoped—and expected—
to receive a fair hearing at the board meeting scheduled
for January 6, 1990, at which a decision about her status,
including continuation of her medical insurance and sick
pay, was to be made.

However, former Hemlock officials later told an investigator that from the time he left her, Derek waged a campaign—carried out by means of letters to chapter leaders
and of personal visits with board members—to discredit
Ann in the eyes of the Hemlock board and staff. He alleg-
edly made calls as well to staff and directors telling them
that Ann was insane, that she was deranged, and that she
should be institutionalized. They also said that Derek had
discouraged board members and employees from contacting Ann, and, when calls for Ann came to the Hemlock
office, he would ask, "Why would anyone want to talk to
that crazy lady?"

It appears that the January 6 meeting was a "done deal"
before it even began.

RITA MARKER

On December 8, 1989, the day after the order to change
the locks had been issued, Hemlock's attorney had written
to Ann's attorney, stating that a majority of Hemlock's
directors had "a great deal of concern about certain actions
and statements made by Ann." Notably absent was any
concern about Derek's actions or statements. If Ann was
to have any credibility at the upcoming board meeting,
the Hemlock attorney wrote, she was to refrain from any
"unauthorized contact with the media and other third par-
ties." In addition, he stated that board members did "not
feel it appropriate" that she discuss her situation with staff.
Although Derek had been discussing Ann with many individuals across the country, there was no mention of similar
constraints being placed on his contacts.

Enclosed with the December 8 letter from Hemlock's
attorney was a "confidentiality agreement"—Ann called it
a gag order—along with a request that Ann sign and return it as soon as possible. It conditioned her continuing to
receive a salary and, far more significantly, her continuing
receipt of health insurance benefits while undergoing radiation and chemotherapy on her agreement that she would
not disclose any information deemed confidential by the
national Hemlock Society. Ann did not sign the agreement
then or later.

Ill from the treatments she was undergoing, Ann was
unable to travel to discuss her side of the story with Hemlock officials who lived in other parts of the country. And
after doing the necessary farm chores each day, she had
no energy to concentrate on anything but survival. Derek,
on the other hand, was not only lining up votes with board

members but also getting his staff ready for the upcoming meeting.

In a letter dated December 14 he had informed Cheryl Smith, the legal assistant who had been with Hemlock only a few months, that he would increase her annual salary by ten thousand dollars, effective on January 1. He also suggested that she was in line for bigger and better things. "As you know," he wrote, "I am asking the Board of Directors to appoint you as executive director from April 1, by which time I trust you will have passed the Bar examination in Oregon." Meanwhile, he had written another memo to his staff in December, announcing that he was planning to resign his posts of president and executive director so that he could devote his time to publications and lectures. He also issued a memo increasing the annual "consultancy fee" for Ralph Mero, president of Hemlock of Washington State, to forty-six thousand dollars.

Derek's private meetings with board members continued until just hours before the January meeting began. He had, by that time, also prepared a three-page statement titled "Why My Marriage to Ann Wickett Failed." Widely distributed to such media as *People* magazine and various newspapers, the statement claimed that Ann had been responsible for destroying his peace of mind; that she had handled "her breast nodule" in an "unacceptable way"; that she rarely accompanied him on business trips and never on vacations to Europe. . . . He wrote: "I gave the matter careful consideration and abandoned the union. I no longer loved her." Derek later said that it had never been his intention to discuss their problems publicly but that he had felt obliged to "counterattack" when Ann had lashed out at him.

The board meeting took place in a conference room at Eugene's Valley River Inn. Ann had asked Julie Horvath to come for support. Ann and Julie had originally met in Los Angeles in 1987, when Julie was giving horseback riding lessons. Though she was much younger, in her early twenties at the time, she and Ann—"Anna" Julie called her—had become very good friends. A former Hemlock member and now a helicopter pilot, Julie described what took place:

"We waited downstairs and had tea by the fireplace for over an hour. Finally Derek came out with a group of people who'd been with him, and it was time for us to go in. Anna had requested that Derek not be present while she spoke to the board. Some people were asked to leave, but board members—including Jean Gillett, Faye Girshe, Don Shaw, and John Westover—were there. Anna's attorney sat on one side of her. I sat on the other. The board members were so hostile, so cold. Nobody asked her how she was feeling. It was like she was an inconvenience, a formality, that had to be put up with. It was a 'state your business and get out of here' thing. No one smiled or gave any sign of encouragement.

"She tried to explain that Hemlock was her organization, too, that she was its cofounder. She told them that Hemlock was supposed to mean caring about people.

"They just glared at her. They said it was their organization, too, and they didn't see why she wanted to drag her personal problems into it. She tried to make them see that this wasn't a personal problem. It was a Hemlock problem, and she, as its cofounder, was seeing it throw people away. But they just didn't care.

"When she said, 'That's all I have to say,' they just looked at her. They dismissed her. They were glad to be done with her. When we left, Anna was shaking. We went to a restaurant to get a sandwich, but she couldn't eat it."

Ann later heard that she'd been granted six months' medical leave.

Julie Horvath said that the only person who had seemed at all open to hearing what Ann had to say was Curt Garbesi, one of Hemlock's legal advisers, who had arrived late after taking a flight from Los Angeles. When he came into the room—Ann had already started to speak—he had been told to leave. When he protested, he was allowed to remain. Garbesi later wrote to Derek saying that he had heard his awkward reception at the meeting had been due to a perception that he was not neutral regarding the problems concerning Ann's relationship with Hemlock. In November Garbesi had sent a letter urging that Ann receive fair treatment.

Within three days of the meeting Derek wrote a memo saying he had appointed Cheryl Smith deputy director—the position Ann had held—and reiterating his earlier orders regarding Ann. He wrote that his previous "ruling" must remain: any request from Ann for information or anything else would have to be cleared through him.

In another memo that day, this one to all staff members, including the Seattle, Washington, and Sarasota, Florida, branches, he wrote that, where public relations were concerned, he was now to be referred to as "*Founder and Executive Director.*" With a few typewriter strokes Derek had transferred Ann's title of deputy director to someone else and had bestowed on himself the role of the sole founder of Hemlock. From then until after Ann's death Derek referred to himself as "founder," with no mention that he and his wife had cofounded the group.

Another person was also stripped of a job and his title following the January board meeting. It was Henry Brod, president of Hemlock of Oregon. Brod had come to Oregon from Florida, where he had worked for Hemlock as an organizer for the Southeast. He had been considered an up-and-coming star in the organization and a potential ally for Derek. However, as the situation between Ann and Derek worsened, he felt that Hemlock was not being fair to Ann. According to Brod, he was forced to resign for two reasons: Derek had begun to see him as a potential ally of Ann's, and he (Brod) insisted that certain financial irregularities within Hemlock be remedied.

CHAPTER 7

■■■

The board meeting left Ann crushed. Before it she had held out some hope that she could still believe the organization she had helped create was somehow good. She had been trying to convince herself of this ever since the deaths of her parents. She had asked herself if Derek had been right all along. Maybe she just wasn't handling it well. Maybe a person could "help" someone else die and then feel no regrets about it. Ann had wanted—needed—to preserve her belief that Hemlock could be what she wanted it to be: a voice for "choice" in dying.

If the board had indicated any concern for her, she might have continued trying to force herself into believing that ideas, which had looked so right to her in theory, could work out well in practice, too. The board meeting shattered these illusions.

Yet even with this final philosophical split with Hemlock, Ann did not contact the media to defend herself against the cruel allegations made against her. It was her friend

Julie Horvath who contacted the press. "I saw my friend being attacked, and I knew I had to do something," Julie said. She explained that Derek and the Hemlock board seemed bent on a crusade to take away any remaining shred of confidence and strength that Ann had. Two days after the board meeting, on January 8, 1990, Julie got in touch with *The New York Times*.

Exactly one month later *The New York Times* ran an article entitled "Right-to-Die Group Shaken as Leader Leaves Ill Wife." In it Ann acknowledged that she had become distanced from Derek and "the world of death and dying" in recent years.

Derek explained that the marriage breakup had been "painful" for him. "I've lost my home; I've lived in a motel for three months," he said. But he'd had to leave. The final blow, he said, had been the "unacceptable way" Ann had handled her breast cancer.

Also interviewed for the piece was Hemlock board member Don Shaw of Chicago. Shaw had conducted the January 6 meeting. He didn't think Derek had abandoned Ann. "She has taken her own route," he said. He referred to her as "a very lonely woman" who was "very disturbed."

While the article did cover problems such as the IRS investigation of the organization that "was born of a wife's death," its major thrust was the breakup of a marriage. This theme was to be the one that ran through subsequent coverage as well. The fact that Ann was having serious second thoughts about the goals of the organization she had cofounded was not adequately addressed in this initial article or, for that matter, in any coverage until after her death.

Some—both men and women—who have reflected on all that took place over the following months question whether the coverage would have been different if a man who had started an organization had expressed misgivings about it. Would the press and the public have delved more deeply into the heart, or lack of heart, in the group? Would there have been closer scrutiny of the direction in which the Hemlock Society was heading? It wasn't until after Ann's death that the broader issues began to be explored.

Derek did his best to contain discussions, focusing on the story as a private matter. He also apparently believed that any interest in the story would soon wane. In a February 10, 1990, memo to all Hemlock directors he wrote, "I'm coping with it, don't worry. It will blow over in a week or two."

But *The New York Times* article had sparked interest. Various magazines and TV shows began to ask for interviews with Ann. Hoping to make her side of the story known, Ann decided that she would do some, though she didn't want to get caught up in any kind of extended public fight with Derek. As she said to me in early February, once the interviews were finished, "hopefully, it's back to peace and quiet and my own journey." She didn't want to get caught up in the "sordid and hurtful" things.

During this time Ann was particularly concerned about the rumor that Derek was drinking a lot. She acknowledged that both of them had been fairly heavy drinkers. Nevertheless, "I find myself wanting to protect him, knowing that all his behavior, even his most despicable, is a product of his fear and terror. How sad, how pathetic," she said.

For her part Ann had stopped drinking when she started cancer treatments. Determined to get well, she had put herself on a good regimen: brown eggs, whole wheat toast, and oatmeal for breakfast; long walks in the fresh air, and no alcohol. Wanting to beat the cancer completely and bent on getting through her difficulties with no "crutches," she decided to join AA. She also decided, at this point, that she was going to learn how to fly.

Ann had always been afraid of flying. Probably related to her agoraphobia, which she had conquered by the mid-eighties, her terror of flying had lingered. "Just walking down the jetway, I'd get sweaty palms," she once told me. "It was awful. I wanted to be relaxed but I couldn't. My legs would quiver. I literally had to force myself to take each step."

She also explained that Derek had been very understanding, not requiring her to fly anywhere unless it was absolutely necessary. It was yet another reason why she remained in the background while Derek became the front man for Hemlock, flying from place to place and attending various conventions.

When Ann got cancer, her terror of being airborne seemed to disappear. "It was as though all the fear of flying I'd had fell away," she said. Never one to do something halfway, Ann didn't just work up courage to be a passenger in a plane. She and Julie checked out flight schools, and by the end of the year Ann would be well on her way to a pilot's license.

In the winter of 1990, however, Ann's plans to concentrate on flying lessons and farm life were derailed. On

February 13 Derek had sent out another version of his "Why My Marriage to Ann Wickett Failed" statement. In this expanded edition Derek referred to the previous November, when Ann had checked herself into the hospital suffering from nervous exhaustion. He distorted the conditions under which Ann entered the hospital, writing that she was "placed" in a psychiatric ward in Eugene for eight days. He also quoted Don Shaw's *New York Times* description of Ann as "very disturbed" and wrote: "Three pscyhologists [sic] and a pscyhiatrist [sic] have told me that Ann suffers from what is called a 'Borderline Personality Disorder.'" (Not until after Ann's death did Derek, when pressed about this allegation by a national Canadian television news program, admit that he knew of no such diagnosis. Ann's doctors had never indicated that she had a "borderline personality.")

In this second version Derek documented his qualifications as a humanitarian. He wrote: "I cared for Jean through her two years of suffering and helped her to die. I have proved my ability to cope with dying as few others have. In my work I deal with it every day. It is ridiculous for Ann to accuse me of lack of compassion." He ended the four-page statement by writing, "Ann frequently signs herself 'Ann Wickett, Ph.D.' It appears on her resume [sic]. She never submitted a thesis."

Ann had scheduled an appearance on *Larry King Live* for February 20. She hoped the show would give her an opportunity to counter this latest volley from Derek and to retrieve her own self-respect. She was to fly to California to tape the show from CNN's Los Angeles bureau. Julie was to meet her at the airport, and I agreed that a few days before the interview, I would call her to go over the "nuts and bolts" of being on TV.

By that time Ann and I had talked on the phone fairly often, feeling very comfortable with each other. It had been a gradual but very real process of "hitting it off" and discussing not only Ann's involvement with Derek and Hemlock but everyday matters as well. On this occasion, since she considered me a TV veteran, Ann asked my help in making sure she came across as calm but assertive on the show.

Although she was nervous about being on national television for the first time, she was eager to do the program to answer Derek's charges and then get on with her life.

But on the Thursday evening before the show, Derek called her and left a message on her answering machine. In a cold, clear, meticulously slow voice he said, "If you continue this stupid fighting one step more, I shall give your sister and nieces a full statement that you committed a crime in helping your parents to die. They will then be able to sue you for the return of the three hundred thousand dollars you inherited. Just live quietly, regain your health, agree to a divorce where we keep our own property, and let's get on with our lives. Otherwise, I fly to Boston. I'm deadly earnest. Think it over."

The call terrified Ann. The money she had inherited from her parents had been used to buy Windfall Farm. Derek was now threatening her with its loss.

She was angry as well. She called me and asked me to listen to the tape. Then she asked me to get a tape recorder and make a copy of it over the phone so there would be a record of it in case something happened to her or to the original tape. "I didn't think he'd go this far," she told me. "This is extortion." It was also an incredibly telling moment. Derek, whose mission in life was ostensibly to make others see that "helping" one's family members die was an act of love, was now trying to use the so-called loving act as a bludgeon to silence his wife. Ann saw his words as another indication of his intent to sabotage her recovery.

"If I lose my farm, I don't have any place to live," Ann said. I told her she could come and live with us. She said that wasn't the issue. "It's my home, my farm, my life. I'm not going to let him do this to me. . . ." She also told me to "use that tape however you see fit."

Derek had been asked to be on *Larry King Live* as well, though his appearance was to be by phone hookup. On the show Ann stayed with her decision to tell her side of the story while not attacking Derek. She told Larry King that one way she had managed to keep her sanity since Derek had left was to spend time trying to understand why he had walked out. "I think that we had both been experiencing some strain and I think, that after thirteen years of marriage, to confront a wife's cancer with a message on an answering machine says a great deal about panic and fear," she explained. "I think he had no idea of the consequences of what he was doing when he left, absolutely none. I think he was running like a panicky animal. It was simply more than he could endure."

Asked by King to explain why he left, Derek responded, "She was unbearable to live with. . . . When her cancer came, her behavior became absolutely unbearable." He described the last four or five years of the marriage as being filled with pain and suffering.

"Why didn't you break up before then?" King asked him.

"Well, I did love her. I cared a lot for her . . . but her behavior over the cancer was absolutely intolerable to me, and unbearable, and that was the straw that broke the camel's back."

King prodded. "But can't you imagine, Derek—how would you feel if you had been told you had a possible terminal illness?"

"Well, I'd feel bad. . . . Now just let me point out that I am not a coward. I nursed my first wife through two years, and she committed suicide and died in my arms. I have proved my staying power. I did it once, and I can do it again."

Later in the show Ann described the threatening phone message Derek had left the previous week. When King asked Derek why he had made that call, he replied, "She was telling all sorts of outrageous stories about me and in a fit of anger I lashed back. . . . I'm not very proud of some of the things I've done. I'm appalled at some of the things Ann has done."

After the show Ann called me from the airport. "I'm so glad that's over. How was it?" she asked. I told her she had done a terrific job. As I had watched the show, nervous for her, I had been amazed that she could remain so calm. She had come across as just the type of person she was— intelligent and vulnerable but able to hold her ground.

Something else had come through as well. As angry as she was at Derek for his increasing cruelty, she still felt an intense desire for everything to be the way it was in the beginning. She missed him terribly. More than a year later she told me, "There's still that little part of me that will always say I still care for him. When Derek left, it's like he took a piece of me. And I'll never be whole again."

Happily for Ann, Derek never followed through on his extortion threat. After *Larry King Live*, however, she began to discuss publicly her misgivings about legalized euthanasia. She told *American Medical News* that, in Hemlock, "there has been so much emphasis on dying when you have a life-threatening illness that measures such as providing a supportive environment are overlooked. . . ." She said she had become convinced that proposals supported by Hemlock—those that would make it legal for doctors to kill terminally ill patients who request such action—could put "subtle but unmistakable pressure on someone to die—to simply get out of the way."

Derek's views were quoted in the same article. Once again he called Ann "mentally ill."

With the appearance of the March 12 issue of *People* magazine, coverage of the story escalated. Humphry told the magazine that he had left Ann because "the ill person owes it to the other person to behave properly. . . . She handled her cancer so badly, I'm sorry to say. She became so neurotic about it that I was falling to pieces. I couldn't take it." The article also made reference to Derek's order that employees not associate with Ann.

This prompted a written response from Jean Gillett, Hemlock's treasurer, who accused the magazine of "biased reporting." She wrote, "Derek hasn't forbidden Hemlock employees from associating with Ann," although Gillett, as a member of Hemlock's board, would almost certainly have been aware of Derek's December memo doing just that. In addition, she wrote that the board backed Derek in his decisions 100 percent. "Ann has made every effort to make a personal problem a Hemlock problem, which it isn't. It's inconceivable to me that anyone would go to such lenghts [*sic*] to air her personal life."

Two weeks later, on the TV show *Inside Edition*, Humphry said, "A tragedy has happened. Lightning has hit me twice." Asked if he had "walked out" on Ann, he said that he had but that she had a "borderline mental illness." He called her "a perfect bitch, unmanageable and hypocritical. . . ."

Growing more and more concerned over all the increased verbal assaults and unusual phone calls she was getting, sometimes in the middle of the night, Ann changed her telephone number to an unlisted one. In that early spring of 1990 she also began seriously to consider filing a lawsuit against Derek and Hemlock.

"What do you think?" she asked me. "Would it help?" I told her that was a decision only she could make but that it really needed to be thought out carefully. If she were to go ahead, she—not anyone else—was the one who would have to bear Derek's and Hemlock's ire. And it would certainly increase if she took legal action.

Uncertain about what to do, and worried about her medical leave—and insurance—which would be up in June, Ann talked to other friends and relatives. I suggested that if she was uncertain, it was best *not* to go ahead with a lawsuit. Ann wasn't convinced. "I don't know," she said. "If I don't do it, everyone will believe that what Derek was saying was true. I can't let that happen. If I do, I'll never be able to get a job."

It was, in a way, a no-win situation. Ann wanted nothing more than to get on with her life. Yet she seemed to believe that to do so, she had to set the record straight. Otherwise doors that she would need to be open if she were ever to be able to earn a living would be closed to her. "Nobody's going to want to hire 'a crazy lady,' " she said. She decided, though, that she would give it a bit more time before she took any steps to initiate a lawsuit. With all that had been going on, and with her divorce to Derek now pending, she knew she needed to conserve her strength for whatever else might come her way.

It was later that year that Ann and I finally got together in person. This would be much different from our polite greetings at euthanasia conferences. During the preceding months we had developed a close relationship by phone. Now, for the first time, we would be meeting as friends.

A previous plan to get together in January, when I was on the West Coast for some speaking engagements, had fallen through when unusually heavy rains had caused flooding, making it impossible to drive from Seattle to Monroe. When I was in Seattle again, we arranged to meet for Sunday brunch in the dining room of the Inn at the Quay in Vancouver, Washington, where there is a wonderful view of the Columbia River. We were to meet at 11:00 A.M. Each of us would have about a three-hour drive to get there.

I arrived a bit early and chose a table way in the corner where we would be able to talk. I was nervous, wondering if we would hit it off in person. Talking on the phone, no matter how comfortably, was one thing. Talking face-to-face was something else.

The first thing I noticed when Ann walked into the room was that she looked terrific. She had lost some weight, and the loss was very becoming to her. She also did not look at all like the aloof sophisticate I had remembered from the Hemlock conferences. While she carried herself with the same elegance, she looked outdoorsy, wearing cowboy boots, jeans, and a turtleneck sweater.

Ann glanced around the dining room and saw me right away. She was carrying a big gift-wrapped box with a bright gold bow on top. Putting it down on the extra chair at our table, she said, "That's for you. Now don't open it till you're on the plane." And without hugs or preliminaries or awkwardness, we started to talk. For me it was like meeting a long-lost sister.

We talked, and talked, and talked—about anything and everything. If we mentioned euthanasia at all, it was to laugh and ask, "Who would have ever thought this would happen?" In discussing our lives, we found out that we both were very much alike—and very different. We had come from opposite sides of the country and the economic spectrum. She was the daughter of a Boston banker while my dad had been a truck driver in eastern Washington. We both had a love of music, loved to read, and had attended girls' schools as teenagers, though Ann had loved her school and I had loathed mine. We both had very strong feelings on just about every social issue and were surprised to find that we agreed on many of them. And we both had avoided elevators and feared flying. Ann had overcome her fear. I had not, although I force myself to fly and to ride an elevator if I have to get to any floor above the eighth or ninth.

After what seemed like only minutes, a waitress came to our table and told us politely that the dining room was closing. We had been there for three hours. So we picked up the box, our jackets, purses, and cups, moved into the lounge, ordered more coffee and tea, and talked some more.

Ann was still worried about what to do about the lawsuit. And though she had finished with her cancer treatments in February and everything looked fine for the moment, in the back of her mind was the knowledge that the cancer might recur. "I'm just taking each day at a time," she told me. "Some days are so beautiful. But others, well, I do get through them.

"It's funny," she continued. "I used to always have to watch my weight carefully. Now I'm just not hungry. I do make myself eat because I know I should. But I just get so tired."

It wasn't until close to seven in the evening that we decided we'd better get headed back. As we walked out to the parking lot, she reminded me again, "Wait till you're on the plane to open the gift." We both laughed.

As soon as I got to the airport, I tore off the wrapping and opened the box. In it was a very old book. Preserved with a special finish, it is permanently open to the page with a poem titled "Friendship." The book is one of my most treasured belongings.

We called each other a couple of times a week after that. Toward the end of April I could tell from her voice that she wasn't feeling good at all. "I'm just tired," she said, but she was more than tired. She was losing even more weight and was completely exhausted.

Ann also had another problem with which to contend. She had found out that her medical insurance was being canceled. In what appeared to have been a bureaucratic mix-up with its insurance carrier, Hemlock had lost its insurance for all its employees. This included Ann as well. However, she discovered this only after she had submitted some medical bills. She was even told that she would probably have to repay some of the insurance money that had been paid out for her cancer treatments.

Once again she checked herself into the local hospital in Eugene. This time the diagnosis was "failure to thrive," a diagnosis usually reserved for infants who have been deprived of love and care. It was, I thought, very appropriate.

Ann was worried about how she would manage once she got out of the hospital. Calling me one day, she was in tears. "I just need somebody to care for me," she said. "It would be so good to know there's someone else in the house. I just wish I could curl up in bed or on my chair and know there would be another person around who'd bring me a hot cup of tea or maybe just walk through the room and smile."

I asked if I could find somebody to stay with her for a while. "Oh, yes," she replied.

I made a couple of calls. One of them was to Janet Smith, a friend who teaches philosophy at the University of Dallas and would be finished with the semester in just a few days. When I told her about Ann's situation, Janet thought of a friend of hers, Susan Selner, a theology student working on a doctoral dissertation, who was an excellent cook and might like to join them as well. Susan found it a wonderful idea.

I called Ann back at her room in the hospital. "Have I got a deal for you! A philosopher and a theologian are absolutely dying to learn how to feed cows. How does that sound?"

"Heavenly." She laughed. "Are you joking?" When I told her I was serious, she immediately said, "Tell them to come. When can they be here?"

It turned out that there would be a few days' gap between the time Ann left the hospital and the time Janet and Susan were to arrive. During those few days Ann was wonderfully cared for by a nurse from the hospital who invited Ann to stay with her family so she wouldn't have to go home alone.

"You'll never guess what I'm doing," Ann said when she called me from the nurse's home. I could hear a piano in the background. "I'm eating cookies and drinking milk, and we're playing the piano and singing hymns. Can you believe that?"

"No."

"Well, we are. I haven't had cookies and milk for years and years. And I definitely haven't done any hymn singing for a long, long time. . . . I'm going to make it. I know I am."

A few days later Ann went home. Janet and Susan arrived, settled in, and, as Ann said later, cooked up a storm, making sure she ate and rested.

Janet and Susan stayed for several weeks. By the time they left, Ann was feeling much better, strong enough to ride her magnificent Arabian horse, Ibn, and playfully shoo Wanda, one of her four cats—King Albert, Beauregard, and Prunella were the others—off the countertops. And the freezer was stocked with homemade lasagna, stews, and goodies of all types.

"I'm going to end up worrying about my weight again," Ann told me happily. "I feel so good." And as she did so often, she added, "I know I'm gonna make it."

Still, there was cause for concern. Another growth had been discovered, this time on her collarbone. Her oncologist told her it was cancerous but contained.

In addition to the growth, the problems with medical coverage for continuing treatment occupied Ann. The insurance company was still maintaining that her policy had lapsed.

Meanwhile, I was scheduled to fly to Holland to attend the eighth biennial conference of the World Federation of Right to Die Societies for an article I was writing on Dutch euthanasia.

"Don't worry. I'll be fine," Ann assured me when I gave her the phone numbers where I could be reached. "Have a great trip and give me a call as soon as you get back."

CHAPTER 8

∎ ∎ ∎

The 1990 world conference of right-to-die societies was being held in Maastricht, a town in the southernmost part of Holland. After flying to Amsterdam, I rented a car for the drive down to Maastricht. Two friends of mine were flying in from London for the conference as well. I picked them up at the miniature, spotlessly clean Maastricht airport, and after depositing luggage, the three of us headed out to the ultra-modern Maastricht Exhibition and Congress Center (MECC), where the meetings were to take place. We spotted the newly opened main conference building as we came over a rise in the road. It might have been mistaken for an oversize airplane hangar had it not been for the gigantic letters—suspended from thick cables running the length of the building's concrete exterior—starkly announcing, 7–10 JUNE WORLD RIGHT-TO-DIE CONFERENCE.

As we approached the main entrance, everything seemed in readiness for the arriving delegates. Sunlight reflected off the gleaming sidewalks; red, yellow, and pink flowers rose to attention along the brick surfaces of the neatly marked parking areas. Sounds of a merry-go-round filled the air, though there were no children and no merry-go-round. The carousel music was spewing from a garishly painted, automated calliope placed beside the entrance.

Inside, the setting was one of quiet elegance. Delegates mingled as a string ensemble played in the background. I was greeted with genuine warmth from the ever-courteous euthanasia leaders. A thick carpet muffled our footsteps as we moved from the foyer into the auditorium for the opening session.

Conference participants from twenty-three countries waited for the session to begin. They had come to the font of euthanasia wisdom to learn from the masters of the craft. Although still technically unlawful, euthanasia is so common in Holland that the Royal Dutch Pharmacists Association has supplied every physician in the country with a booklet carefully outlining the most efficient ways to kill patients. So respectable has the practice become that only six months before the Maastricht meeting a British paper had reported that a physician had been reprimanded by the Dutch Medical Disciplinary Board (the Dutch counterpart of our American Medical Association) for *not* providing euthanasia to a patient. For those present, Holland seemed like the perfect place to glean practical advice for implementing ongoing efforts to expand the "right to die."

Mrs. Pit M. M. Bakker, president of Nederlandse Vereniging voor Vrijwillige Euthanasie (NVVE), the Dutch euthanasia society, was scheduled to welcome officially delegates to the conference. Ponderous, white-haired, and ruddy-cheeked, she took her place onstage and moved to the podium.

She intoned the welcome in a booming voice, reminding all of the importance of this moment in the history of the Dutch euthanasia movement. She expressed the customary gratitude to all who had planned and subsidized the event, thanking the Dutch Ministry of Social Affairs, Health, and Culture and the General Dutch Lottery for their donations. She also thanked the French and Swiss euthanasia organizations that were providing translators for those who did not speak English, the official language of the conference, and thanked the media representatives who, it was expected, would carry the message far and wide.

Then she became stern, castigating in absentia the board of the Deutschen Gesellschaft für Humanes Sterben, the German euthanasia society, for not being in attendance. "There is no reason for their absence," she said. The German boycott of the meeting stemmed from a two-year-old controversy that had surfaced at the international group's 1988 conference in San Francisco. There the president of the German euthanasia society, Hans Atrott, had vociferously opposed allowing doctors actually to administer euthanasia. If physicians were allowed to give the deadly dose or lethal injection, it would "come to the point of the Nazis in the past," he had argued. His group favors "self-administered euthanasia" by such means as cyanide.

Mrs. Bakker continued: "Considering the establishment of Europe 1992, right-to-die societies the world over must work together" to see to it that their goals are pursued in a united Europe.

"I *will* be in contact with the German society after this Congress," she promised. And no one who heard her could doubt that when Mrs. Bakker said she would do something, it was as good as done.

That said, she introduced one of the organizers of the conference. He spoke briefly, welcoming all the participants, and then turned to the men and women seated at the table onstage and introduced Derek Humphry to the gathering.

This was Derek Humphry's moment. Since 1984 he had sought high office in the world body. At the 1986 conference in Bombay, India, he had been elected vice-president, the title he had held at the 1988 conference in San Francisco, after which he automatically advanced to a two-year term as president. Although this was largely a ceremonial title with no real power, for the man who had once been an obscure London journalist worried about what he would do if his newspaper closed, it was a considerable achievement. He was opening and presiding over an international gathering of doctors, lawyers, ethicists, and policy makers—all movers and shakers seeking to change laws around the world.

Derek carefully stood up from the table and slowly walked to the podium. He cleared his throat.

"It is my great honor as President to open this eighth international conference. . . . This congress represents thirty groups from nineteen nations." The official participant list consisted of twenty-three countries; Derek's figures may have reflected the fact that, as of December 1989, there were thirty member organizations from nineteen countries.

"The first world congress was held in Japan in 1976 with a mere six groups from four nations attending. This statistic shows more than anything the recent growth of the movement for the right to choose to die."

A few latecomers came and took their places.

"Some of the larger countries, like Australia or America, each have four or five groups. . . . Although some of the groups differ in their ethical and legal approach, all believe in the right of the terminally ill person to choose voluntary euthanasia at life's end.

"We meet in our congress every two years, in different parts of the world, to exchange ideas, report progress, discuss strategies, offer model laws. . . ." Someone coughed. Papers were rustling, programs were being read, conference packets examined. Contrary to his usual winning way with the audience, Derek seemed nervous, not "on."

"I believe the right to choose to die with dignity is the ultimate civil liberty," Derek continued. "If we cannot die according to our personal wishes, then we are not free and democratic people."

The audience listened politely as he went on to chronicle the history of euthanasia: how the Greeks and Romans had allowed a choice of death as a matter of honor; how, with the rise of Christianity, the issue had become taboo; how the British and American euthanasia societies had started. . . .

Pausing for a sip of water and still a bit nervous, he resumed his speech. He described how, after her case had been decided, Karen Ann Quinlan had been kept alive by a respirator for eight years. (Actually the respirator was removed after her case had been decided, and she lived for another nine years.) He discussed the progress of Living Will laws, saying that the first one took effect in California in 1978. (He was two years off; it had been 1976.) But the inaccuracies didn't seem to make a difference. No one was taking notes.

"This congress is being held in the nation which has, with great courage, humanity, and legal skill, made the most progress towards lawful physician aid-in-dying. Visitors like myself hope to learn a great deal within the next few days."

It was clearly time to close.

"We are definitely not about murder or killing. . . . This movement is about compassion and love for our fellow man and woman."

I thought about Ann listening to his farewell message on the answering machine just when she was starting chemotherapy.

"It is about caring."

I thought about Ann at home alone in Monroe, Oregon, worrying about finding a way to get medical coverage to continue her cancer treatments.

"As we debate many complicated topics over the next few days, let us never lose sight of the main target: helping human beings to suffer less," he concluded.

It was over. This had not been Derek's typical audience of—as some have described it—little gray-haired ladies to whom the subtle nuances of euthanasia did not mean very much. These were euthanasia professionals who could not be easily impressed by a retelling of the events of *Jean's Way* or charmed by Derek's winning combination of a nice smile and a British accent. Derek was not scheduled to give another presentation, and at the close of the three days of meetings Britain's Jean Davies, the group's vice-president, would automatically take over the helm.

Intense dedication to their mission characterizes the euthanasia faithful. The movement has its saints, revered by the true believers, and its special evangelists, who proselytize with fervor. And the Netherlands is its heaven. At the Maastricht conference one American delegate grasped the microphone and, in a voice quivering with emotion, exhorted all who were listening to "be thankful" for the guidance being offered in the Dutch euthanasia "paradise."

People from every corner of the world were present at the deliberations in Maastricht. Representatives had come from New Zealand, South Africa, Colombia, Japan, India, and a host of other countries. The Americans in attendance included a veritable who's who of U.S. euthanasia circles. They included Ronald Cranford, a Minnesota neurologist who often appears as an expert witness in right-to-die cases; Sidney Rosoff, chairman of the Society for the Right to Die; Donald McKinney, of Concern for Dying; John Stanley, head of the Appleton Consensus, an international working group formulated to deal with issues of medical ethics and cost containment; and Margaret Pabst Battin, a University of Utah philosophy professor, sought after as a speaker at ethics conferences around the world.

Among the movement's evangelists who delivered sermons to those in attendance was Dr. H. S. Cohen, a Dutch general practitioner who works closely with the euthanasia society in his country. Cohen is short, slightly paunchy, and moves with an electric energy, punctuating his sentences with choppy hand gestures. At this conference he spoke about euthanasia's being a necessary part of good medical care.

"Don't you ever get any opposition to what you're doing?" he was asked.

"Sometimes," he said. "But it's very, very rare. Occasionally someone will come up to me, point a finger and say, 'You're the doctor that kills people,' " he added, mimicking the accuser.

He paused, tugged on his little beard, and with an eye-crinkling grin said, "I just tell them, 'I only kill my friends.' "

Adept at handling confrontation, he is also a master of persuasion. Dr. Cohen is brought in by the Dutch euthanasia organization if someone has called to say that a particular doctor is unwilling to administer euthanasia. Dr. Cohen then asks the colleague in question to meet and discuss the issue.

This task of personally contacting and coaxing the recalcitrant into compliance involves no heavy-handed tactics, just gentle, friendly, reasonable, doctor-to-doctor dialogue until there's an understanding that administration of death is "part of good spiritual care."

"It takes time," he said, "but it's well worth it . . . a previously uncommitted doctor may become a very active euthanasia advocate. Talking with an unwilling physician helps not only the patient but often leads the doctor to talk with all his patients in the future," Cohen explained.

"Isn't there ever any abuse?" someone asked.

With just the slightest show of irritation, Cohen dismissed the possibility, saying that the Dutch medical establishment is of such high integrity that it is "not corruptible." Then he went on to discuss the need to make the option of death more readily available and more widely known.

"Euthanasia should have a firm place in school discussions, just like any other right. It should be discussed along with other important issues like voting rights," he said. "It's never too early to think about euthanasia. . . . It's a way of life . . . just another exercise in medical ethics."

Cohen made it clear that doctors and nurses have a responsibility to bring up euthanasia as an option to patients who could benefit from it.

Offering the "right" to euthanasia has to be done delicately, though, Dr. H. Bakker-Winnubst, a physician who directs a large nursing home in Holland, told conference participants.

"It takes courage and diplomacy," she said, because patients in nursing homes are very dependent and very willing to go along with whatever a doctor suggests. "Many patients are apt to say, 'Yes, Doctor, whatever you say.' Now this doesn't mean we should avoid the issue. But it means we need to use good timing and great care when we bring up the subject," she explained.

One doctor very willing to bring up the choice of euthanasia is Dutch anesthesiologist Pieter Admiraal, who insists that there can be "no terminal care without the possibility of euthanasia." He is perhaps the foremost euthanasia practitioner in the world. He has appeared internationally on radio and television and, of course, is virtually always a featured speaker at euthanasia conferences. Perhaps more influential, though, is his quiet involvement in policy planning that has had a ripple effect throughout the realm of medical ethics.

To cite but one example, in March 1989, euthanasia promotion in the United States received a significant boost when a "report," published in the *New England Journal of Medicine*, concluded that it is morally acceptable for doctors to give patients suicide information and the necessary prescriptions for the deadly dose. Called the "strongest public endorsement of doctor-assisted suicide ever published in a major medical journal," the report became front-page news across the United States.

One of the report's twelve physician authors, Ronald Cranford, stated, "We broke new ground, and we were very aware we were doing it. We felt it was an opportunity to make a statement that's very controversial and stand by it." He acknowledged that assisting suicide is "the same as killing the patient."

His observation is accurate. The influence physicians hold in society as well as the control they have over information supplied to patients gives them great power. The very act of providing a prescription for a lethal dose of medication serves as confirmation that the patient is better off dead. Although viewed as respectable because it takes place in the professional physician-patient relationship, it could be likened to lifting a person to the narrow ledge of a tall building and then saying, "It's okay to jump."

At the time the report was released, few people were aware that the panel had been convened by one of America's leading euthanasia organizations, the Society for the Right to Die, not by some impartial group. Even fewer knew that four of the twelve panel members served on

Ann, a shy, sensitive little girl,
grew up in Boston

Ann and Derek married
in a London Registry office
just six months after they
met through an ad Ann
had placed in a personal
column

After their marriage, Ann
and Derek went to Rules,
the restaurant where he
had taken the doctor who
provided the lethal dose of
pills for his first wife

Ann and Derek in happier days

Derek took time from his work at Hemlock for fun and family

Dr Christiaan Barnard at the 1984 World Federation of Right-to-Die Societies conference in Nice

Right: At its 1986 conference, Hemlock announced its sponsorship of the Humane and Dignified Death Act in California, its first attempt to legalize aid-in-dying

Below: Betty Rollin and Derek Humphry after Rollin's keynote address at the 1986 Hemlock conference

Dr H.S. Cohen of Holland takes tea during a break at
the World Federation of Right-to-Die Societies conference
in Maastricht, June 1990

At the Maastricht conference in 1990, Dr Pieter Admiraal
stressed the need to include euthanasia in any program
which provided services for the terminally ill

Windfall Farm, Ann and Derek's peaceful home in Monroe, Oregon

Ann loved animals and raised Fiona from a tiny lamb
who had to be bottle-fed

Ibn, Ann's magnificent Arabian horse

Ann escaped to the wilderness whenever she could

Ann and her son Bill had their first and only reunion in the summer of 1991

Ann with the author in Steubenville, Ohio

Ann's last trip to the Oregon coast

either the board of directors or the advisory committee of the society. Cranford, also on the panel, had previously written that "physician-assisted suicide may not only be permissible, but encouraged" in the future.

The report also set the stage for euthanasia as a "treatment" for nondying patients who are considered "hopelessly ill." Perhaps most noteworthy and least known was the fact that in addition to the twelve physicians listed as authors of the groundbreaking document, a thirteenth physician had been present for the deliberations during which the report was formulated. The thirteenth, unnamed physician was Pieter Admiraal.

Admiraal is held in esteem that borders on veneration by the euthanasia elite. Introducing him to the audience assembled in Maastricht, Dr. Cohen said, "Here is this humble man who just calls himself simply Pieter, like the other one who opens the gates of heaven for those who suffer down here."

Admiraal wears the mantle well. His voice is soft, soothing. He is a bit on the heavy side, and his slightly rumpled appearance gives him the look of everyone's grandfather or beloved family doctor. With him caring for you, you would feel secure. He tilts his head slightly to the side, so you know he is really listening. He appears concerned but kindly, never hasty, never rushed.

"I work as an anesthesiologist in the Reinier de Graaf Gasthuis in Delft," he said. "As many of you know, I was the first in the Netherlands to speak openly about practicing euthanasia."

Methodically he presented the main considerations regarding euthanasia and shared his more than twenty years of experience. He stressed the team approach in which doctors, nurses, and pastors are equal in the decision-making process, although the ultimate responsibility lies with the doctor.

"The family suffers," he said. "They ask themselves how much longer it will last, and an eventual request for euthanasia by the family is understandable. But it is only the patient who can ask for it. In cases where the family opposes the patient receiving euthanasia, the request is nevertheless carried out.

"Many patients at this stage of their illness have totally detached themselves from their families, and they long for an early mild death.

"About ten percent of our terminal patients ask for euthanasia," he said. But this is not because of pain. "Pain is very seldom a reason for euthanasia in our hospital. Patients in our hospital ask for euthanasia because of a total loss of human dignity."

Once the final decision has been made, euthanasia is carried out quickly, generally by administration of a combination of pentothal (which causes a patient to go into a deep sleep) and curare (an agent that paralyzes the muscles of the entire body, including the respiratory muscles, so the patient dies of suffocation).

Asked about the cost incurred in providing this "treatment," Admiraal said, "It is about five guilders—the price of the pentothal and curare." (That is about $2.75.) He added, "I think society can assume this because a single day in a hospital costs five hundred guilders."

Patiently he responded to many of the other questions

posed from the audience and would, no doubt, have been willing to answer all had time allowed. It seemed as though just having the opportunity to ask him a question was considered an honor by those in attendance.

Regarding the future, he said there must be more consideration given to "how to handle the problem of euthanasia on babies with a handicap and comatose and demented patients." Although the Royal Dutch Society for the Promotion of Medicine had already suggested some guidelines in these cases, he predicted that for political reasons it would take a few years to settle the issue.

At the end of the question-and-answer period, Admiraal was asked about training of doctors. He explained that euthanasia is not dealt with in Dutch medical schools but is addressed in a later phase of training that is required of all future general practitioners.

Without a doubt, Admiraal is an effective speaker and advocate for euthanasia. In addition to presenting the practice as a necessary option, he inspires the "folk" to go out and bring the word to others.

Among those wishing to use Admiraal's expertise to meet euthanasia needs in his own country was Japan's delegate, Katsutaro Nagata, who asked for guidance and a specific "strategy" to spread thoughts on euthanasia.

"We in Japan are now looking for better ways to give terminal care and to conduct euthanasia," he said. Admiraal assured him that he was willing to go to Japan and talk things over. By the close of the Maastricht meeting the 1992 conference of the World Federation of Right to Die Societies had been scheduled to take place in Tokyo.

Smaller, but no less significant, steps taken by groups in other countries were shared at the meeting as well. For example, John Balfour of Australia reported that one Australian medical society had adopted the Dutch criteria for euthanasia a few months earlier. "Unfortunately this is one of the smallest medical associations in Australia," he said, "but still, it is a great step forward."

A Hemlock official spoke of promoting another important development in the United States—groups that meet regularly to support those who are planning suicide. Similar efforts, the official noted, are also directed toward supporting those who have assisted a suicide.

Although suicide support groups had long been discussed quietly, it took until 1990 for them to be promoted publicly.

Among those who suggest that suicide advocacy may be a legitimate counseling position has been philosopher Margaret Pabst Battin. A speaker at many ethics conferences in the United States and throughout the world and the author of numerous articles and books, Battin has served as philosopher in residence at a Veterans Administration medical center and travels around the country giving ethics seminars for medical students. She has also spoken very persuasively for more than ten years about the benefits of suicide.

In April 1981 she urged those attending meetings of the American Association of Suicidology to consider making suicide advocacy a component of suicide prevention programs. She said that such advocacy would add a "new sensitivity" to the work of suicide prevention. Her paper was reprinted in the January 1982 edition of the *Hemlock Quarterly*.

Although she acknowledged that suicide prevention was praiseworthy, Battin said that it "may very well not be humane" in some cases. Openness to the possibility of supporting suicide would offer the benefit of a more accepting, more reasonable, and more caring atmosphere, she claimed.

She urged a "genuine interaction and exchange" between the two different responses to the potential suicide. "After all, suicide advocacy, like suicide prevention, is humanitarian at root. Each has—or should have—the interests of individual human beings at heart," she said.

When Margaret ("call me Peggy") Battin stands at a podium, her pleasant, conversational style has the informality of a next-door neighbor chatting over coffee. Her wholesome appearance, with open smile and round face softly framed by brown shoulder-length hair, lends warmth to her down-to-earth presentation style. Using a "some say this, while others say that" format, she draws conclusions that seem eminently reasonable when offered.

Four years after introducing the concept of suicide advocacy as humanitarian, Battin expanded on her views at Hemlock's 1985 conference, which I attended.

She acknowledged that dying "relatively early, relatively easily, in a way in which you won't impose a burden on others" was a real possibility if euthanasia was legalized. This, she said, should concern us. But she also claimed that society's expectation of an early death would have good results: The law would support active euthanasia, medical assistance would be openly and readily available to bring about death, and families would benefit because there would be adequate support for it. Assistance from churches would also be expected.

With concern on her face and in her voice, Battin addressed the possible external pressures that could be exerted on people making death decisions.

"Will these societal expectations, in effect, destroy options?" she asked. "Will persons not desiring death be able to resist these expectations?

"The question," she continued, "is not how we can avoid emergence of these expectations, because they probably will emerge. But the question is, how does one respond to them?"

Those least capable of withstanding the pressure to request euthanasia or commit suicide would be people who have been the least self-determining throughout their lives, Battin suggested. She noted that particularly vulnerable would be a woman who has lived for her family and has always been concerned about the needs and comfort of others.

"There will be an interest in avoiding the burdens of care and large bills," she pointed out. "We may wish to comply with this interest.

"A problem that needs further reflection," she noted, "is the philosophical claim that the very ill and the very old have 'had their time' or 'had their share.'" She suggested there may be validity to this attitude.

Having carefully placed the benefits and possible drawbacks before the audience, Battin concluded that even if the euthanasia option created undue pressures for some people, this still was not a reason to abridge the right of those who did choose euthanasia in the first place.

"Sure, there is reason to fear, but the fact that people will have a choice is the most important thing," she concluded.

Two years later, in March 1987, an article in the Washington *Times* described Battin as saying that suicide assistance might be warranted for elderly people worried about the prospect of extreme old age and lack of resources.

In 1988 a lengthy piece by Battin and psychiatrist Stephen K. Yarnell was published in the journal *Psychiatric Annals*. The piece extolled the changes in a society that was moving toward a more accepting attitude regarding euthanasia and suicide. "Most will agree, after a long struggle against religion, that the world can be described in terms of facts," the authors wrote. "It seems to us—and we think this is a fortunate thing—that we are moving away from an absolutist, taboo ethics to a consequentialist ethics emphasizing the greatest good for the greatest number. . . ." Legalization and support of a "socially respected way of coming to the end" will, they maintained, be of tremendous benefit.

It was with this impressive background as a champion for euthanasia and suicide that Margaret Pabst Battin, the only American on the program, gave the closing address at the Maastricht conference. With a beaming smile, she thanked all who had made the days at the conference so very special. Then, shaking her head with regret, she said, "I would like to examine the problem of going home.

"It is a problem that arises not only because of the delights of Dutch hospitality and the richness of Dutch art and the picturesque nature of the Dutch landscape. It is a problem that arises because here, in Holland, we discover that voluntary active euthanasia can, in fact, be practiced in accord with a patient's wishes.

"We are beset with envy as we see the tranquillity and naturalness of a practice that is still violently disputed every place else in the world.

"We ask ourselves about 'going home' and about whether we can take what we see here in Holland with us."

Always the teacher, she went on to mention the possible problems that confront other countries in the implementation of what works so well in Holland, cautioning that these problems should not prevent anyone from forging ahead.

"We all have homework to do. When we're back home, we need to think carefully about the exact nature of what's suited to our own particular countries."

And now it was over.

It had been a heady week, as participants drank in the intoxicating visions of elegant, graceful death by day and the rich sights and delicacies of the two-thousand-year-old city by night. Death by choice had been lauded over steaming cups of coffee. Tiny sandwiches were absent-mindedly consumed during intense discussions on the relative merits of using a clear or an opaque plastic bag over one's head to achieve "self-deliverance." Legal strategies had been debated over wine and lavish dinners.

Now, however, it was time to come down from the mountain, put aside the affable debates, and get to the task of bringing a bit of euthanasia paradise to the far corners of the earth.

CHAPTER 9

■ ■ ■

The rush to bring the "benefits" of Dutch euthanasia practices to the rest of the world is assumed to be the noblest of endeavors for many in the movement. Yet there is a dark side to Dutch euthanasia that until very recently has remained largely unexamined.

Euthanasia in Holland looks well controlled on paper. The fact that euthanasia is still technically illegal—conviction carries a penalty of twelve years' imprisonment—would appear to keep abuses to a minimum. There are also strict guidelines, developed in response to court cases over the last twenty years, stating the conditions under which euthanasia can be administered. However, those guidelines have been constantly broadened and have served only to give doctors more power rather than less. In actual practice, safeguards intended to protect patients are illusory, and the only restraints are those imposed by the euthanasia practitioners themselves.

The landmark court case that foreshadowed the current

situation occurred in 1973, when Dr. Geertruida Postma, a general practitioner, was charged with killing her seventy-eight-year-old mother by lethal injection. Dr. Postma's mother, although neither terminally ill nor in unbearable physical suffering, had undergone a number of debilitating illnesses and was experiencing severe mental suffering. According to Dr. Postma, her mother had repeatedly said she wanted to die. At her trial Dr. Postma referred to her mother as a human wreck and said she had acted out of compassion, only wishing she had ended her mother's life earlier. A nurse from the facility where Dr. Postma's mother had been a patient also testified that the elderly woman had told him that she wanted to die. The nurse described the woman as a difficult patient who lacked the will to live.

Convicted, Dr. Postma received a one-week suspended sentence and a week's probation. In its opinion the court relied heavily on expert testimony by the district's medical inspector, who set forth certain conditions under which the average physician thought euthanasia should be considered acceptable. Among them were the requirements that the patient must be considered "incurable," the suffering must be subjectively unbearable, the request for termination of life should be in writing, and there should be adequate consultation with other physicians before euthanasia is carried out.

Inclusion of these conditions in the court's decision in the 1973 case became the cornerstone for the subsequent expansion of euthanasia as an acceptable option. Dr. Postma's case became the rallying point for further changes.

Two euthanasia groups were formed to pursue even

greater acceptance of the practice. One group, in northern Holland, was headed by Dr. Postma in cooperation with a social worker and his wife; the other, formed in The Hague, was headed by Dutch lawyer Adrienne van Till.

Other cases followed, each expanding the conditions under which the practice of euthanasia would not be punished. The turning point, giving the widest leeway to the practice of euthanasia, was an opinion rendered by the Rotterdam court in 1981. It listed a minimum of nine criteria that must be met if euthanasia is to be excused:

1. There must be unbearable suffering on the part of the patient.
2. The desire must emanate from a conscious person.
3. The request must be voluntary.
4. The patient must have been given alternatives and must have had time to consider them.
5. There must be no other reasonable solutions to the patient's problem.
6. The death does not inflict unnecessary suffering on others.
7. More than one person must be involved in the decision.
8. Only a physician may actually euthanize the patient.
9. Great care must be exercised in making this decision.

An additional requirement is that every instance of euthanasia must be reported to the local prosecutor. As it exists today, the Dutch legal system accepts the defense of force majeure—similar to the defense of necessity—in any prosecution for euthanasia. In such a defense it is claimed that all available options are unacceptable but that the least unacceptable has been chosen. While the illegality of the action does not change, two factors make the legal status of Dutch euthanasia a moot point: The vast majority of euthanasia deaths are falsely listed on death certificates as deaths resulting from natural causes, and of those few that were reported during the three years ending in 1990, only one case went to trial.

At the same time that the guidelines have been disregarded, they have also been broadened. One of the most telling expansions of the boundaries of "acceptable" euthanasia came in a 1986 judicial decision that recognized "psychic suffering" and the "potential disfigurement of personality" as acceptable grounds for euthanasia.

In some quarters concern about involuntary euthanasia was growing. By 1990 the Dutch Patients' Association, a disability rights group, had begun distributing a small wallet card for members to carry. The card specifically states that it is "intended to prevent involuntary euthanasia in case of admission of the signer to the hospital" and that "no treatment be administered with the intention to terminate life." The card is now seen by many as a necessity, considering the current climate of acceptance for ending lives considered to be low in quality.

Reports of euthanasia being administered to people with diabetes, rheumatism, multiple sclerosis, AIDS, and bronchitis and to accident victims are not uncommon. Reckless, even casual, performance of the practice—often without the patient's knowledge—has been noted. In 1991 this was corroborated by information released in a book titled *Regulating Death*. The book was written by Dr. Carlos Gomez, a medical resident at the University of Virginia Hospital, who personally interviewed physicians throughout the Netherlands, gathering information on their practices and attitudes. His research indicated that the official guidelines governing euthanasia were both unenforced and unenforceable.

Some of the pressure to administer euthanasia may also be attributed to inadequate pain control and inadequate comfort care for terminally ill patients in the Netherlands. This lack of care had been noted in a 1988 report by the British Medical Association, which had undertaken a study of Dutch euthanasia at the urging of British right-to-die activists.

The situation in Holland serves to illustrate the devastating effect that acceptance of euthanasia can have, even where basic health care is available to all. The Dutch government guarantees medical care to all citizens. Yet health coverage for all has not alleviated the universal fear of pain and fear of being without comfort care. Indeed, even where medical *treatment* is available to everyone, once euthanasia has been accepted in policy or practice, little emphasis is placed on the needs of noncurable patients. And euthanasia becomes an inexpensive and certain means of ending both pain and the problems of providing care.

As of mid-1990 there were only two hospices operating in all of Holland, and services at them were very limited.

In a speech at the 1990 Maastricht conference, Dr. P. Sluis, chairman of the Dutch Hospice Movement, stated, "As an organization, we are not against euthanasia." He explained that a big problem for Dutch hospices is a time limitation on care. A person with a life expectancy exceeding three months is not eligible for hospice services. This presents a real dilemma when a patient lives beyond the predicted three months.

Sluis described how he had once solved this type of dilemma by removing insulin from a diabetic hospice patient who had outlived his three-month limit. "I had to decide whether I would take responsibility for the patient," he explained.

The first official confirmation of the prevalence of involuntary euthanasia in the Netherlands came on September 10, 1991, when the long-awaited government report *Medical Decisions About the End of Life* was released. Popularly known as the Remmelink Report (named after the chairman of the committee that issued it), the study documents the degree to which doctors have taken over the decision making on questions of euthanasia.

It is ironic that a practice that is described as giving greater control to patients has instead given doctors unprecedented power. In Holland it is primarily the doctors—often without consulting either the patient or the patient's family—who determine who will die at their hands.

A sampling of the data found in the Remmelink Report gives a clear indication that physician-induced death is out of control in Holland, a country of 15 million people. Of the 130,000 deaths each year:

- Twenty-three hundred people die as the result of doctors killing them upon request.

- Four hundred people kill themselves with medication provided by their doctors for this purpose.
- One thousand people—an average of three each day—die from involuntary euthanasia. These cases, accounting for 0.8 percent of all deaths in the country, are deaths in which doctors prescribed, provided, or administered a medication with the specific purpose of causing death, even though the patient had made no explicit request for euthanasia. Of these patients, 14 percent were fully competent, while 72 percent of them had never given any indication regarding termination of life.
- In addition, eighty-one hundred patients died as a result of doctors deliberately giving them overdoses of pain medication, not for the purpose of controlling pain, but to hasten the patient's death. The decision to administer the intentional overdose was *not* discussed with 27 percent of the fully competent patients who died in this manner.

The findings of the Remmelink Report indicate that Dutch physicians deliberately end the lives of 11,800 people each year by administering or providing lethal doses or lethal injections. This accounts for 9.1 percent of annual deaths.

These numbers do not include the cases in which doctors withheld or withdrew life-sustaining medical treatment from patients with the intent to cause death and without the patients' consent. Nor do they include involuntary euthanasia carried out on handicapped newborns, children with life-threatening illnesses, or psychiatric patients.

It is particularly tragic that Holland, where such abuses are now documented, was the only country occupied by the Germans in World War II whose physicians refused to participate in any way with euthanasia programs. At that time Dutch doctors refused an order to take even the seemingly benign step of concentrating their efforts solely on restoring the "physical efficiency and health" of their patients. They recognized that obeying an order to attend to only those patients who had a good chance of full recovery would be the small first step away from the principle of caring for all patients. And they recognized where that first step would lead. The German who had issued the order was later tried for war crimes and executed.

Throughout the entire Nazi occupation Dutch physicians did not recommend, nor did they carry out, a single case of euthanasia. As Malcolm Muggeridge wrote in his essay "The Humane Holocaust," it took but a few decades "to transform a war crime into an act of compassion."

CHAPTER 10

■ ■ ■

A t the beginning of the same week that right-to-die leaders from around the world were meeting in Maastricht, another development on the euthanasia front occurred in the United States. It was the emergence of Jack Kevorkian, later to be known as Dr. Death.

Kevorkian, a sixty-two-year-old unemployed—not retired, as some reports have stated—pathologist from Royal Oak, Michigan, had been unsuccessfully trying to find the right person to test his new machine. This "killing machine," as it was called in a Detroit *Free Press Magazine* article in March 1990, was made from scrap aluminum, a toy car that Kevorkian had torn apart for its pieces, and various and sundry other scraps scavenged from garage sales and flea markets.

On June 4, 1990, Kevorkian parked his rusty old Volkswagen van at a campsite near Detroit. Later in the day, with his sister's help, he hooked up Janet Adkins to his machine. The fifty-four-year-old woman had been diag-

RITA MARKER

nosed with Alzheimer's disease a year earlier. She and her husband, Ron, both Hemlock members who lived in Portland, Oregon, had seen Kevorkian on the Phil Donahue show. After arrangements had been made with Kevorkian, both had flown to Michigan for her death.

Jack Kevorkian's contraption, which utilized three solutions—saline, a sedative, and potassium chloride to cause heart stoppage and death—worked. Janet Adkins was dead by nightfall.

The trial run was not without its problems, however. In his eagerness Kevorkian spilled the sedative as he was pouring it into one of the machine's bottles. As Janet Adkins waited in the old VW—probably staring at the sky through the windows framed by new curtains Kevorkian had personally made to spruce up the death van—Kevorkian drove the ninety-mile trip home and back to get more. Just to be sure that nothing else went wrong, he brought back some extra tools—needle-nosed pliers to do some "fine tuning" on the machine.

That done, the procedure was ready to go. But then the doctor, who had not worked with a living patient in years, couldn't get the needle properly inserted into Mrs. Adkins's vein. Four tries later, and with blood on his hands and spattered on his trousers, Kevorkian had finally hooked up Janet Adkins to the machine. According to Kevorkian, he activated the saline, and then Mrs. Adkins herself tripped the mechanism that activated the other, deadly dose.

His work finished, and with Janet Adkins dead, Kevorkian notified Ron Adkins, who had been waiting at a motel for word of his wife's death, the medical examiner, and the sheriff. Kevorkian was on his way to the front pages of newspapers around the world.

As the story of Janet Adkins's trip to Michigan unfolded, it became known that Kevorkian had never spoken to Mrs. Adkins until the weekend before her death. All arrangements—even the initial call to Kevorkian after he had appeared on *Donahue*—had been handled by the husband of the victim, who "did not want to be a burden to her husband and her family."

According to friends, when the vivacious and talented Janet Adkins—who had played the piano and climbed mountains—received the diagnosis of Alzheimer's disease, she had been shattered. At her family's urging, she entered an experimental program for the disease. Later, when it became obvious that nothing was available to stem its progression, she continued to handle her illness with aplomb.

Her husband, however, was unable to cope with the situation. He explained later that it was he, the healthy spouse, who couldn't sleep at night. He noted again and again that his wife had always been the strong one in the family. The Adkins children confirmed this as well. Janet Adkins had always taken care of the emotional needs of her husband and children. They all had depended on her.

When Janet Adkins expressed her willingness to die and get out of the way, she apparently received strong support from those closest to her. The Reverend Alan G. Deale, the Unitarian minister who presided over her memorial service, called the concept of planned death "an idea whose time has come." He explained that he had discussed the decision with Mrs. Adkins and her family but that he had not felt it was his job to try to talk her out of committing suicide. Her husband apparently felt the same way. In interviews following his wife's death never did Ron Adkins say he had tried to change her mind. At every step of her way to the Michigan campsite Janet Adkins had been told that hers was the right decision. The fact that she really wanted to die went unchallenged.

Where did that leave Janet Adkins? Did she feel, up until the very last, that she had to be the care giver? Did this place her in the untenable position of handling both her own needs and those of her family? Is it possible that she may have wanted someone to let her know she was loved for who she was rather than for what she could do? And was it also possible that Janet Adkins found herself so horribly isolated by self-expectations or the unspoken needs of others that she felt the only honorable road to take was that which led to a machine in the back of a rusty van? Was this burden of continuing to appear strong so others could lean on her as deadly as the lethal solution that entered her veins in Jack Kevorkian's van?

We will never know for sure what motivated Janet Adkins, but we do have a great deal of evidence regarding the plans of Jack Kevorkian.

For years this slight gray-haired man has had a fixation with death—the death of others. He speaks in italics, as he bluntly pushes for moving away from what he calls the "emotionalism over the Nuremberg codes."

As a second-year resident physician Kevorkian approached condemned criminals, suggesting that they donate their organs. More recently he has speculated about starting death row medical experiments and offering the option of death to prisoners with sentences of three years or more. (Even his attorneys did not like this last one.)

While no American journals printed his proposals for a "bioethical code for medical exploitation" prior to his achieving notoriety, he did manage to have several articles published in the mid-1980s *Medicine and Law*, an English-language German periodical. In one such article, published in 1986, he discussed future plans to make euthanasia more beneficial to society. He called this "positive euthanasia," a process by which "subjects," including infants, children, and the mentally incompetent, would be used for experiments "of any kind or complexity."

"If the subject's body is alive at the end of experimentation," he wrote, "final biologic death may be induced. . . ." Among the methods of death induction are the "removal of organs for transplantation, a lethal dose of a new or untested drug to be administered by an official lay executioner," and "a lethal intravenous bolus of thiopental solution, injected by an official lay executioner."

In August of the following year Kevorkian received some limited publicity when *Health Care Weekly* unveiled the feisty doctor's plans for a new medical specialty called obitiatry, a name appropriately similar to "obituary." Kevorkian, described in the article as a personal friend of Dutch Dr. Pieter Admiraal, had even then designed business cards for his future practice. His card read: "Jack Kevorkian, MD . . . Bioethics and Obitiatry . . . Special Death Counseling, By Appointment Only."

Kevorkian, though, remained essentially an unknown eccentric tinkering with his machines and writing his so-called bioethics codes until mid-1989. It was then that he tried to have an advertisement for his death gadget published in the Oakland County (Michigan) Medical Society *Bulletin*. When the seven-member medical society board unanimously turned down the ad, news services reported on the macabre product. This gave Kevorkian the exposure he wanted, and talk shows picked it up from there.

Following Janet Adkins's death, Derek Humphry applauded Kevorkian. In a phone interview from Holland, Derek referred to Kevorkian as a "brave and lonely pioneer," and Hemlock's national office issued a press release stating, "Hemlock would prefer that actions like those of Dr. Kevorkian were clearly made legal and not subject to ambiguity." The Society for the Right to Die commented on the case the same day. "He's pushing the boundaries," stated Rose Gasner, an attorney for the group. "It's uncharted legal territory." Gasner's organization was apparently waiting to test public reaction before deciding what its public stance would be on the case.

Kevorkian was charged with murder on December 3, but eleven days later Judge Gerald McNally of the Oakland County District Court in Michigan dismissed the charges. McNally later called for caution in passing any specific law opposing assisted suicide. "I think there's a place for it [medically-assisted suicide]," he told a Michigan reporter. "I'm confident this thing Kevorkian is spearheading or leading is not a false trend. Those trends are irreversible and you have to go along with it."

McNally explained that the "right to die is the most personal decision you'll ever make" and compared choosing suicide with other decisions made on an everyday basis.

Whether it is the choice of dinner entrée or the choice of death, it is the choice itself that counts, according to McNally. "You want to eat fish or chicken or beef. Whether you exercise choices or not gives life dignity. Those choices should be available," he said.

Even though murder charges against Kevorkian were dropped, his status and that of his machine remained an issue for the courts. A temporary injunction preventing him from using the device was issued, and the Oakland County prosecutor's office commenced action to make the injunction permanent. In issuing the temporary injunction, Circuit Court Judge Alice Gilbert stated that it was necessary to protect public health and welfare.

An outraged Kevorkian responded that just the opposite was true. "[T]he voluntary self-elimination of individual and mortally diseased or crippled lives taken collectively can only *enhance* the preservation of public health and welfare," he wrote.

The Hemlock Society's Michigan chapter sought to get in on the action, requesting to become a party to the case. When the organization was turned down, it filed a Silent Intervenor brief on behalf of Kevorkian, saying that permanently prohibiting him from using his "mercy machine" would have a "chilling effect" on the doctor-patient relationship.

Hemlock's views did not prevail, and on February 5, 1991, Judge Gilbert ordered that the temporary injunction be made permanent. In her thirty-four-page opinion she stated that "patient self-determination does not encompass self-extermination effectuated by a physician." Describing Kevorkian, Judge Gilbert wrote: "The multiple eccentric, unorthodox, and controversial remarks made by Dr. Kevorkian provide convincing evidence that he has a flare for flamboyancy, a propensity for media exposure, and seeks recognition through bizarre behavior. His arrogance coupled with unabashed disregard and disrespect for his profession and its current professional and ethical standards reveal that his real goal is self-service rather than patient service."

Kevorkian waited less than a year before defying the injunction. On October 23, 1991, he used a new and updated model of his invention in a secluded cabin in Oakland County, Michigan. The victims this time were forty-three-year-old Sherry Miller and Marjorie Wantz, who was fifty-eight.

Sherry Miller had been diagnosed with multiple sclerosis in the late 1970s. She was divorced in 1983 and had told a friend that "she felt she was becoming a burden on people." She first contacted Kevorkian in 1990.

Marjorie Wantz was described in initial news reports as suffering from "an incurable and painful genital tissue disease." She met with Kevorkian only two times before her death.

In a motel room on the night before their deaths, Kevorkian made a videotape of the women stating their desire to die. Plans called for both women to use the device that had come to be known as Kevorkian's death machine.

The following day preparations for Mrs. Wantz's death went smoothly, but Kevorkian ran into difficulty when he tried to hook Mrs. Miller up to the IV. With both women still alive at the cabin, Kevorkian drove back into town to get supplies to provide an alternate method of death for

Mrs. Miller. Four hours later he returned with a cylinder of carbon monoxide. He then rigged up a lever to activate the gas by taping a screwdriver to the handle of the canister. A mask was placed over Mrs. Miller's face, and when the screwdriver was removed, the gas was turned on. Mrs. Wantz had died shortly before, following activation of the levers on the death machine.

Commenting later on Mrs. Miller's death from carbon monoxide poisoning, Kevorkian's attorney, Geoffrey Fieger, said, "The gas offers a simple, painless, odorless death. Better than that, it leaves you looking good. . . . Your complexion looks beautiful and pink."

As for Mrs. Wantz, her husband stated that his wife wanted to die because of severe vaginal pain, but Kevorkian never examined Mrs. Wantz's vaginal area and saw her medical records in the motel room only the night before her death. Furthermore, upon autopsy, Mrs. Wantz's body showed no evidence of disease.

Although neither Marjorie Wantz nor Sherry Miller had been terminally ill, their deaths prompted much discussion of terminal illness and the fear of pain. Call-in programs and commentaries were filled with statements from people who said they would prefer death to excruciating pain. This reflects a prevalent belief that pain—particularly cancer pain—cannot be controlled and leads to the often stated view that the only option for some patients is pain or euthanasia.

Yet medical journals are full of articles reporting advances in pain control that make it clear that all pain can be alleviated and that which cannot be totally eliminated can be brought within tolerable limits. In 1990 the World

Health Organization released results of a six-year study involving 401 cancer patients. The study showed that "cancer pain can be treated satisfactorily until death." Successful treatment of such pain includes not only easing the pain itself but providing additional medication to eliminate other symptoms as well. Control of pain does *not* require that a patient be placed in a drug-induced oblivion.

Medical journal articles acknowledge that mitigating the fear of pain is also extremely important. Euthanasia advocates, however, erroneously claim that patients are condemned to excruciating deaths, thus exacerbating the very fear that makes pain management more difficult. To support their claims, they often introduce anecdotal evidence of patients who did not receive necessary pain management. As a solution they suggest euthanasia.

These claims should not be dismissed. Some physicians do not do their jobs well; other physicians have not kept up on the latest advances in patient care. But while the claims of the euthanasia advocates should not be dismissed, their solution to the problems should be. We would be doing far better to demand that doctors upgrade their training in comfort care and in current, highly effective pain control techniques than to empower them with the right to kill pain by killing patients.

Empowering doctors in this manner continued to be Hemlock's proposal following the deaths of Marjorie Wantz and Sherry Miller. As it had at the time of Janet Adkins's death, the Hemlock Society applauded Kevorkian. A press release, issued the day after Wantz and Miller died, stated: "Dr. Kevorkian's motive was purely humani-

tarian. . . . Dr. Kevorkian has done the nation a service. . . ."

On December 18 the medical examiner listed homicide
as the cause of the deaths of Wantz and Miller. During the
time that a grand jury was investigating these two latest
cases, Kevorkian once again made news when an article he
had written appeared in the *American Journal of Forensic
Psychiatry*. The thirty-five-page piece contained an elabo-
rate outline for dividing the state of Michigan into zones
that would be overseen by specialists who would review
cases of people requesting death. He suggested that his
Michigan plan could serve as a model for a national network of suicide clinics.

On February 5, 1992, a grand jury indicted Kevorkian
on two counts of murder in the deaths of Wantz and Miller.
He was arrested and charged that day.

Three months later, while Kevorkian was awaiting trial
on these charges, yet another disabled woman died after
receiving his services. On May 15 fifty-two-year-old Susan
Williams, who had multiple sclerosis, died from carbon
monoxide poisoning. Kevorkian had provided the canister
of gas and was present when she died. Her death, which
was later ruled a homicide, came less than two weeks after
a "Dear Abby" column printed the address where letters
could be sent to protest Kevorkian's prosecution for the
deaths of Miller and Wantz.

Meanwhile, by the end of 1991 Derek Humphry and the
Hemlock Society had begun an effort to distance themselves from Kevorkian and his activities, calling him "the
loose cannon of the euthanasia movement" and "a con-

fused man." No doubt seeing the need for distance as a necessity in Hemlock's bid to change the law on mercy killing around the country, Derek claimed that Hemlock had sent emissaries to Kevorkian as far back as October 1991 (prior to the deaths of Wantz and Miller), asking him not to use his machine again. Kevorkian's attorney denied this, calling Derek an "absolute liar."

CHAPTER 11

■ ■ ■

In June 1990 Jack Kevorkian was just beginning to make headlines. At that time it was difficult to predict just how much he would capture the attention of the American public and further confuse the issues surrounding euthanasia.

I spent the summer writing about all I had learned in Holland, which, at that point, seemed more threatening than Kevorkian. And I also spent even more time talking to Ann.

By that summer Ann had decided to go ahead with her lawsuit against Derek and Hemlock. She had also decided that she wouldn't use the attorneys who had represented her in her divorce proceedings. She didn't think they were as sharp as they could have been and was dissatisfied with their work. To help clear her name, she felt strongly that she needed a firm that would aggressively pursue her interests.

Finding new lawyers and preparing for the lawsuit took

up much of her summer, as did getting her medical insurance reinstated.

She was finally able to work out a deal directly with the insurance company in which she obtained the medical coverage on her own, but she had to pay a very high premium rate. Nevertheless, knowing that she did have medical insurance took a great load off her mind.

She did find time to enjoy herself that summer, too. She went river rafting for the first time, going down the Salmon River in Idaho with a friend and his brother. Both men were naturalists and experienced campers, and Ann had a great time, sending me "Ann in the Wilderness" pictures.

She also took up fly fishing, went horseback riding for hours on end, and prepared herself for the preventative and reconstructive surgery that was to take place in September. The surgery went well. Ann called me from her hospital room in great spirits. "I thought I'd look like Dolly Parton, but I guess I'll have to settle for being another Lily Tomlin," she quipped.

When Ann returned home from the hospital, friends from AA provided support, and one came to look after her for a week. This was a great help to her because following the surgery she had a hard time using her arms. Getting out of bed, for example, was difficult; she had to roll out of the bed, taking care not to lean a certain way. Not until several months later did she feel free to move her arms without difficulty.

The lawsuit against Derek, the National Hemlock Society, Hemlock of Washington State, and its leader, Ralph Mero, was filed in Lane County, Oregon, on October 19, 1990. Derek, in interviews following the filing, said the only reason for the suit was the divorce. It was, however, far more than that. The complaint was for libel, slander, outrageous conduct, negligent infliction of emotional distress, and breach of fiduciary duty. In the suit Ann specifically claimed as well that Derek's actions had been intended "to impede and oppress [her] recovery from cancer itself" and "to induce [her] despair and [her] suicide." Derek's response to this was that Ann's claims were without merit, prompted by her acrimony.

In November Ann finally started flight school at the Eugene airport. She had sold some farm equipment to pay for the lessons, and as she later wrote to Janet and Susan, the two women who had taken such good care of her in the spring, "it was white knuckle at first." But she persisted and loved it.

As the end of the year rolled around, Ann received news that made all the ups and downs and cruelty she had endured over the previous months fade into the background. A registered letter came from the Adoption Disclosure Department of Toronto's Social Services. Calling it the best news of her life, Ann found out that Ian, the son she had relinquished for adoption twenty-two years earlier, was looking for her.

The agency began what was to be an extensive screening process by phone before she and Bill, as he had been renamed by his adoptive parents, could eventually meet. The process was very slow and deliberate, and Ann accepted it willingly, careful not to press too hard for information or to expect too much. Although she was ecstatic at the news, she didn't want to dwell too much on it; knowing Bill was alive and well was enough for the moment.

Just before Christmas she came to visit us before going on to a cousin's house in Virginia. When I picked her up at the Pittsburgh airport, she was bubbling over with talk about Bill, and I couldn't resist teasing her.

"Just think, with a twenty-two-year-old son, you may even be a grandmother," I told her.

"Whoa. I'm just getting used to being a mother again," she said.

During her stay with us Ann seemed aglow in the overwhelming realization that she was in contact with her son. She had, after all, given up hope of ever seeing or hearing from him again. Now the prospect of their eventually seeing each other made her tremendously happy.

We trimmed the Christmas tree, took walks on the nearby university campus, relaxed, and read. My family loved having her. My husband, Mike, joked with her, our youngest son said he didn't mind letting her use his room as long as she liked, and she was even introduced to Chips, the ferret, and to Mandy, our Chihuahua terrier, who curled up on Ann's lap and fell asleep.

"I never would have imagined at this time last year that I could be so happy again," Ann said as we were getting dinner one evening. A few days later she left for Virginia. It had been a happy time for us, too, and for Ann a wonderful ending to a year that had begun on such a bad note. Sadly it was to be her last Christmas.

The first few months of 1991 held promise of a new beginning for Ann. She had met a number of people at a weekend conference—a workshop on building self-esteem—and one person, in particular, made a strong impression on her. She called to tell me about him.

"His name's Rick," she told me. "I don't know how to describe him except to say he's like a big teddy bear. I really like him." Then she went on to tell me that he was very quiet and that he was an emergency room physician at a nearby hospital. "He's really special," she said.

They had arranged to get together soon after that, but Rick had to cancel because of work. "I hope he's not getting cold feet about seeing me," Ann told me. "He's so sweet and so shy. . . . I'll just take it slow and easy." Within a few months they were seeing a lot of each other.

During this time Ann was thinking a lot about the much-anticipated meeting with her son. The Adoption Disclosure Department had done quite a bit of screening by phone, and by the middle of February Ann had sent off a picture of herself with a short "life history" to be used in the gradual reintroduction process. And she had received a letter from him, forwarded by the agency as the next cautious step in the procedure.

From the letter she found out that the tiny fellow she had wrapped in a blanket and said good-bye to more than twenty years earlier, was still blond and blue-eyed. But now he was six feet tall. He was a student at a fine arts conservatory in Montreal, majoring in film. He played the piano, the cello, the drums, and enjoyed the outdoors, as she did. And most important, his adoptive home in Toronto was with a warm and caring family.

When she received her first set of pictures—Bill as a little boy, Bill as a teenager, Bill at his graduation—she made color photocopies and sent them to me with a note saying, "My kid! Isn't he handsome." She wrote to Janet and Susan, too. "His letter was extraordinarily articulate and literate," she noted, bubbling over with motherly pride.

Even while talking about him, however, she was always sensitive to his adoptive parents and extremely grateful to them for being family to him. "They're the ones who took care of him when he was sick, picked him up when he was learning to walk, did all of the things that really make you a parent. But I'm so thankful that they're willing to share him with me now. I'll never try to take their place. I couldn't do that. But, oh, it's so wonderful just to know he's alive and happy and he wants to see me."

After the first of the year Ann began to write again. Although she genuinely liked to write, she also did it for financial reasons, realizing that she needed an income of some sort to support herself. Among her writing projects was a story that she believed needed to be told. It was the story of Hemlock. She had even selected a title for it— "Hemlock Unraveled." It was not to be only about the Hemlock Society itself but, far more important, about the image that Hemlock had perpetuated and that she, as its cofounder and deputy director for almost a decade, knew so well. She wanted to inform others—through her own personal experience—that what she had promoted for so long and what she had carried out in practice was not a good, kind, and compassionate solution to suffering. It was, instead, a deadly deception that, if accepted, led only to more suffering.

She was going to use her own story and hurt, not to "get

back" at Derek or Hemlock but to illustrate how, in real life, there is often "more to the story" than just a loving decision to "help" someone die.

While she maintained that it was possible that someone might opt for suicide, she had come to feel strongly that any involvement or "assistance" from others should remain illegal. The possibility that help in committing suicide could become legally available, she believed, would put pressure on the person to die. She reasoned that even though to all observers it might appear that a person really wanted to die, he or she could be responding more to the pressure than to anything else. Ann's firm belief that her mother really had not wanted to die lent strength to her argument.

Ann returned again and again to her own experience and what she felt to be intense pressure to die and get out of the way. She explained that if aid-in-dying had been legal at the time of her cancer diagnosis, she probably would have requested it—not because she wanted to but because she would have thought it was what she *should* do. Applying her own experience to the woman who is neither assertive nor well educated, she was convinced that such a woman could be overwhelmed by the pressures and expectations of others.

She had come to feel that any attempts to legalize aid-in-dying were misguided and dangerous. And she believed that by sharing her own pain and grief, she would help others avoid going through what she had endured.

Sometimes she read bits and pieces to me over the phone. I remember one part very well. It was a short passage in which she described a book she had once read, one that she said came very close to what she had felt. In the book a husband sits beside his dying wife. His hand, around which his wife's hands are encircled, is closed tightly around a little kernel of happiness. The kernel of happiness is his knowledge that very soon his wife will be dead, and he would be free to be with his mistress.

Knowing that someone wants you dead, Ann said, is more lethal than cancer as it spreads and kills.

Several months later Ann asked if I would be willing to write the book instead. She felt strongly that what she had to say needed to be told. However, she couldn't face the prospect of immersing herself in the Hemlock/euthanasia scene to the degree that would be necessary to write about it. She wanted to concentrate her writing on more positive topics. I questioned whether it would be wise for me to write such a book since my very strong opposition to euthanasia could lead readers to assume that the book was biased. But when she urged me to do so, I agreed, saying it was something we had a very long time to work on.

It was wonderful to see Ann working and planning ahead for new things in her life during that winter of 1991. Janet and Susan later shared a letter with me that Ann wrote during that time in which she told them of her new positive outlook on life. She wrote that her life had miraculously returned. She was now getting the threads of her life together and doing simple things she hadn't done for more than a year: rearranging furniture, buying flowers. She ended the letter saying how glad she was to be alive.

Unfortunately that happy period was brought to an abrupt end in early spring. Ann had gone into the hospital for some more surgery. The surgery was routine, a follow-up to the procedure that had been performed the previous fall, so she hadn't been particularly concerned about it. Indeed, everything seemed fine until a few days after the surgery when she was back at home. She began feeling ill. She told me that at first she felt as if she had the flu.

It was Sunday. Rick remembered it well. He'd called Ann earlier in the day, and she told him she felt awful. He had to go into work, and when he called her several hours later, she told him she felt even worse. Rick convinced her to get to the hospital just to be on the safe side. There she found out that she didn't have the flu. She had an infection from the most recent surgery, but no amount of insistence could keep her at the hospital. She told the doctors that she would get better faster at home. After some intravenous antibiotics she went back to the farm.

Rick had to work that evening as well, and he couldn't get over to the farm, so he kept tabs on her by phone. She assured him she didn't have a fever. But she hadn't used a thermometer to check. As Rick described it, "She had put her hundred-and-three-degree hand on her hundred-and-three-degree forehead."

By Wednesday night she knew something was seriously wrong, yet she didn't want to go back into the hospital. Rick wouldn't take no for an answer. "Go. Right now," he ordered. By then she had a massive infection, one that couldn't be treated with antibiotics. "I want to go back home," she pleaded, not wanting to believe that this was happening to her.

"Look, either you stay and get better or you go home and die," Rick told her.

She stayed. Her doctor arrived a few minutes later, and

she was rushed into emergency surgery, where her reconstructed left breast was removed.

Late spring of 1991 was difficult for Ann. Recovering from major surgery for a second time in less than a year, Ann found herself with a new worry. Tests had come back showing a liver problem of some kind. At first Ann assumed it was an indication of the cancer spreading to her liver, but this turned out not to be the case, and for yet one more time she set about regaining her strength and getting on with living.

CHAPTER 12

■ ■ ■

The year 1991 had begun as auspiciously for the Hemlock Society as it had for Ann. During that time Hemlock had thrown its support behind another significant case of a husband "helping" his wife to die—this time with the plastic bag method, which Hemlock has advocated as one of the preferred methods of "self-deliverance."

The previous August sixty-nine-year-old Virginia "Ginger" Harper of Loomis, California, had flown to Michigan with her husband, Bertram, taking along a copy of the Hemlock Society's instructions for "self-deliverance." She had been diagnosed with incurable cancer only two weeks before, after several earlier encounters with the disease. In a motel room near Detroit's Metropolitan Airport, Mrs. Harper took a lethal mixture of drugs and alcohol and put a plastic bag over her head.

If she had died then, the story would no doubt have ended, but Mrs. Harper removed the bag—not once but several times. It was not until after she had fallen asleep that her husband placed the bag over her head for one last time, securing it with rubber bands. Then, as he looked on, she died. An autopsy showed that Ginger Harper died of asphyxiation rather than a drug overdose.

Bertram "Bob" Harper was charged with murder, and his legal fees were paid for in part by the Hemlock Society. Harper admitted covering his wife's head with the plastic bag, but the defense claimed that suffocating a spouse with a plastic bag was "an act of love." Hugh Davis, Harper's attorney, went so far as to compare the plastic bag over Ginger Harper's head with the veil she had worn on her wedding day.

Throughout the court proceedings in the spring of 1991 Harper contended that his wife was primarily concerned about the quality of her life. As evidence of her wish to live only if she had no impairments, he produced a letter she had written years earlier. Ginger Harper had stated: "I want to establish these facts. I beg my husband, Bob Harper, to either terminate my life or help me terminate my life in the event of any sort of disabling disease or accident happens to me. I trust his love, his wisdom and his intelligence implicitly. I trust him totally. . . ."

On the CBS newsmagazine program *Whose Side Are You On?*, which aired later that year, Harper was asked if he had, at any time, tried to talk his wife out of suicide, if he had ever told her that he loved her and didn't want her to leave him, or if he had even suggested that they check with a doctor to see if the pain she was experiencing could be alleviated with medication. To each of these questions, Harper responded with an emphatic no.

Even more disturbing than that was the revelation that

Ginger Harper had tried to commit suicide a full year before she was diagnosed with terminal cancer—and no one in her family had urged her to get any type of counseling.

In May a Michigan jury found Harper, who had worn the Hemlock pin bearing the insignia "Good Life, Good Death" throughout his trial, not guilty. Also in Michigan, on the same day, another man was sentenced to four years in prison—for causing the death of a cat.

Even more significant for Hemlock than victory in the Harper case that spring was Hemlock's new legislative push—Initiative 119, which was Hemlock's effort to legalize aid-in-dying in Washington State. In January the initiative had been certified as having received sufficient signatures to be placed on the ballot in November. Banking on Washington voters' past willingness to pass controversial legislation, Hemlock was pushing hard for a change in the law. The Seattle *Post-Intelligencer* described the measure as "an attempt to update the state's decade-old Natural Death Act." Natural Death Act was the name of Washington's Living Will law.

In Initiative 119, called the Death with Dignity Act, the question to be put to the voters was simply: "Shall adult patients who are in a medically terminal condition be permitted to request and receive from a physician aid-in-dying?" Buried in the very small print of the initiative was the meaning of "aid-in-dying," defined as a "medical service" that would end a patient's life in a "dignified, painless and humane manner."

Although the exact method for delivering the "aid" was not specified in the proposal, its supporters did acknowledge that it would probably be accomplished by means of a lethal injection or drug overdose. An attempt was made to downplay this as much as possible. "Try not to go into methods of aid-in-dying such as lethal injections" was the advice given in a speakers' packet formulated by the Friends of Initiative 119, an umbrella group for the measure's supporters. Instead speakers were advised to say that Initiative 119 was needed to "protect our rights as patients." Audiences were to be told that the measure was needed to correct flaws that had been discovered by members of the medical community in the state's outdated Living Will law.

Nowhere in the wording of the initiative was it made clear that the state's homicide laws would change. The naked truth that what was called aid-in-dying in the initiative was currently called first-degree murder in Washington—and virtually every other state in the Union—was missing from news coverage as well. One national news program merely described the initiative as a proposal "to clarify language in Living Wills."

In addition to downplaying the lethal injection—direct killing—aspect of the measure, its proponents attempted to portray doctors who would provide the new "service" as caring, compassionate physicians. This image was significantly enhanced in March of that year.

It was then that Dr. Timothy Quill, a professor at the University of Rochester's School of Medicine and Dentistry in New York, wrote an emotionally charged defense of doctor-assisted suicide. His account of a patient's suicide was published in the *New England Journal of Medicine*.

Recounting the story of his patient of eight years—

known only as Diane—Quill skillfully blended timing, tone, and right-to-die jargon in a manner that achieved maximum impact. According to his account, Diane was an extraordinary person who had overcome many problems, both personal and medical. When faced with the diagnosis of acute leukemia, however, she was convinced that she was going to die and that she "would suffer unspeakably in the process." Her fears were affirmed by Quill, who wrote, "There was no way I could say any of this would not occur."

Quill acknowledged that he had long been an advocate of the right to die. (Although not mentioned in his article, his involvement with a euthanasia group goes as far back as 1976, when he developed a program supported by the Euthanasia Educational Council.) Fearing that she might achieve an "ineffective suicide," Quill referred Diane to the Hemlock Society and only a week later wrote a prescription for her, knowing that the medication "was an essential ingredient in a Hemlock Society suicide."

The Quill article had an essential component of the "ethically correct" posturing that was becoming effective in the euthanasia debate. That component was the requisite expression of regret. In the growing number of articles advocating euthanasia and physician-assisted suicide, hastening a patient's demise has taken on the aura of a praiseworthy deed as long as the medical professional pays at least lip service to discomfort with the decision.

Unlike the flamboyant and abrasive Jack Kevorkian, Quill did just that. News reports described him as having undergone an "agonizing struggle." He actually referred to an "uneasy feeling" about crossing the line between allowing death and causing death. It was his sentimental description of his final meeting with Diane though that won over commentators across the country. "In our tearful goodbye, she promised a reunion in the future at her favorite spot on the edge of Lake Geneva, with dragons swimming in the sunset," he wrote.

Not only did the *New England Journal of Medicine* publish the piece, but its editor in chief, Dr. Arnold S. Relman, endorsed Quill's actions. He told a writer for the *Medical Ethics Advisor* that he and his colleagues had been "deeply moved" by the account and had considered themselves "fortunate" to print the "very poignant" story. Relman pointed out as well that there were many differences between Quill's article and the "Debbie" article that had run in the *Journal of the American Medical Association* in January 1988. Among the differences, he noted, was the fact that there was no way to know if the Debbie story had been true. The Quill story, on the other hand, was signed. According to Relman, because it was signed, it was verified.

Relman may have been mistaken. While there is no doubt that Quill signed the article, there are definitely some questions about the accuracy of the account. Could it be that the Diane story was a fiction-based-on-fact account, masterfully orchestrated by a writer who sought to move the euthanasia debate forward? Some inconsistencies and contradictions make this seem possible.

For instance, Quill wrote, "I called the medical examiner to inform him that a hospice patient had died. When asked about the cause of death, I said, 'acute leukemia.' He said that was fine and that we should call a funeral director." A spokesperson from the medical examiner's office denied this, saying, "He [Quill] wrote that, but he did not make any such call."

Quill also claimed that he had given acute leukemia, rather than suicide, as the cause of Diane's death so that she would be spared the bodily invasion of the autopsy that would follow a reported suicide. His claim of protecting his patient from postmortem bodily invasion was destroyed when it was disclosed that Diane's body had been found at a local community college, where it was being used as a teaching cadaver.

Despite the questions and inconsistencies in his story, Quill became the role model for the "new ethic." His admirers included Dr. Timothy Johnson, medical editor of *Good Morning America*, who said that if Quill's actions were considered legally wrong, the legal system should be changed.

Dr. Louis Weinstein, a University of Arizona medical school professor, said he thought that what Quill did "was an act of love," although it was "a very difficult thing to do." So convinced was Weinstein that doctors should make some patients die that he penned his own modernized version of the Hippocratic oath, called the "Oath of the Healer." It appeared in a letter to the editor in the *Journal of the American Medical Association*:

> In the eyes of God and in the presence of my fellow students and teachers, I at this most solemn time in my life do freely take this Oath, whereby I shall pledge to myself and all others the manner in which I shall live the rest of my days. . . .
>
> I shall always have the highest respect for human

life and remember that it is wrong to terminate life in certain circumstances, permissible in some, and an act of supreme love in others. . . .

The Quill case was just the type that Initiative 119 supporters needed. Quill had put forward a good face for doctors who "assist" patients to die, and his actions would serve as a catalyst to keep euthanasia before the public in polls, commentaries, and television shows.

By the spring of 1991 magazine articles and talk shows about euthanasia had grabbed the attention of the public and were appearing with more and more frequency throughout the country. A typical example was the question "Should doctors do this?" asked by *Longevity* magazine in its June 1991 issue.

The magazine had run a survey asking, among other things, "Is it ever proper for a doctor to assist a patient in committing suicide, if the person may be years from death and not yet physically suffering greatly?" Of the respondents 57 percent said yes, only 26 percent said no, and the remaining 17 percent didn't know. The survey results were reported in an article that referred to the Quill case and also included interviews with Jack Kevorkian, Derek Humphry, and me.

Kevorkian used the occasion to call for development of his specialty of obitiatry, saying that general practitioners could then refer suicidal patients to an obitiatrist for death assistance. "Such a specialist would be highly respected in the profession, with a great deal of experience, perhaps retired," he said. (He later elaborated on this specialty in his February 1992 article in the *American Journal of Forensic Psychiatry* and during an interview on ABC's *20/20* with Barbara Walters.)

Derek Humphry used the opportunity to predict that Washington's Initiative 119 would pass in November and that Oregon and California would soon be part of the move toward changing the law. He explained that Hemlock wanted to "reform the law. . . . The physician could then assist without being prosecuted. The family would be informed only as a matter of decency." He stated, "We are within sight of achieving change."

My reactions to the survey differed markedly from those of Derek and Kevorkian. What I told the magazine was that the results reflected an elitist view held by many who are upscale and comfortable, an attitude that considers those who are dependent or sick to be inconvenient and disposable.

I believe that such a view, which stems more often from lack of awareness than from any malice, demeans the many people who desperately want and need to be cared for and cared about, treating them as though they were invisible and their struggle for the resources to obtain basic medical care as somehow unimportant. The support that has been given for assuring the right to be dead, if rechanneled into working for the right to medical coverage for everyone, could truly make a difference on policy makers.

Discussions similar to the *Longevity* article were taking place on talk shows, with both sides of the issue generally getting a hearing. In my dealings with the media I've found that producers really try to be fair when they put together shows on a controversial issue, although actually doing it is difficult, if not impossible. But one national show early that summer was far from fair.

I had been called and asked to do the show along with "several other people who would present personal experiences." It wasn't until after the show's taping began that I found out that I would be presenting one side and the "several other people" were five individuals who favored legalization of euthanasia.

One guest was a woman who had "helped" her husband die by pouring a huge amount of vodka into his feeding tube. Another had given her sister a mixture of cocaine, codeine, and other drugs, combined with tea and vodka; she had followed that by putting a plastic bag over her sister's head. She had obtained the directions for this procedure, she said, by reading *Let Me Die Before I Wake*. The third and fourth guests were a father and his son; the father had "aided" his wife's death in a four-hour process that started with an overdose of morphine, followed by an insulin injection, and ended with his injecting air bubbles into her vein; the son agreed that his mother, who had been diagnosed with stomach cancer two months earlier, should die, and he had "documented" her death by photographing it. The fifth and final guest was a woman who explained to the audience that although she had refused to assist her brother's suicide when he was dying, she had since changed her mind and if she had it to do over, she now would be willing to help him kill himself.

When—finally—I was brought on the set to present a "different viewpoint," only a scant few minutes of taping remained. I had very briefly described my concerns when the host invited a tiny, frail white-haired lady dressed demurely in a navy blue and white dress to the microphone. As an "audience participant" she pleaded with viewers to support the efforts then going on in Washington State to pass Initiative 119.

I recognized her right away. She was Trudi Dallos, the leader of a New York Hemlock chapter. So committed is Trudi Dallos to Hemlock that not long after the program aired, a newspaper article described her daily routine: "Trudi Dallos starts each day with a cup of coffee and *The New York Times* obituary page—looking for the names of people who called asking for information on how to kill themselves. Peering through her glasses, she searches the small type for evidence that anyone acted on the materials she sent them—a book and a chart describing how best to overdose on pills and the merits of a plastic bag."

Yet even though I knew who this timid-looking woman was, there wasn't time to explain that to the audience. Since I'd had very little time to speak, I deliberately interrupted her to make a few comments just as the show was ending.

Immediately afterward I realized how disastrous the whole show had been. I called Ann from the airport while I was waiting for my flight back home.

"How'd it go?" she asked.

"Awful," I told her. "No, not awful. Terrible. Worse than terrible." I told her about Trudi Dallos. "No one's going to know who she was. They'll think I was verbally beating up on a little old lady."

"I bet you did fine," Ann said. "You watch it and see," though she knew the show wasn't going to be aired for a few weeks. "Look, you did the best you could," she said when I didn't seem convinced. "Don't feel bad about it. . . .

Go home. . . . Get Mike and the kids and go out to the camper and forget about it."

Throughout our friendship it seemed to me that Ann and I managed to give each other a boost when we needed it most. I took her advice this time, too.

Despite the continuing struggles with her health, Ann was in an upbeat mood during this period. By early summer of 1991 she had recovered enough from her near-fatal infection to go back to her flying lessons and to riding Ibn. Her relationship with Rick appeared to be going well, too. They found a beautiful place to camp and hike—the Three Sisters Wilderness Area in western Oregon, which was to become Ann's favorite place. And most important of all, her son, Bill, was finally coming to visit in August.

Ann's anticipation had grown all year. With everything she had found out about Bill, she was already very proud of him. But she was concerned, too, wondering if he would be proud that she was his mother.

She met Bill at the airport, and from what she told me, there was a special bond from the very beginning of the reunion. Ann felt none of the strangeness one would expect between a woman in her forties and a young person meeting for the first time in more than twenty years. It was mother and son, who almost on sight bridged a two-decade gap.

They spent two fantastic weeks together. Rick, Ann, and Bill took the family dogs and went to Cape Perpetua on the Oregon coast, a ruggedly beautiful place with a spell-binding view of waves crashing against the massive boulders on the beach.

They watched whales playing in the water from eight

hundred feet above the sea. They walked on the shore together, tossing driftwood into the shallow water for one of the dogs to retrieve, and waded at the spot where the Yachats (pronounced Ya-hots, Indian for "at the foot of the mountain") River flows into the ocean. Ann and Bill drove up to the Three Sisters Wilderness Area and then went back to the farm, where she taught him to ride a horse.

They spent time learning about each other during those few short days, and a lot of catching up was done. "I can't believe how much alike we are," Ann said to me afterward. "The way he tilts his head, his little gestures, so many things. . . . I'd know he was my son even if someone hadn't told me so."

When I spoke with Bill later, I found him to be very much like Ann: intelligent, quiet, with a wry sense of humor and deeply sensitive. We talked about how much the trip had meant to him also and how very much he admired his mother. Bill was to be fiercely protective of his mother's reputation after her death and wanted to do everything he could to set the record straight.

Although no specific date was set for their next visit, it was assumed that this was the first of what would be many reunions. A few days after Bill had left to go back to Canada, Ann called me. "I'm so happy," she said. "Bill just phoned. He said he misses me. Can you believe that? He misses me."

As happy as she was, within a few weeks Ann had to get back to some of the less pleasant aspects of her life: deciding what to do about the farm and preparing for the litigation against Derek and Hemlock.

She knew she couldn't continue doing all the farm work on her own. She was going to have to make arrangements for some help. It would have been needed even if she were in perfect health, but she was facing still more surgery as a follow-up to the complications she'd had the previous spring. The added expenses were a problem, too, but Ann felt that job hunting was out of the question for the moment since she believed that first she had to "clear her name" and regain her professional credibility.

For that reason the litigation was particularly important to her. Hemlock, Ann said, had offered a settlement, but that in itself was not enough. She believed deeply that her life depended on what she saw as the need to strip off the labels Derek had applied to her with his frequent statements about her "mental illness." She was certain she could prevail at the trial—until *Final Exit* hit the best seller list.

CHAPTER 13

■ ■ ■

On August 18, 1991, Derek Humphry's book *Final Exit* topped *The New York Times* best seller list in the "Advice, How-to and Miscellaneous" category.

The book's cover was adorned with endorsements from author Isaac Asimov, former Colorado Governor Richard Lamm, physician and ethicist Frederick Abrams, theologian Dr. Joseph F. Fletcher, and author Betty Rollin. Rollin—whose *Last Wish* about how she "helped" her mother die, was then in the filming stage of a made-for-TV movie—also wrote the foreword to *Final Exit*.

Many commentators attributed the success of Derek's new book to some great societal need to control death. University of Minnesota ethicist Arthur Caplan called its success a "statement of protest of how medicine is dealing with terminal illness and dying." But as *USA Today*'s founder, Al Neuharth, later wrote, the success of the "poorly written although easy-to-read book" may, more accurately, have been ascribed to "hype." Derek agreed—

at first. Quoted in the *Journal of the American Medical Association* in November, he said, "The media have made this book happen." Yet several months later he wrote that there had been "no hype" or advertising to promote the book.

The book had been published in April by Hemlock, but its promotion and distribution were handled by Carol Publishing, whose goal was to make it a best seller. Carol Publishing concentrates largely on sensational nonfiction. It is owned by thirty-four-year-old Steven Schragis, who operates with the conviction that the way to sell books is to make it easy for reporters to write about them. He told *The New York Times* that when he publishes a book, he asks himself if the book itself "is interesting or controversial enough to provoke a feature in the Los Angeles *Times* 'View' section."

But in addition to his business interest, Schragis considered *Final Exit*'s success something of a "personal crusade," since both he and his wife are Hemlock Society activists. This crusade led him personally to handle the book's publicity. It was Schragis who sent letters to newspaper and magazine reporters. It was Schragis who contacted TV stations and news editors. And it was Schragis who, when he received no response, continued to push. He was committed and undaunted.

According to one published account, in a prepublication blitz Schragis sent numerous letters to editors and journalists at magazines, newspapers, and TV stations extolling the virtues of the book. In one such letter, to the publishing reporter of the *Wall Street Journal*, he wrote that bookstores were surprisingly receptive to *Final Exit*. He explained how the book would make a good news story since its acceptance by mainstream bookstores signified just how well the voluntary euthanasia movement was growing.

He received no response. According to the *Journal of the American Medical Association*, Derek himself admitted that three hundred review copies had been sent out, but they had not resulted in one review. Derek has claimed that fifteen thousand copies of *Final Exit* were sold during its first three months. But according to a press release put out by the Carol Publishing Company later that summer, only eight thousand copies of the initial forty thousand print run were distributed to bookstores around the country. The press release further stated that of those eight thousand copies, "under" two thousand books had been sold from April through mid-July. Another account stated that the figure was closer to one thousand.

Schragis, meanwhile, was not deterred, continuing to write letters. And then, on Friday, July 12, his labors finally paid off. The *Wall Street Journal* ran a major story on the book titled "Suicide Manual for Terminally Ill Stirs Heated Debate." Its lead sentence declared that controversy was brewing over "an explicit new self-help book." That one article acted "as a match to tinder," its writer, Meg Cox, said later.

Final Exit was off and running.

Hype over the book spawned book sales. *Good Morning America, CBS This Morning*, and the *Today* show scheduled interviews with Humphry. CNN and network nightly news programs devoted time to it. Orders poured in, and within days the remaining copies of the first run of forty thousand books had sold out.

Increasing book sales generated yet more hype. By mid-

August the book was a best seller, within a month several hundred thousand copies had been sold, and the book was available in libraries almost everywhere.

In most interviews Derek stuck to the "self-deliverance manual for only the terminally ill" description of the book. However, in an interview for a British newspaper, a momentarily unguarded Derek Humphry had been more candid. "It tells you how, where and when to kill yourself or someone else. It breaks the last taboo. Follow my instructions for a perfect death, with no mess, no autopsy, no post-mortem," he had told the London *Sunday Express*.

The book does just that. It not only gives step-by-step instructions that any suicidal teenager can follow but also offers explicit directions for any person planning to kill someone else. Written in large type—to make it easier for the elderly to read and follow its directions—the book contains a drug dosage table—previously distributed by Hemlock in pamphlet form—with specific brand names and lethal amounts. It also includes suggestions for obtaining and storing drugs and tips on ways to avoid criminal prosecution.

A couple of pages after the table, and after more than one hundred pages of instructions and suggestions for achieving death, four sentences tell the reader not to use the chart if he or she is "unhappy" or cannot "cope" with life. Such a person, Derek writes, should seek help. And where does Derek Humphry—the writer who has so carefully detailed the instructions on how to kill—suggest that one get such help? He is not terribly specific, offering only generalizations, which are followed by a sanctimonious statement about not "wasting" a life. This advice, it would seem, might be in the book more for the purpose of protecting the writer than the reader. Including that caveat also enables Derek to say, as he has again and again, that his book is not for anyone who is depressed.

A sampling of the catchy chapter headings and the almost flip tone of the advice offered is an indication of just how casually the author views suicide. "Self-Deliverance via the Plastic Bag" efficiently describes just what needs to be done to make sure that oxygen in the bag will be replaced with carbon dioxide and nitrogen. It also states that man "cannot live on carbon dioxide and nitrogen alone."

Not to be neglected is the decision about whether one should choose a clear or an opaque plastic bag for suffocation. It's a matter of preference; Derek would opt for the clear one because he likes the world that he would be leaving. He also describes how to practice with the bag so that a person can get comfortable with the whole process.

A section on "Going Together" has nothing to do with dating; it is a reference to double suicide. An etiquette section, "Letters to Be Written," contains a sample suicide note and the advice that if you end your life in a place such as a hospital or a motel, you leave a written apology, and perhaps a tip, for the "inconvenience" you have caused. Going out "Hollywood Style"—with air injected into the vein—is not recommended since if it works, it is probably detectable at an autopsy. Also, it would be difficult to achieve in the elderly, whose veins are "tricky to get into."

The horrors of German euthanasia programs are dismissed in one paragraph. Derek assures readers that physicians who had been involved were duly punished. He also claims that the German victims' deaths were "swift," although he makes the point that this is small consolation to the relatives of those who were put to death.

He tries very hard to show his fairness by examining the pros and cons of whatever he is discussing, but this tactic only serves to give more ideas to those who may be vulnerable. In looking at cyanide, for example, he dwells at length on its merits, and though he concludes that it should not be used because it is a very painful and violent way to die, the reader learns that it is nevertheless very effective.

Self-execution with firecrackers, rattlesnakes, electricity, guns, ropes and other methods are included in a section on "Bizarre Ways to Die." Derek states that if he hadn't written this section, his mail from those readers who felt "cheated" would have increased significantly. He turns thumbs down on shooting oneself; while it could be appealing because of its speed, certainty, and painlessness, it is "messy." But he does find death by freezing acceptable because he admires the person who would go to such lengths to commit suicide.

For those less physically fit, such as quadriplegics and the elderly—who have "terminal old age"—Derek foresees a delay before there is total acceptance of euthanasia. Once Hemlock manages to get aid-in-dying laws on the books, however, he predicts that there will be a "more tolerant" view toward such cases. He clearly calls for eventual expansion of eligibility for euthanasia to those who have become "incompetent."

Once *Final Exit* hit the best seller list, accolades were given its author for his courage in writing what some called a "long overdue book" that met the needs of people "desperate for such information." *The New York Times* syndicated columnist Anna Quindlen wrote that she read *Final Exit* out of curiosity but planned to keep it for possible future use.

Not every commentator shared that assessment. In a scathing review of the book in *Commentary* magazine, Dr. Leon R. Kass, a respected medical ethicist, described Derek Humphry's tone:

> Above all, the author is calm, cool, and collected, and marvelously matter-of-fact. His confident voice of experience guides us through every step of the process, allaying anxieties, dispelling doubts, showing us exactly how-to-do-it. Adopting a tone and manner midway between the Frugal Gourmet and Mister Rogers, Humphry has written a book that reads like "A Salt-Free Guide to Longer Life" or "How to Conquer Fear in Twenty-two Easy Lessons." The reader, blinded by blandness, nearly loses sight of the big picture: this self-appointed messiah is indiscriminately and shamelessly teaching suicide (and worse) to countless strangers.

Soon what some might call "results" of the book began to be reported. Three British Columbia citizens used methods described in the book to kill themselves. Two of the victims were in their late twenties; the third was under fifty. None was terminally ill. The vice-president of the Goodbye Society of Vancouver, British Columbia, which is associated with Hemlock, denied any connection between the book and the deaths, saying, "It seems almost impossible for someone who is in a depression to follow the Final Exit."

On September 9, 1991, a seventy-nine-year-old Buffalo Grove, Illinois, woman killed herself by overdosing on prescription drugs. Left on her nightstand was a copy of *Final Exit*. In response to reports about her death, Humphry told an Illinois reporter, "It bothers me not one whit that a terminally ill person would be found with this book on her nightstand. That's what this book is for." The woman had severe arthritis. In California, a twenty-nine-year-old woman was found dead in a Contra Costa motel room, a plastic bag taped around her head. She had suffered from chronic fatigue syndrome.

In early October the International Anti-Euthanasia Task Force office received a particularly tragic call from Southern California. There a thirteen-year-old girl had found her mother dead, with a plastic bag over her head. Near the dead woman was a copy of *Final Exit*, with passages highlighted. The woman, who had been seeing a counselor for emotional problems, had not been terminally ill.

Books have been "blamed" for many things, and certainly blaming books for actions is fraught with danger to the rights of free expression. For example, novels and news reports regularly contain explicit and gruesome descriptions of suicides and murders. But to blame their writers for other deaths that might occur after someone has read them is unfounded.

Final Exit, however, is neither a novel nor a news report. It is, and has been promoted by its author as, a "how to" book. Deaths related to the book are not tragic unforeseen events; they are the outcome of its explicit directions. Derek himself has said that hundreds of people have relied on his writing to take their own lives. Yet he maintains that he feels no regret or responsibility for such deaths.

Regarding *Final Exit*, the public should be aware of what the book contains and of its potential danger. This awareness should extend to recognizing that in recent years it has been *Final Exit*'s author who has spearheaded attempts to change the law to legalize both assisted suicide and euthanasia under the label "aid-in-dying."

In terms of sales the 170-page bed stand manual of death was a success. From the time the *Wall Street Journal* article appeared in July until mid-November 1991, sales of *Final Exit* had reportedly earned over two million dollars for Hemlock.

Ten years earlier, in *Let Me Die Before I Wake*, Derek had used folksy stories as a means to show people how to commit suicide or kill someone else. By the time he wrote *Final Exit*, he had dropped the folksy stories, presenting the options in stark detail. Though different in their approach, both books have the same underlying theme: Killing can be compassionate, and it can benefit the killer as well as the victim.

In *Let Me Die Before I Wake* there is a story about a woman who has smothered her mother. Called Mary in the story, the woman describes her feelings of ambivalence and recounts the "pep talks" she gave herself: "I can do this. . . . This is an act of compassion. It is not an act of brutality."

Reflecting on her actions after her mother is dead, Mary realizes that she has gained strength from the experience. If she can kill her own mother, she can do anything, she says, and she repeats this to herself whenever she needs to.

The fictional Mary saw killing her mother as a source of strength. And in the book's concluding chapter, written by Hemlock's Gerald Larue, such death benefits were reinforced. Larue explained not only that he had never heard of anyone who had regretted aiding an "act of self-deliverance" but that one of the saddest comments he had ever heard was that of a man who had *not* helped a friend to die. By contrast, according to Larue, those who had done so experienced feelings that were "almost euphoric."

When I first read *Let Me Die Before I Wake*, it was long before I met Ann. And it was long before the deaths of Ann's parents. Even then I found the glorification of killing so grotesque and the suggestion that it could be a source of strength and self-esteem so horrifying that it chilled me to read it. Now, as I reread it, I think of Ann— about how very different she was from the fictional Mary.

Yet Ann, along with Derek, had marketed *Let Me Die Before I Wake*. She had written, and Hemlock had sold, *Double Exit*. And though she had split with Hemlock by the time *Final Exit* was published, if she had been treated a little more humanely by Derek during her illness, she might have participated in the publication of that book as well. Both she and Hemlock tried for a long time to convince anyone who would listen that killing in the name of compassion is a decent, noble act.

But in the long run Ann realized that the one person she couldn't make believe that was herself. In her heart she could not reconcile what she had done.

CHAPTER 14

■ ■ ■

It was just before noon on Friday, September 6, when the phone rang. I hadn't heard from Ann for about a week and was thinking about giving her a call. But I had put it off, concentrating on several writing and research projects for which the deadlines were fast approaching.

"This is Ann," said the voice on the other end when I picked up the call.

I thought it was one of my former students named Anne, whom I still talk to fairly often. It sounded as if she were laughing.

"Ann?"

"I'm so afraid." Then I realized that it wasn't the student. It was Ann Humphry, and she was sobbing uncontrollably. "Oh, Rita, I'm so scared. I'm afraid of losing everything. My son. My farm. My—"

"Wait. Tell me what's wrong? What's happened?"

"I'm so tired. I just can't face any more surgery. Any

more doctors. Any more attorneys. I just want to check out. . . ."

By then I was really alarmed. She seemed so frightened. It was the second anniversary of her discovery of the lump in her breast, and I had never heard her sound so down. But she had called, I told myself. That was a good sign.

"Look," I said, "pack your things. Get on a plane and come over. Please. Let's deal with this together."

"Really? Is that okay?"

"Of course it's okay. It's more than okay." I was relieved she'd been willing to consider it.

"I'll call the airline right now. I'll get back to you," she said.

A few minutes later she called again. "I can't do it. I just checked, and it's over a thousand dollars unless I wait a week. They said I'd have to buy the ticket at least a week in advance to get it any cheaper. I can't wait that long. Do you have a ticket I can use?"

I did have one frequent flyer coupon that I was going to use for a trip to Ann's that we had planned for late October or early November. I called the airline. The earliest available date for a flight from Eugene to Pittsburgh was Sunday; I made the reservations and called her back, quickly giving her the flight numbers. "I'll run over and pick up your tickets right now and send them out by Fed Ex tonight," I told her. "You should have them by noon tomorrow. I've got to get going right now or I won't make it to the airport in time to get them out tonight. Say a quick prayer I don't get stopped for speeding."

I grabbed a Fed Ex envelope, hopped in the car, and

drove as fast as I could to the airport, where I got the ticket and put it in the express box right there. Then I called Ann. "The little red Yugo made it," I told her.

She laughed and said, "What do I owe you?"

"How about a few prayers that I get my work finished this weekend?"

"You've got 'em," she said. "I feel better already."

"So do I."

She was supposed to get into Pittsburgh early in the evening on Sunday, but the connecting flight out of Chicago was canceled. It wasn't until around ten-thirty at night that she finally landed.

"I just couldn't handle it alone the other day," she told me on the drive home. "I really need to talk about it, but I want to get some rest first. Can we just do whatever— whatever you and Mike and the kids would be doing—for the next few days?"

Looking back, I think she really wanted—and needed— to talk then. But as always, she was very concerned about "being a burden"—a phrase that I wish could be deleted from the English language. And since she knew I was busy with work, she was thinking about my need for time, not her need for rest.

It was close to midnight before we got home. Mike was waiting up for us. My sons were already asleep, though the youngest had prepared his room for her, cleaning and making up the bed with his favorite sheets.

"Hi, kiddo," Mike said, giving her a big hug.

"Hi. Are you too tired to see a tape?" she asked, taking out a videotape of her son's visit. Ann had bought a video camera sometime before, and once she got it, she video-taped everything. It became a great hobby for her, and Bill's visit, of course, had not escaped the camera.

As the three of us sat watching the tape, Ann did a running commentary. "That's my kid. . . . Isn't he great? . . . Look how well he rides. . . ." Gazing at the TV screen, she looked like any other proud mother watching her child. Mike and I both felt relieved; she seemed so much better than when I had talked with her two days earlier.

Ann slept late the next morning and joined me for a casual lunch with a reporter for whom I had just done an interview. After lunch she took a spare typewriter up to her room to do some writing of her own. Within a few hours she had completed a draft of the first few pages of what was to be a magazine article about her experiences in giving Bill up for adoption and being reunited with him years later. When she showed it to me, she remarked about how good it felt to be writing a story with a happy ending.

That evening, as we sat in the kitchen peeling carrots and slicing up vegetables for stir fry, she said, "Do you know what I want to do while I'm here? I want to go to one of those stores that puts letters on shirts. I'm going to get a sweat shirt that says, 'It's a Boy,' on it. My son may be over six feet tall, but he's still my boy." We decided we'd go to the mall later during the week.

She seemed her old fun-loving and relaxed self the next day. Early that morning, while she was still asleep, a call had come in from a local television station. It was doing a piece on *Final Exit* and asked if I would be willing to discuss it. I agreed.

The TV people arrived a little after nine o'clock. A camera was set up. The newscaster sat on the sofa, her back to the staircase that leads to the bedrooms. I was seated at the other end of the sofa, able to see the steps from the corner of my eye. We began discussing all that had been standard in the many "response interviews" I had done about Derek's book—its content, the Hemlock Society in general, Derek's "helping" his first wife, and his behavior toward his second wife. Then, just as the reporter was in the middle of another question, I caught some movement on the stairs.

I realized immediately that I should have put a note up at the top of the steps saying that there would be people from the television station downstairs. But it was too late. Ann was halfway down the stairs before she noticed the cameraman. She stopped, hesitated for a second, made a funny face to make me laugh, then continued down the steps, passing behind the reporter and ignoring the cameraman on her way to the kitchen.

I dashed into the kitchen a few minutes later, after the crew had left. Ann was sitting at the table, chuckling. "I'm sure glad you didn't introduce me," she said, dissolving into laughter. "That sweet young reporter sounded so intense. And she didn't even have a clue who walked right past her. She just missed the biggest story of her life." It was good to see her laughing.

That evening Ann and I finally had a chance to begin talking about what was really on her mind. We had driven in a separate car to join my husband and sons for a picnic at our camper located at a campground about twenty miles from the house. As we drove home, she began to talk about the upcoming depositions in her lawsuit against Derek and Hemlock.

The law firm had assigned a young attorney to take Derek's deposition. "Derek will run circles around them," Ann said. "I know him. And I know how he can handle these things. . . . I've tried to tell my attorneys. . . ." She was convinced that Derek would be able to twist everything if an inexperienced attorney handled the deposition.

"I've got to convince them," she said. "But I'm so tired of all of this. I don't want to get into a battle with my attorneys. . . . It seems like it's just one thing after another . . . and now, now Derek has the money he's gotten from his book to call in the big guns.

"I'm no match for him. . . . I know Derek and Hemlock are going to do everything they can to destroy me, and I can't face that. I'm so tired of losing. . . . I'm so tired of thinking that everything's going better and then having it come crashing down again. . . ." I couldn't blame her for feeling so frustrated. Even in those short months that we had been friends, it seemed as though whenever things were going well for her, something else happened that threatened to take it all away.

"Have you thought about just dropping the lawsuit?" I asked her, wondering if the pressure associated with it was bad for her at the moment.

She responded adamantly. "No way. I'm not going to do that. I've said there were two things I wanted to live for: seeing my son and getting through this lawsuit. I've done one, and my attorneys have said the suit could go on even if I'm dead. That lawsuit is *not* going to be dropped."

We drove around, talking for a long time. When we arrived at the house, she stopped before getting out of the car and said, "I'm going to do some more writing in the morning. Then can we just spend the afternoon talking?" And that's what we did.

It was only then that I realized how frightened Ann felt, that she had been putting on her I'm-feeling-better face until she knew I was done with my work. She seemed desperate, far more alone and far more emotionally exhausted than I'd imagined. Facing her were more surgery and the looming specter of the litigation. She also felt, she said, the certainty that Derek was going to fight hard—harder than ever—now that he had all the money he had earned from *Final Exit*.

Underlying it all, though, was the overwhelming sense of guilt she felt over the deaths of her parents. She told me again and again that she knew her mother hadn't been ready to die, how she could never forget it, and how wrong it was. "I don't think it's any coincidence I got cancer," she said.

"Wait a minute," I told her. "Cancer isn't a punishment. It's an illness. It's been over a year . . . you're doing okay . . . you can—"

"I just want to go and be with my parents," she cried. "Don't you see? For someone to really beat cancer, they need support. Sure, I know you're here for me. But you've got your family, and I live thousands of miles away. . . . Julie cares about me, but she's got her hands full . . . and Rick, I'm afraid that if I lean too hard on him for help . . .

"Rita, you and I both know ... I've read a lot about cancer recovery. I've tried to make myself strong. Look at me. I've learned to take care of myself or at least thought I had. ... I've gone river rafting; I've learned to fly; I've gotten to know my son, and I'll always be grateful for that ... but to *really* beat cancer, to *really* recover, there has to be that strong, strong support. When Derek left, he took that from me. He took a part of me that I need to really recover. And I can never get it back again. ...

"I need someone to love me. I want someone to take care of me. ... And I don't have that. You have Mike and your family. ... I don't have that. ... But I can get out now before Derek can do any more to me. At least I'll be doing it myself. I won't let him hurt me anymore."

Hearing her talk about "getting out," I realized how much greater her anguish was than I had wanted to admit. She had been so good at putting on her cheerful demeanor when she first arrived, I had convinced myself that perhaps I was overreacting in being so worried about her. Now, though, I saw how wrong I'd been.

As we talked, I urged her at least to consider moving in with us for a while.

"Don't you see?" she asked. "What if I offered you a million dollars for the task force but told you you'd have to leave your family? Would you take it?" I told her I wouldn't.

"You're offering for me to move here," she said, "and that means a lot to me. But I couldn't do that, just like you wouldn't leave your family. I can't just leave my place, my farm, my animals. I'd be giving up everything that I have. . . ." I said that was different and that, if she killed herself, she'd be leaving her farm and her animals anyway.

"But *I'd* be doing it," she answered.

"I've given it a lot of thought," she went on. "I wanted to get some professional help. I know I need that kind of support to get me through this. But I can't do that." I asked her why.

"Remember what Derek did when I checked myself into the hospital in Eugene after he left? Remember how he used that? Remember how he's twisted any counseling I've ever had to make it sound like I'm unstable? Do you realize what he'd do now if he heard I was getting any type of counseling? He'd have a field day.

"He's got access to media. Now more than ever. Who would take the word of a 'crazy lady' against that of a best-selling author?" she asked.

"But getting counseling and support and recognizing that you need it is a sign of stability," I said.

"Sure. You know that. I know that. Derek knows it, too. But that's not going to stop him," she said.

Complicating matters even further was the fact that her medical insurance was through a small carrier. In order for the company to cover any counseling, she would have to find a counselor within Oregon. Practically speaking, that meant the Eugene area, where in the small-town climate word traveled fast. Derek, more likely than not, would find out.

There was nothing I could say that seemed to change Ann's feeling that she was trapped in a no-win situation. I tried pushing her to drop the lawsuit; suggesting that she put off surgery for a while; begging her to come live with us; reminding her how bleak things had looked before yet how they had gotten better. . . .

I tried the "we'll look back on this next year and realize what a bad time this was" approach. I tried to help her see that there wasn't anything she could do now to change her parents' deaths and that anyone could be forgiven for anything, that she needed to forgive herself. I tried to convince her to meet with a psychologist in Steubenville; she wouldn't even consider it. I also tried to help her see that if she killed herself, she would be benefiting Derek. And I realized how inadequate my efforts had been.

On the second to the last evening before she was to leave, Ann was resting on the couch, having come down with a bad cold earlier in the day. I told her I had to run over to my office for a few minutes. Instead I went down the street to my daughter's apartment. From there I phoned a friend whom I'll call Aaron. Aaron is an oncologist in a nearby city who devotes a large part of his practice to dealing with depression in cancer patients. While, in the past, I had been very careful to get Ann's permission before discussing her situation with anyone, I felt I had to make this call without asking her first.

I told Aaron what had been going on. He said he would be glad to talk to Ann. He knew of her and was willing to do whatever he could. I explained the insurance situation as well. Since he was in a group practice, he would be required to bill her if he saw her at the office, so he suggested that both of us come to his home for dinner.

The drive would take only about an hour and a half,

and there would be no record of the visit. It sounded good to me.

I went back to the house and told Ann what I had done.

"No," she said. "I know you want to help me. But I don't want to tell another person. I wouldn't be able to keep seeing him. It would only be a one-time thing. I need ongoing support, but I can't get it because Derek would use it. . . . I'm tired. I'm tired of trying to explain. . . ." She went up to take a nap, and I called Aaron to thank him for his willingness to help.

Hanging up the phone, I felt so powerless. It had been difficult enough watching Ann blame herself for everything that had happened to her; knowing there was nothing more I could say or do to change things made it even worse.

The next morning I had reason to feel a little more hopeful. Ann knew that I was going to Italy with my husband for a week on a working vacation. I asked her to promise not to do anything until I got back. "I don't want to go unless I know you'll be all right," I told her. She said she'd try, though she couldn't promise anything—I now recognize that was her way of trying to communicate how bad she still felt—but then she got out her checkbook and wrote a check. "This is for you to come out to my place," she said. "If you get a ticket a week in advance, it'll cover it." Then she added, "I wish it could be more." She wanted me to put it in the bank right away.

Like so much during that week, every time I saw what I considered a positive sign, I convinced myself that things really weren't as bad as they seemed. Despite everything,

Ann did look more rested now than when she had first arrived. And she had seemed eager about her writing projects while she was here, beginning her article about Bill and giving me a list of people to talk to for the book on euthanasia that she wanted me to write. Handing me that check and talking about my visit seemed another good sign that she was planning for the future.

I drove her back to the airport on Saturday. When we got there, she said, "You don't have to come in."

"I want to," I told her.

We went to the boarding area, sat down, and waited. For a couple of minutes neither of us said a word.

"Penny for your thoughts," I said.

"Penny for yours."

"I feel like I'm having a bad dream or watching a movie. It's a prison scene. There's an execution scheduled, and everyone's waiting for the phone to ring—for the governor to call and stop it. . . . I feel so helpless," I told her.

She smiled and said, "I'll call you tomorrow night."

A few minutes later her flight was called. We got up and gave each other a big hug. "I love you very, very much. Please be here when I get back from Italy," I told her.

"I love you, too. I'll call you tomorrow night," she said. She walked up the ramp. At the top she turned and waved. Then she disappeared into the jetway.

As I drove home from the airport, I was still very worried. Although matters didn't seem as thoroughly hopeless as they had two days before when I'd called Aaron, Ann still seemed very fragile. I debated whether I should call anyone. Rick came to mind. But I had talked to him only a few times and really didn't know him well at all. I had no idea if he knew about Ann's thoughts of suicide. I thought of calling the cousin whom Ann had visited the previous Christmas, but I had never talked with her. Besides, what would she do? Would she—or Rick—tell Ann I had called, and would Ann somehow feel I was going behind her back? It had been one thing to call Aaron—Ann was here, and I didn't feel that I had violated her privacy—but if I called someone after she had left, I was worried that Ann might think I was betraying her in some way.

The only person I could talk to was Ann's friend Julie. I called her when I got home. She had talked to Ann, too, and knew everything. She assured me she would keep in touch with her while I was away.

After talking to Julie, I again debated whether I should call Rick or Ann's cousin and decided not to risk it. It is a decision I have regretted ever since.

Much to my relief, Ann called the following night, sounding much more positive. She told me not to worry, that things were better. In fact, she had decided to go on a river-rafting trip with Rick. She promised that she would give me a call when she got back.

She did go on the trip and called almost a week later when she returned. She seemed to be in a good mood, and I really thought she was going to be all right. We phoned each other several more times, and then, on Saturday, September 28, the night before Mike and I left for Italy, I called to give her the phone numbers where I could be reached there. It was the last time we talked.

CHAPTER 15

■■■

Mike and I had been in Italy for several days, yet not one message had come in from either home or the office. That was highly unusual. Although there weren't phones in the rooms where we were staying, we were sure the main desk would have notified us if anyone had called.

To be on the safe side, I placed a call to the office myself. It was Thursday. Michelle, the office manager, answered.

"I'm so glad you called. I tried all day yesterday to get you," she said, explaining that both she and my daughter—who was watching her little brothers while Mike and I were away—had been trying to reach us. "Every time either of us got through, they'd say, 'No English,' and hang up," she said.

"What's wrong?" I asked, immediately picturing that one of my sons was sick or had been in an accident of some kind.

"You've got to call Ann right away. It has something to

221

do with her lawsuit. If you can't get hold of her, call her attorney." She gave me his number.

Wondering if Ann had also tried unsuccessfully to reach me by phone, I dialed her number but couldn't get through, so I called her attorney. He informed me that the day before his firm had withdrawn from Ann's case.

I couldn't believe it. "Why? Why in the world would you do that?" I asked him.

He explained it had been over a disagreement in the handling of the case. He assured me that it had nothing to do with its merits; the case was still viable, so Ann could still find another law firm.

I knew right away what Ann must have felt when she had been told about the withdrawal; it was just one more piece of heavy artillery that Derek could use. While the case wasn't dropped, he'd make it sound as if it had been. He would imply that the case itself, not its handling, was the reason for the withdrawal.

The attorney also told me that he had been on vacation when the firm's decision to withdraw had been made. I thought I could sense that he regretted the decision, but at that moment I didn't care one bit how he felt.

"She's been hanging by a thread, and you've just cut the thread," I told him, and hung up. I tried Ann's number again. It seemed an eternity for the call to go through. When someone answered, it wasn't Ann. It was Pam Wilson, a woman from town with whom Ann had become friendly. She had talked about plans for Pam to live in a trailer on the property.

"Ann's been gone since last night," Pam said. "I'm just getting ready to call the police." She told me that she and her ten-year-old daughter had come over the night before, after Ann had called her. Ann had told her she had to go away and wanted her to come and watch the place. Ann had given her Julie's phone number, leading Pam to assume that Ann had left for Los Angeles because Julie was sick or needed to see Ann for some reason. Pam and her daughter had stayed at the farm overnight. But then she had received the day's mail. In it was a note from Ann, mailed the previous day, instructing Pam on what to do with the animals and asking her to take good care of the farm. . . .

"Go ahead, call the police right away. I'll check back with you in a few hours," I told her. I hung up and called Ann's attorney back. I told him she was missing. I also said a few more things that were neither professional nor polite but that did express what I was feeling.

Mike knew as soon as he saw me that something was very wrong. He put his arms around me. "Ann's missing," I said. I think we both knew that she was already dead. But we kept hoping.

Late that night, when I got hold of Pam again, she told me that Ann's truck was gone, along with her horse trailer and her horse, Ibn. By this time Rick was at the house, too. He thought she might have gone to the Three Sisters Wilderness Area, one of their favorite spots, where she had taken her son, Bill, only weeks before.

In the next few days I called Ann's farm over and over. I talked with Pam, with Rick, and later with Julie, who'd come up from Los Angeles, and Bill, who'd flown down from Montreal. They all were waiting. I told them that I would call a couple of times a day and also made arrangements so they would have an easier time calling me if they needed to.

Bits and pieces of information came in. Someone had seen Ann driving her truck into the Three Creeks campground in the Three Sisters area on the night she had left Monroe—just as Rick had guessed. She had saddled her horse and ridden west out of camp. Less than two hours later Ibn had returned to the camp without either a saddle or bridle. It appeared as though he had just wandered back.

Search-and-rescue workers combed the trails and an area a hundred feet wide on either side of them. On the second day of the search, a horseshoe had been found on one of the trails. When Ibn had wandered back into camp, he had been missing the right rear shoe.

When four days had gone by since she'd left and Ann still hadn't been found, we became a little more optimistic. I think all of us hoped that maybe she would just walk out of the woods somewhere and say, "Hey, I changed my mind." But we really knew better.

A half hour before noon on Tuesday, October 8, 1991, a search-and-rescue team member who had ridden his horse a couple of hundred yards off the trail spotted a saddle and saddle pad behind a tall pine on the top of the ridge just above Snow Creek Ditch. Ann's body was next to it.

Dressed in her green corduroy riding pants, her black knee-high riding boots, and a rose-colored ski parka, she was lying with her head on a canvas saddlebag, facing north toward the north and middle of the Three Sisters mountains. The sheriff said it looked as if she had just gone to sleep.

Ann had not gone to sleep. She had killed herself. The police reports starkly describe the scene:

> [The officer] discovered 6 empty pill containers, (Vesparax) in her right hand coat pocket. . . .
> [At the scene, there was] ½ gallon of Chivas Regal Scotch whiskey about ⅓ gone. Near the bottle was a seal, indicating the bottle was opened when Humphrey [sic] reached the area. Also nearby the body was a one gallon milk bottle nearly full of water. The green plastic cap for the milk bottle was on a log in front of the body. . . .
> Humphrey's remains were then given to Tabor's Desert Hills Mortuary.

Bill, Rick, Julie, Pam, and two of Ann's cousins received the news at the farm. Rick was the one who called me in Italy to let me know that her body had been found.

She wasn't going to walk out of the woods. The searing moment when I knew for certain that she was dead will always live with me in memory. And I've thought often of the lines written so long ago by Thomas Hood, about another tragic suicide:

> *Take her up tenderly,*
> *Lift her with care;*
> *Fashion'd so slenderly,*

Young, and so fair!
· · · · · · · · · · · · · ·
Take her up instantly,
Loving not loathing.
· · · · · · · · · · · · · ·
All that remains of her
Now is pure womanly.

The Ann whom I had respected as a skillful adversary and had come to love and care deeply for as a friend would never again be on the phone saying, "Hi, Rita. It's Ann—guess what?" No more would we laugh about the fact that we always seemed to know when the other was going to call. And she was never again going to say, "I'm going to make it. I know I am," or, "It's so good to be alive."

I called and talked with Rick, with Julie. . . . Even though there had been five days to prepare, to know what to expect, there was for all of us now a numbness, a finality, allowing no hope, however small. Knowing what to expect and hoping it won't prove true are far different from knowing, at last, that hope is gone.

The rest of my time in Italy passed by in a blur. I watched people. Tourists sauntered by in the streets. Teenagers laughed, shoved, snapped their fingers to the beat of their music. Cars were backed up in the heavy traffic. . . . But it seemed as if everything moved in slow motion. I had a sense that this was all somehow unreal.

Apparently for Derek Humphry, the days immediately following the discovery of Ann's body were filled with making statements about her to the press.

This was the man who, eighteen months earlier, had

said, "I don't wish to reconcile with Ann. I've never thought about a reconciliation. . . . If you want the absolute truth, since 1984, I have had a mistress, other than Gretchen, in another city. . . ." This was the man who, only weeks before Ann's death, had told a reporter, "I married in haste and repented. After the first year, I knew it was bad but I tried to make it work." His comments had led the article's writer to conclude, "What it comes down to is, he didn't love her."

Now, quoted in various newspapers, Derek seemed to be trying to convey how caring and how hurt *he* was. A sampling of his statements:

"I would have liked to have spoken with her," (after claiming Ann had refused to speak to him since their marriage broke up).

"It's not within the philosophy of the Hemlock Society that you take your life if you're unhappy or you have a setback."

"I don't feel accountable. I feel tremendously sad. All her sisters [*sic*] and friends have called me. I don't find that people blame me."

"It's extremely painful to have lost two wives. It's like a Greek tragedy . . . but I shall press on with my campaign."

Even though there had never been any diagnosis of Ann's having the "borderline personality" or other disorders with which he had often labeled her, Derek reiterated his previous statements about her instability, embellishing as he went along:

"A year after our marriage I realized I'd married someone with severe mental problems. . . . [S]he was in constant psychological care. We spent thousands of dollars on care for her. I was told she had a borderline personality disorder. It was more a manic depressive condition."

"Some of us, when we are terminally ill and in an unbearable state, want to die. And some of us, like poor Ann Wickett, who have a lot of private demons, want to die. . . . The complexities of her recent life were too much for her. In the real world, there are some people whose minds are so tortured that they cannot go on."

On Thursday, October 10, I flew back from Italy to Detroit for a speaking engagement that had been booked long in advance. I did not cancel the speech since I knew that I deal better with difficult situations by keeping as active as possible.

As soon as I got to the hotel, I called the farm. Bill answered. "My mom left an envelope for you," he told me.

"She did?"

"Yeah. Do you want me to open it?"

"Please."

I heard him take a quick breath. "Oh my God. It's a note to Derek. She's written something to you on the bottom. Do you want me to read it to you?"

He sounded shaken. There is something about reading such a letter aloud that makes it even more difficult emotionally. I thought it would be too hard on both of us.

"No. Don't read it aloud. Can you put it in express mail for me?"

He said he would. We went on to talk more, first about Ann and then about Derek.

"I can't believe the things he's saying about my mom.

Doesn't he have any sense of decency? . . . He hurt her so much while she was alive. . . . He's still trying to hurt her. . . . Won't he ever stop?" Bill and the others who were gathered at the farm wanted to issue some type of statement. We worked on a press release by phone. It read: "We are shocked and appalled by the statements made by Derek Humphry. . . . We grieve her death because certainly, to all of us, it is a needless loss of a remarkable woman. We hope that all this tragedy will cause people to wake up and to realize what Derek Humphry and the Hemlock Society now stand for."

The statement was issued under the names of Julie Horvath, friend and former Hemlock member; Robert William Stone, son; Nancy Raymo, cousin; Pam Wilson, friend; and Rita Marker, friend.

When we issued the statement, I thought it would be the extent of my public comment on Ann's death for many months. I wanted to take that long to wait, to reflect and to heal from the loss of my friend.

However, a few days later, on Monday, October 14, that changed.

Monday, October 14, was the Columbus Day holiday. Around ten o'clock that morning our doorbell rang. There stood the UPS man with the express envelope Bill had sent to me. I opened it and at once understood why Bill had been so shocked when he read the enclosed note from his mother, Ann, to me.

I sat down, read Ann's note slowly, and handed it to Mike to read. Then I put it away, but a few minutes later

Derek:

There. You got what you wanted.
Ever since I was diagnosed as
having cancer, you have done
everything conceivable to pre-
cipitate my death.

I was not alone in recognizing
what you were doing. What you
did--desertion and abandonment
and subsequent harrassment of
a dying woman--is so unspeakble
there are no words to describe
the horror of it.

Yet you know. And others know too.
You will have to live with this
untiol you die.

May you never, ever forget.

Ann

Rita: My final words to Derek. He is a killer. I know. Jean actually died of suffocation. I could never say it until now; who would believe me? Do the best you can.

Ann

I took it out again to reread. I knew Ann meant that I should tell her story, but it seemed too soon. I resolved to give it careful thought and to discuss her message with friends before I made a final decision.

Two hours later the phone rang. It was Dr. Joseph Stanton calling from Boston. "Have you seen today's *New York Times*?" he asked. When I said I hadn't, he told me that Derek Humphry had taken out a half page advertisement, boldly headlining it SUICIDE, A STATEMENT BY DEREK HUMPHRY and giving his title, "Executive Director of the Hemlock Society, Author of *Jean's Way* and *Final Exit*." Dr. Stanton then read the ad.

The casual reader could well have been taken in by the ad, which began, "I am saddened to learn that my former wife, Ann Wickett Humphry has taken her life during a period of despondency. My colleagues and I at Hemlock mourn the death of one of our founders, and our condolences go to her family." He went on to recount her literary and academic accomplishments; then he said she "was dogged by emotional problems." Noting that she was beautiful and talented and could be wonderful company, he said that "her depressions were so serious that she had to be hospitalized. . . ." Once again he was attempting to distort the fact that *she* had checked *herself* in and out of the hospital when experiencing emotional exhaustion. Describing suicide as "a basic liberty," he explained that "nobody could temper her private demons." He concluded by asking, "What organization does not have casualties? Emotional illness knows no boundaries."

Hemlock's mailing address and telephone number appeared at the bottom of the ad.

Was the advertisement intended to promote Hemlock or to be a sincere eulogy to Ann's memory? Apparently it was neither. Asked later why he placed that ad, Derek replied, "Damage control."

To those who knew Ann well, the ad was a cruel assault

on her memory. As soon as I heard what Derek said about her, I decided to make her note public. Ann could no longer speak for herself, but her note spoke for her. I contacted three journalists whom I respected. I told them of the note's existence and explained that I was prompted to release it after seeing Derek's *New York Times* ad.

Interest in Ann's final note forced the media to take a fresh, closer look at Hemlock and the euthanasia movement in general.

Ann had also made a videotape with Julie Horvath just two days before her death. Julie had gone up to be with her for a few days during the weekend I left for Italy. The tape shows Ann discussing her feelings about her parents' deaths, Derek, Hemlock, and the euthanasia movement in general. Excerpts from the videotape were later shown on various television programs.

That is what Ann wanted. Would that the media interest that has been shown since her death had been evidenced while she was alive.

Articles containing information from the note Ann had left for me, including one in *Vanity Fair* that printed a copy of the entire note, discussed Ann's allegation that Jean had died of suffocation. Derek has steadfastly maintained that the accusation is totally false. There is, of course, no way of proving the actual cause of Jean's death. I question, though, whether the method itself is of any but aesthetic importance. Whether Jean died from the lethal drugs Derek mixed into her coffee, as he has consistently maintained, or from a pillow he placed over her face, the fact remains: Derek Humphry intended to become a widower on that March day in 1975.

CHAPTER 16

■ ■ ■

On October 23, 1991, I went to Ann's farm in Oregon for the first time. It was close to the date that we both had planned for me to be there, but it was for a far, far different reason. Bill had already returned to school in Canada, but Pam, Rick, Julie, and I were having a memorial service for Ann at the farm she loved. Other friends of Ann's, including neighbors from the surrounding area, would be there for dinner beforehand.

I had agreed to pick Julie up at the airport in Eugene; then we would stop at the grocery store to get a few needed items and head on out to the farm. Driving the last few miles, I thought back to all the times Ann and I had said we would get together at her house for a few days. We had promised ourselves endless games of Scrabble, which we both loved and she always won, and maybe—if I were especially brave and Ann especially patient—she would teach me to ride a horse. There would never be any of that now. . . .

Julie's flight from Los Angeles got in just a little before three in the afternoon. We stopped in Junction City to buy the groceries, and by the time we got to the farm, a typical western Oregon rain was falling. It was almost a mist—liquid sunshine, as it's called in Oregon. The mist had turned to heavy rain by evening, as the house began to fill with people who had also been Ann's friends. Because of his work schedule at the hospital, Rick arrived after everyone else.

Although it was the first time many of us had met one another, the atmosphere was of a great big family getting together for Thanksgiving. (There was even a turkey in the oven.) It was the comfortable feeling of being among friends, even though the one person who had brought us all together wasn't there.

In the kitchen, warm from the oven, one woman mashed the potatoes as she talked of first meeting Ann. Another, stirring the gravy, said, "Oh, and I remember . . ." The bright blue teakettle began to steam. Someone moved it to another burner and joined in the conversation.

The rugged trestle table in the dining area was soon covered with salads and desserts many had brought. We filled our plates and carried them past the big fireplace and up two steps into the living room. There we all sat—on the sofa, chairs, cushions, the floor—and shared our memories of Ann.

After dinner some of the women took their umbrellas and walked down toward the pond where Ann's ashes had been scattered. By about nine or nine-thirty most of the people had gone. Only Julie, Rick, Pam, Pam's ten-year-old daughter, Lindsay, and I remained. A few minutes later Lindsay went off to bed.

Rick put another log in the wood stove and lit the candles he had brought, using two bottles as candlesticks. We all chuckled, commenting that Ann would have liked that "rustic touch." For the next three hours the four of us shared more memories. Julie showed us her *Anna Banana* book, a children's storybook she and Ann had laughed about so many times in the past. She also talked about the videotape she and Ann had made two days before Ann's death and how she had thought Ann would be okay when she returned home to Los Angeles. Rick talked of speaking to Ann about their plans for the weekend just the day before she died. Pam, who had come to know Ann through the feedstore where Ann bought supplies for her animals, talked about how much Ann had meant to her. And I told them about the baseball game she and I had played at dusk in an open field, winning by one run against the other team, made up of my ten- and twelve-year-old sons.

We shared the loss each one of us felt and knew that things could never again be quite the same. We discussed what we thought Ann would want us to do—to let the truth be known—each in our own way, not pushing, but not being intimidated either.

As the last log turned to embers, Julie softly read the closing lines of T. S. Eliot's "Choruses from 'The Rock' " from one of Ann's favorite books.

And we said good-bye to Ann.

CHAPTER 17

■ ■ ■

During the month following Ann's death, Derek accurately observed that Washington State was in the international spotlight. As November 5, 1991, drew near in that state—voting day for Initiative 119, Hemlock's aid-in-dying measure—he said, "The world is watching what happens in Washington and, if they are not convinced by that, then I think California will make the point next year." Vowing to fulfill his goal of changing the law throughout the country, he said, "We are hoping for the domino effect."

Euthanasia proponents were predicting victory as voting day approached. They had raised more than $1 million for the campaign, giving them a formidable five to one fund-raising advantage over opponents. Total expenditures—by both supporters and opponents—set a record for a state ballot measure in Washington.

Surveys were indicating a potential landslide win for Initiative 119 and medically induced death. The Tacoma

Morning News Tribune conducted a poll of likely voters during the closing weeks of the campaign and found that 61 percent of potential voters supported the measure while only 27 percent opposed it. The remaining 12 percent were still listed as "undecided."

On Sunday, November 3, two days before Washington voters were to make their decision, the Boston *Globe* ran a front-page story, "Poll: Americans Favor Mercy Killing," which carried results of a poll sponsored by the *Globe* and the Harvard School of Public Health. The poll indicated that 64 percent of respondents thought doctors should be allowed to directly and intentionally kill patients by means of lethal injection or drug overdose. Release of that poll, timed to hit the national media on the day before the crucial vote, seemed a rather transparent attempt not only to report public opinion but to shape it as well.

When the citizens of the state of Washington cast their ballots, however, they refused to bestow on doctors the legal right to kill patients. In a record-breaking turnout Evergreen State voters said no to Initiative 119 by a 54 to 46 percent margin.

Derek Humphry has long attempted to make it appear as though opposition to aid-in-dying emanates from religious zealots who "shriek 'murder.' " Portraying opponents in this way has been common among those who promote aid-in-dying. It depicts those who disagree with euthanasia as people who seek to advance their own religious agendas and impose sectarian views on society. If this were true, it would be a violation of the principles on which our country was founded. But it is *not* true.

It is important to note that people on both sides of the

euthanasia controversy claim membership in religious denominations. There are also individuals on both sides who claim no religious affiliation at all. But it is even more important to realize that this is not a religious debate. It is a debate about public policy and the law.

Legislation that prohibits salesclerks from stealing company profits also coincides with religious beliefs, but it would be absurd to suggest that such laws be eliminated.

Those who want to change laws related to euthanasia have confused matters by seeking to transform a matter of public policy into one of sectarian debate.

The fact that the religious convictions of some euthanasia opponents parallel what has been long-standing public policy does not disqualify them from taking a stand on the issue. Throughout the history of our country and, indeed, in the entirety of modern history, doctors have been restrained by laws from killing their patients. The necessity for having such laws has been and should continue to be argued on the basis of pure reason, completely apart from any singularly religious doctrine.

In Washington polls taken within days of the defeat of Initiative 119 indicated that fewer than 10 percent of those who opposed the measure had done so for religious reasons.

Acknowledging that other factors were at work, Derek Humphry stated later that the measure had lacked safeguards and that he believed this had been a major factor in its defeat.

More than anything else, however, Washington voters realized that passage of aid-in-dying legislation would transform Dr. Jack Kevorkian's self-execution machine

into standard medical equipment, and the practice of patient killing would become just another medical service.
This dose of reality turned the tide in the closing days of
the campaign. Washingtonians clearly did not want to turn
the medical degree into a license to kill.

From the closing months of 1991 through most of 1992
Hemlock embraced another initiative campaign. Known as
Proposition 161, the Death with Dignity Act, this fresh
assault on California was coordinated by Californians
Against Human Suffering, the group previously known
as Americans Against Human Suffering. Interestingly
enough, a new label—"assistance-in-dying"—was used in-
terchangeably with "aid-in-dying" on the petitions, though
"aid-in-dying," defined as "a medical procedure that will
terminate the life of the qualified patient in a painless,
humane, and dignified manner," remained the operative
phrase.

In his officially prepared summary of the proposal Daniel E. Lungren, California's attorney general, noted, "This
measure would result in some unknown savings due to
decreased utilization of the state Medi-Cal program and
other public programs, including county programs." His
point was well made. People killed by doctors will never
again use any government program.

Derek Humphry signed another appeal letter, asking
for help in obtaining the necessary signatures to place the
measure on California's ballot in the fall. An advisory
board for the measure included such well-known individuals as Betty Rollin, Bertram Harper, and Episcopal priest
Malcolm Boyd (author of *Are You Running with Me, Jesus?*).
Initial endorsements included the California Psychological

Association, the Beverly Hills Bar Association, the Gray
Panthers, and Los Angeles KABC Talkradio. The California chapter of the National Organization for Women assisted in signature gathering by making it possible for
petitions to be sent to each of its thirty thousand members.
The 1992 campaign also differed from the one in 1988 in
that it hired professional signature gatherers instead of
relying on volunteers.

The events leading up to the November vote on the
California initiative—Proposition 161—weren't the only
important developments on the euthanasia front in 1992.
In February there was a failed attempt to pass a resolution
endorsing aid-in-dying by the American Bar Association.
That resolution, which would have sparked lobbying efforts in legislatures across the country by the 370,000 members of the ABA, was strongly opposed by the ABA's
Commission on Legal Problems of the Elderly for a number of reasons.

"The proposed right to choose aid-in-dying freely and
without undue influence is illusory and, indeed, dangerous
for the thousands of Americans who have no or inadequate
access to quality health and long-term care services," the
commission stated in its seven-page memorandum of opposition. Emphasizing the illusory nature of such a "right,"
the commission said, "The lack of access to or the financial
burdens of health care hardly permit voluntary choice for
many. What may be voluntary in Beverly Hills is not likely
to be voluntary in Watts. Our national health care problem
should be our priority—not endorsement of euthanasia."

Declaring that aid-in-dying is "intentional killing,"
John H. Pickering, the commission's chairperson, said the

proposal could result in the application of "subtle pressures" to hasten death. On February 3 the ABA House of Delegates voted overwhelmingly to defeat the resolution.

In late March the long, torturous story of Nancy Beth Cruzan finally seemed to reach its end. The severely brain-damaged young woman had been cared for at the Missouri Rehabilitation Center in Mount Vernon, Missouri, for seven years, after a car accident in 1983 had left her totally disabled. Her food and fluids were provided by a gastrostomy tube, even though she could chew and swallow at the time the tube was inserted. Tube feeding had been initiated to make her long-term care easier.

A narrow ruling by the U.S. Supreme Court in June 1990 had temporarily blocked her family's attempts to deny her food and water. The ruling held that it was not unconstitutional for a state to require clear and convincing evidence of an incompetent person's wishes before eliminating treatment or care. In August of that year Ms. Cruzan's parents had once again instituted court proceedings, claiming that new witnesses had come forward with the required clear and convincing evidence: In a casual conversation at work twelve years earlier, Ms. Cruzan had supposedly indicated that she would not want to live if she were severely disabled. Finally, on December 14, 1990, a court order authorized the removal of her food and water. Nancy Beth Cruzan had died of dehydration the day after Christmas 1990.

But this was not the end. In an obscene exploitation of a dependent and disabled young woman, Ms. Cruzan's last days were captured on film by a television crew as she lay dying in her hospital room. It was part of *Frontline*'s continuing coverage of the entire case. That particular segment was shown on PBS on March 24, 1992, titled *Frontline: The Death of Nancy Cruzan.*

During the same period articles seriously considering the implementation of euthanasia appeared in both professional and popular publications. At the beginning of the year the *New England Journal of Medicine* published an article by Dr. Guy Benrubi of the University of Florida Health Science Center, who proposed the practice of what one might call safe killing. Although he acknowledged that there is concern "about how to set aside the role of healer and assume the role of terminator of life," Benrubi suggested that it could be done by certified specialists, "skilled in relieving suffering and, when necessary, terminating life painlessly." He proposed involvement of psychiatrists—to evaluate potential recipients of euthanasia—but noted that "the psychiatrist would not have veto power over the decision to perform euthanasia." That final decision "would be left to the patient and the anesthesiologist," he wrote.

In the "My Turn" column of its March 2, 1992, issue, *Newsweek* magazine printed one of the most blatant calls for involuntary euthanasia to appear in more than fifty years in any popular publication. "A Gentle Way to Die," written by Katie Letcher Lyle, who was identified as a freelance writer "actively involved as a volunteer on three boards advocating on behalf of the handicapped," suggested that severely retarded individuals have their lives terminated in the same manner as animals destroyed by a veterinarian.

Lyle asked readers to "consider Henry, 40, six feet tall, strong, affectionate, loves action movies, his IQ in the profoundly retarded range." She explained that Henry is troublesome and "has already cost American taxpayers roughly $1.5 million" and that he has no prospect for a good life. Her solution? Death for Henry.

The summer of 1992 saw a major change at the Hemlock Society. In August, the Reverend John Pridonoff, a Congregational minister from San Diego, replaced Derek as Hemlock's executive director. Hemlock had announced six months earlier that Derek was planning to retire so he could devote more time to writing and lecturing. He would retain a nonsalaried position with the title of "Founder and Consultant." In the announcement, Derek explained it was time for the group's management to be handled by someone else. "I shall still be in the forefront of the campaign to change the laws on euthanasia through public speaking and my writings," he said.

True to his word, Derek did devote a great deal of time campaigning for California's Proposition 161. However, on election day, November 3, California voters defeated the aid-in-dying initiative. The margin of 54 to 46 percent was the same as that in the previous year's Washington state defeat.

Discussing the measure's outcome, euthanasia proponents noted that efforts to legalize physician-assisted death would continue, with Oregon as one possible site of the next attempt. Ten days after the vote Derek wrote, "Undoubtedly, we in the Hemlock movement will try an initiative again. . . . In fact, plans are under way in Washington and Oregon." He also called on President-elect Bill Clinton to establish a presidential commission on the right to die.

There should be no doubt that the battle over euthanasia

will continue. I believe, though, that efforts of euthanasia supporters will not be limited to campaigns similar to those that took place in Washington and California but will include attempts in courts, state legislatures and policy making boards of professional organizations as well.

It also seems likely that the full aid-in-dying package (physician-assisted suicide *and* physician-administered death) will be incrementally promoted. For example, Dr. Timothy Quill, whose 1991 story about providing a patient with the means to commit suicide was widely discussed, and two other physicians have proposed guidelines for making assisted suicide a part of medical practice. Their proposal is limited to providing an overdose to hopelessly ill patients who can self-administer the lethal medication. The guidelines suggest that family members be encouraged to be present for the actual suicide. Ironically, the authors acknowledge that, if such guidelines are adopted, there would be a need for support and careful monitoring of those involved "since the emotional and social effects are largely unknown but are undoubtedly far-reaching."

As for Jack Kevorkian, the dismissal of murder charges against him in the deaths of Marjorie Wantz and Sherry Miller has been appealed. The case could eventually determine whether a physician's actions which are directed at ending a patient's life will be considered medical treatment. The International Anti-Euthanasia Task Force has filed an amicus brief in the case which may not be decided until well into 1993.

As I consider the developments of 1992 I realize how quickly time has passed.

It's been more than a year since Ann's death. Often during the first year I'd catch myself looking back, thinking "last year at this time, we were. . . ." And, sometimes, I'd find myself going to the phone to call her. There are so many little things that serve as reminders of our friendship: She gave me the trivet that I put kettles on when they come off the stove; I still have the almost finished container of tea bags we bought; the score sheets from our games are still in the Scrabble box.

Looking back is one thing. Looking forward is another. I wish that, as friends, we still could be saying "next year at this time. . . ." But that is not to be. All I can do is what Ann said in her last note to me when she wrote, "Do the best you can."

I know now what a deep personal effect the suicide of someone close can have. My friendship with Ann, brief though it was, meant a great deal to me. And I miss her very, very much.

AFTERWORD

■ ■ ■

At a Hemlock conference held in Denver in November 1991, a table held a display of greeting cards intended for people who are ill. Their messages were not the expected statements of concern or well-wishing. Designed by a Hemlock member and endorsed on the conference program as cards to be given to the terminally ill, one card in particular exemplified the core of the movement that would remove the last shred of hope remaining to a person faced with a life-threatening illness.

The greeting card was of heavy cream-colored bond, embossed with tiny blossoms. Its edges elegantly ragged in the style of an invitation, it carried the message "I learned you'll be leaving us soon."

Problems face all of us as we attempt to deal with illness, disability, aging, and our own mortality. Fear of pain and fear of suffering are genuine and cannot simply be wished away. Yet to see a person who is terminally ill and blithely say, "I learned you will be leaving us soon," represents the ultimate in abandonment. The idea of killing the incurable, once before, was advanced as a remedy that has come to be known as part of the Final Solution. We pledged, "Never again!"

What, then, can we do constructively?

In the many discussions surrounding euthanasia, the need to provide better pain control is a central issue. That there exists today the technology to control pain is recognized, but the inadequacy of up-to-date training in pain control within the medical profession is also commonly acknowledged. A requirement that physicians devote part of their continuing education to pain control techniques prior to the renewal of their medical licenses could be a sustantial step toward eradicating the fear that doctors will not alleviate pain.

It is important to remember something else. Recent high-profile cases of assisted suicide have involved disabled, not terminally ill, people. Most debate about aid-in-dying has focused on people who are terminally ill but, as severely disabled people have pointed out, laws such as those that failed in Washington and California would affect them immediately.

There is a deeply rooted prejudice in our society against those who are severely disabled. This prejudice manifests itself in many ways, including the lack of necessary services. Many severely disabled people who could live full independent lives find themselves virtually incarcerated in hospitals and nursing homes because there is little or no funding for independent living. No national policy exists for training attendants to help with daily needs. And, while the Americans with Disabilities Act made great strides in opening up job opportunities, there are no centers for training severely disabled people to enter the work force.

An assumption that one is "better dead than disabled" frequently results in inadequate psychological support for those with disabilities. A severely disabled person who exhibits suicidal behavior and depression is likely to be given saccharine pronouncements by able-bodied professionals who encourage the "rational choice" that has been made.

Psychologists who are disabled have not only the professional training but also the personal experience which allows for greater insight into the needs of disabled persons seeking help. Yet, in celebrated cases related to death requests from disabled people, this wealth of expertise goes virtually untapped. According to Dr. Carol Gill, a clinical psychologist and president of the Chicago Institute of Disability Research, "Views of experts who are disabled are rarely sought or recognized by the legal system, medical establishment or media. One might wonder if people with disabilities have credibility only when asking to die!" This disregard for professional expertise coupled with the current tendency to comply with a disabled person's suicide request is nothing more than an act of discrimination which would not be tolerated if directed toward members of other minority groups.

Establishing programs and policies to meet the need for counseling, for independent living opportunities, and for job training where appropriate should become a priority in a society which professes concern for all citizens.

Efforts to assure that each and every person has access

to health care are absolutely imperative. Recognition of the limitations of medical technology and curative measures is of great importance as well.

There does come a time when enough is enough, a time when continued attempts to cure are not compassionate, wise, or medically indicated. Yet when cure is no longer possible and curative treatment is stopped, when a justifiable "no code" is in place, that person at the "edge of life" remains a person with the innate human dignity vested in each and every human being. Killing is a destructive answer; caring never is.

This nation's founding documents affirm that *all* are created equal and are endowed by the Creator with certain unalienable rights. We would do well to reflect on all that this entails as life approaches its natural end. As a reflection on this, printed as an appendix in this book, is the magnificent declaration "Always to Care, Never to Kill."

APPENDIX

---■■■---

The following is a condensed version of a declaration on euthanasia, produced by the Ramsey Colloquium of the Institute on Religion and Public Life in New York City. The colloquium is a group of Jewish and Christian theologians, ethicists, philosophers, and scholars who meet periodically to consider questions of ethics, religion, and public life. It is named after Paul Ramsey (1913–1988), the distinguished Methodist ethicist, who was a pioneer in the field of contemporary medical studies.

This version of the declaration, which also appeared in the *Wall Street Journal* of November 27, 1991, is printed with permission of *First Things* magazine.

"Always to Care, Never to Kill"

We are grateful that the citizens of Washington state have turned back a measure that would have extended the permission to kill, but we know that this is not the end of the matter. The American people must now prepare themselves to meet similar proposals for legally sanctioned euthanasia. Toward that end we offer this explanation of why euthanasia is contrary to our faith as Jews and Christians, is based upon a grave moral error, does violence to our political tradition, and undermines the integrity of the medical profession.

In relating to the sick, the suffering, the incompetent, the disabled and the dying, we must relearn the wisdom that teaches us *always to care, never to kill*. Although it may sometimes appear to be an act of compassion, killing is never caring.

The well-organized campaign for legalized euthanasia cruelly exploits the fear of suffering and the frustration felt when we cannot restore to health those whom we love. Such fear and frustration is [*sic*] genuine and deeply felt, especially with respect to the aging. But to deal with suffering by eliminating those who suffer is an evasion of moral duty and a great wrong.

Deeply embedded in our moral and medical traditions is the distinction between *allowing to die*, on the one hand, and *killing*, on the other. That distinction is now under attack and must be defended with all the force available to us.

Medical treatments can be refused or withheld if they are either useless or excessively burdensome. No one should be subjected to useless treatment; no one need accept any and all life-saving treatments, no matter how burdensome.

When we ask if a treatment is useless, the question is: "Will this treatment be useful for this patient; will it benefit the life he or she has?" When we ask if a treatment is burdensome, the question is: "Is this treatment excessively burdensome to the life of this patient?" The question is not whether this life is useless or burdensome. We can and should allow the dying to die; we must never intend the death of the living. We may reject a treatment; we must never reject a life.

Once we cross the boundary between killing and allowing to die, there will be no turning back. Current proposals would legalize euthanasia only for the terminally ill. But the logic of the argument—and its practical consequences—will inevitably push us further.

Arguments for euthanasia usually appeal to our supposed right of self-determination and to the desirability of relieving suffering. If a right to euthanasia is grounded in self-determination, it cannot reasonably be limited to the terminally ill. If people have a right to die, why must they wait until they are actually dying before they are permitted to exercise that right? Similarly, if the warrant for euthanasia is to relieve suffering, why should we be able to relieve the suffering only of those who are self-determining and competent to give their consent? Why not euthanasia for the suffering who can no longer speak for themselves?

Once we have transgressed and blurred the line between killing and allowing to die, it will be exceedingly difficult—in logic, law, and practice—to limit the license to kill. Once the judgment is not about the worth of specific treatments but about the worth of specific lives, our nursing homes and other institutions will present us with countless candidates for elimination who would "be better off dead."

In the face of such danger, we would direct public attention to four sources of wisdom that can teach us again always to care, never to kill.

Religious Wisdom

As Christians and Jews, we are not authorized to make comparative judgments about the worth of lives or to cut short the years that God gives to us or others.

We are to relieve suffering when we can, and to bear with those who suffer, helping them to bear their suffering, when we cannot. We are never to "solve" the problem of suffering by eliminating those who suffer. Euthanasia would inevitably tempt us to abandon those who suffer. This is especially the case when we permit ourselves to be persuaded that their lives are a burden to us or to them. We may think we care when we kill, but killing is the rejection of God's command to care and of his help in caring.

Moral Wisdom

We can, if we wish, renounce many goods or give them into the control of another. Life, however, is not simply a "good" that we possess. Our life is our person. To treat our life as a "thing" that we can authorize another to terminate is profoundly dehumanizing. Euthanasia, even when requested by the competent, attacks the distinctiveness and limitations of being human. Persons—ourselves and others—are not things to be discarded when they are no longer deemed useful.

We can give our life *for* another, but we cannot give ultimate authority over our life *to* another. To turn one's life into an object that is at the final disposition of another is to become less than human, while it places the other in a position of being more than human—a lord of life and death, a possessor of the personhood of others.

Human community and the entirety of civilization is premised upon a relationship of moral claims and duties between persons. Personhood has no meaning apart from life. If life is a thing that can be renounced or taken at will, the moral structure of human community, understood as a community of persons, is shattered. The result is a brave new world in which killing is defined as caring, life is viewed as the enemy, and death is counted as a benefit to be bestowed.

Political Wisdom

"We hold these truths," the founders of our political community declared, and among the truths that our community has held is that the right to life is "unalienable." All human beings have an equal right to life bestowed by "Nature and Nature's God." Government is to respect that right; it does not bestow that right.

This unalienable right places a clear limit on the power of the state. Except when government exercises its duty to protect citizens against force and injustice, or when it punishes evildoers, it may not presume for itself an authority over human life. To claim that—apart from these exceptions—the state may authorize the killing even of consenting persons is to give state authority an ultimacy it has never had in our political tradition. In that tradition it is recognized that government cannot authorize the alienation of a right it did not first bestow.

Institutional Wisdom

Legalized euthanasia would inevitably require the complicity of physicians. In a time when the medical profession is subjected to increasing criticism, when many people feel vulnerable before medical technology and practice, it would be foolhardy for our society to authorize physicians to kill. Euthanasia is not the way to respond to legitimate fears about medical technology and practice. It is unconscionable that the proponents of euthanasia exploit such fears. Such fears can be met and overcome by strongly reaffirming the distinction between killing and allowing to die—by making clear that useless and excessively burdensome treatment can be refused, while at the same time leaving no doubt that this society will neither authorize physicians to kill nor look the other way if they do.

Conclusion

This fourfold wisdom is rejected at our moral peril. By attending to these sources of wisdom, we can find our way back to an understanding of the limits of human responsibility, and of the imperative to embrace compassionately those who suffer from illness and the fears associated with the end of life. Guided by this wisdom, we will not presume to eliminate a fellow human being, nor need we fear being abandoned in our suffering. The compact of rights, duties, and mutual trust that makes human community possible depends upon our continuing adherence to the precept, *Always to care, never to kill.*

HADLEY ARKES, Amherst College
MATTHEW BERKE, *First Things* magazine
MIDGE DECTER, Institute on Religion and Public Life
RABBI MARC GELLMAN, Hebrew Union College
ROBERT GEORGE, Princeton University
PASTOR PAUL HINLICKY, Lutheran Forum
RUSSELL HITTINGER, Catholic University of America
THE REV. ROBERT JENSON, St. Olaf College
GILBERT MEILAENDER, Oberlin College
FATHER RICHARD JOHN NEUHAUS, Institute
on Religion and Public Life
RABBI DAVID NOVAK, University of Virginia
JAMES NUECHTERLEIN, *First Things* magazine
MAX STACKHOUSE, Andover Newton Theological School

NOTES

■ ■ ■

Chapter 1
Page
23 "Death was stalking the Humphrys . . .": Cal McCrystal's Notebook, "The Woman who Chose to Die in the Wilderness," London *Independent on Sunday*, October 13, 1991.

Chapter 2
27 sensing his need for closeness yet being embarrassed by it, too: Ann Wickett, *Double Exit* (Hemlock, 1989), p. 31.

31 "slap-up dinner": Cal McCrystal, "Love, Death & Loathing on the Road to Windfall Farm," London *Independent on Sunday*, April 8, 1990.

32 Derek and Jean's pact: Derek Humphry and Ann Wickett, *Jean's Way* (Hemlock Publication, distributed by Grove Press, 1984), pp. 62–63.

32 never talked about it again: Ibid., p. 63.

32 Nine months passed: Derek Humphry, "Who Will Help Another to Die," *Hemlock Quarterly* (October 1982), p. 6.

33 "Is this the day?": Humphry and Wickett, op. cit., p. 108.

33 Jean's death: Ibid., p. 113.

33 "tender and rare love story": Quote from Ed Orloff of the San Francisco *Examiner* which appears on the back cover of *Jean's Way* (1984 edition).

33 "He *told* her that it was": For more than twelve years Derek said that his words in response to Jean's question had been "Yes, my darling, it is" (Humphry and Wickett, op. cit., p. 108). These words, without any alteration, were used each time he told Jean's story—in print, on radio and television shows, and at conferences. However, in the summer of 1992, after it had been pointed out that his words made it clear that *he* had been the one who decided when Jean should die, he changed the words. He now says that he responded to her question by telling Jean that if she wanted to die, he couldn't disagree: "Playboy Interview: Derek Humphry," *Playboy* (August 1992), p. 57.

33 Derek's sexual release elsewhere: Humphry and Wickett, op. cit., p. 82.

34 Jean's stunned reaction: Ibid.

34 An example of Derek's new variation of Jean's death is an interview done with him on WJON Radio, Minnesota, August 29, 1991.

36 "idiocy of the present law": "Briton Jailed for Aiding Suicides," San Francisco *Examiner*, October 31, 1981.

36 Description of Reed's trial and codefendant's actions comes from the San Francisco *Examiner* article and also from "Trial Damages Chance of New Legal Base for the Right to Die," London *Guardian*, October 31, 1981.

38 "I don't mean to change the world . . .": Melissa Steineger, "Free to Die," *Northwest* (*Sunday Oregonian Magazine*), March 12, 1989, p. 9.

38 "one of the last great social reforms . . .": Dana Tims, "Hemlock Society Founder to Push for Legalized Euthanasia from Oregon Base," *Oregonian*, August 4, 1988.

39 "putting to death of nonvolunteers . . .": " 'Mercy' Death Law Proposed in State," *New York Times*, January 27, 1939.

39 "euthanasia primarily in cases of born defectives . . .": " 'Mercy' Death Law Ready for Albany," *New York Times*, February 14, 1939.

39 1941 poll: O. Ruth Russell, *Freedom to Die: Moral and Legal Aspects of Euthanasia* (New York: Human Sciences Press, rev. ed., 1977), p. 89. According to Russell, former chair of the Department of Psychology at Western Maryland College, "This poll played a part in the decision of the Euthanasia Society to continue to limit its program to voluntary euthanasia, even though some polls of general public opinion had shown that about as many persons favored euthanasia for grossly defective infants as for incurable adults" (p. 90).

39 "newborn versus older defectives": Ibid., p. 89.

40 Kennedy's plan for child euthanasia: Foster Kennedy, "The Problem of Social Control of the Congenital Defective," *American Journal of Psychiatry*, vol. 99 (1942), pp. 13–14.

40 Information on contributions to Euthanasia Educational Fund from 1967 to 1974: Derek Humphry and Ann Wickett, *The Right to Die: Understanding Euthanasia* (New York: Harper and Row, 1986), p. 88.

41 Information on Chicago meeting: "History of Euthanasia in U.S.: Concept for Our Time," *Euthanasia News*, vol. I, no. 4 (November 1975), p. 3.

41 Abigail Van Buren's name was on the printed listing of Advisory Committee members for the Euthanasia Educational Council and on the letterhead of Concern for Dying.

42 The sole case was *Barber* v. *Superior Court*, 147 Cal. App. 3d 1006, 195 Cal. Rptr. 484 (1983).

Lack of need for a law to allow doctors to remove treatment has been noted by others as well: ". . . the myth of the incarcerated physician and the specter of the large civil verdict haunt our nation's intensive care units. . . . It doesn't seem to matter that this has only happened once in the entire history of American jurisprudence and, in that case, the indictment was quashed prior to trial." (Armstrong and Colen, "From Quinlan to Jobes: The Courts and the PVS Patient," *Hastings Center Report* [February–March 1988], p. 38.)

43 "walk before we can run . . . who shall speak for those who are incompetent . . . wait until the general public accepts . . .": *Dilemmas of Euthanasia: Excerpts from Papers and Discussions at the Fourth Euthanasia Conference*, New York Academy of Medicine, December 4, 1971 (New York: Euthanasia Educational Council, 1972), p. 42.

44 Information about the split between Concern for Dying and the Society for the Right to Die is a composite of what Ann told me and material published in "CFD Severs Ties with Society for the Right to Die," *Concern for Dying Newsletter*, vol. 6, no. 1 (Winter 1980).

44 Hemlock's name: In 1988 the Hemlock Society amended its articles of incorporation, officially changing its name to the National Hemlock Society, but it is still commonly referred to as Hemlock or the Hemlock Society.

44 Suicide death of Richard Scott: Scott, an emergency room physician turned trial lawyer, died on August 6, 1992 of a self-inflicted gunshot wound. In addition to being a founding member and first legal counsel of the Hemlock Society, he had served on the advisory committee of Concern for Dying. In Scott's obituary that appeared in the October 1992 *Hemlock Quarterly*, Derek Humphry described Scott as "part of the team in California that drafted and got passed into law the world's first Living Will [law]" and as "the guiding hand behind *Let Me Die Before I Wake*, which was a 'how-to' self-deliverance book ten years before *Final Exit.*"

45 Larue's lead article: Gerald Larue, "Hemlock: Introducing Ourselves," *Hemlock Quarterly* (October 1980), p. 1.

46 Ann's first editorial: *Hemlock Quarterly* (October 1980), p. 5.

46 Use of Hollywood publicist by Hemlock: *Hemlock Quarterly* (January 1983), p. 8. In addition to promoting the book, the publicist, Irwin Zucker, of Los Angeles, was used to "help promote the Society's aims on radio and television." For his services, Hemlock paid Zucker seventy-five dollars for every radio or television show that he arranged for a Hemlock staff member. This information was contained in a letter of August 23, 1989, by Derek Humphry to Pablo Solis of the Internal Revenue Service, p. 3. The letter was prepared in response to an audit that Mr. Solis was conducting regarding Hemlock's tax-exempt status.

47 Skinner's comments on *The Merv Griffin Show*: "Hemlock Society in Humor, Literature and Comment," *Hemlock Quarterly* (January 1984), p. 3.

Chapter 3

50 Among the articles about the euthanasia document were "Un Manifeste pour l'Euthanasie," *Le Monde*, September 20, 1984, and "Des Médecins Offrent la 'Mort Douce' aux Malades," *France-Soir*, September 20, 1984.

50 Results of the survey of French physicians: "Malade Condamné: 81% Des Généralistes Choisiraient l'Euthanasie," *Tonus* (September 18, 1984), pp. 16–21.

51 "We dispose of an old dog . . .": *Hemlock Quarterly* (April 1984), p. 2.

58 "servants of society . . . obey the wishes of society": Diane Gianelli, "Would Aiding in Dying Make MDs Hired Killers?," *American Medical News* (February 16, 1990), p. 3.

63 Schwartzenberg's expanding euthanasia practice: David P. Schenck, "Requiem for Life: A Review," *BioLaw Update* (April 1987), pp. U:411–412.

63 One-year suspension from the French Medical Association: Sylvia Hughes, "Doctor's Suspension Stirs French Debate over Euthanasia," *New Scientist* (July 28, 1990), p. 22.

Chapter 4

66 "mentally ill": Diane Gianelli, "Right-to-Die Leaders' Divorce Dispute Spotlights Rift in National Group," *American Medical News* (February 23, 1990), p. 16.

66 "very disturbed": Robert Reinhold, "Right-to-Die Group Shaken as Leader Leaves Ill Wife," *New York Times*, February 8, 1990.

66 Information on Hemlock revenue and Ann and Derek Humphry's income: IRS Form 990 for year ending December 31, 1985, filed by Hemlock, May 15, 1986.

67 "No substantial part of the activities . . . attempting to influence legislation . . .": Articles of Incorporation of Hemlock, a Nonprofit Corporation, filed March 10, 1981, Office of the California Secretary of State.

67 "supporting voluntary euthanasia . . . change antique laws." *New York Times Book Review*, September 8, 1985.

67 "we shall launch legislation. . . .": The fact that Derek has been so involved in attempts to change U.S. law is a matter of curiosity since according to Ann, Derek remained a British citizen. As a noncitizen he cannot vote for the proposals that he works to place on the ballot.

68 Description of Hemlock's program: IRS Form 990 for year ending December 31, 1985, filed by Hemlock, May 15, 1986.

68 Derek's brother had died in a British hospital following a medical accident that occurred during a minor medical procedure. See Cal McCrystal, "Ann Humphry's Final Exit," *Vanity Fair* (January 1992), p. 142. Derek later described the family difficulties and his brother's death in an interview with *Playboy* magazine. He said that 1986 (the year Ann's parents died) was a "year of disaster." *Playboy* (August 1992), p. 58.

70 Order and method of payment for Vesparax are composite of what Ann told me and a receipt from the Zurich, Switzerland, pharmacy for purchase of Vesparax charged to Derek Humphry's Visa card.

70 Derek's storage of lethal drugs: Derek Humphry, *Final Exit* (Eugene, Ore.: Hemlock Society, distributed by Carol Publishing, 1991), p. 70.

71 "so she would not see the gun": District Ct. App. 11FLW 1008, May 9, 1986.

71 "premeditated mercy": Strat Douthat, "Fearful Seniors Debate 'Mercy Killing' Case," St. Cloud (Minn.) *Daily Times*, September 23, 1985.

73 "and I am somewhere back in ankle socks and braids . . .": Wickett, *Double Exit*, loc. cit., p. 92.

73 "residue of two strangers' lives": Ibid., p. 111.

73 Betty Rollin, *Last Wish* (New York: Linden Press/Simon and Schuster, 1985).

76 The gift was listed on IRS reports as an August 5, 1986, loan to Americans Against Human Suffering. IRS Form 990 for year ending December 31, 1986, filed by Hemlock, May 5, 1987.

77 Receipt by Hemlock of $50,000 from a Florida donor to launch the political campaign: "Thank You for the Funding," *Hemlock Quarterly* (July 1986), p. 1.

77 Description of Hemlock's relationship to Americans Against Human Suffering included the reference to AAHS as "Hemlock's affinity group" in an "Urgent Gram" fund appeal from Derek Humphry, October 1987, and as a "sister organization" in the *Hemlock Quarterly* (July 1988).

Additional confirmation of the close ties include:

"AAHS is the political wing of the Hemlock Society and has our full backing in its campaign to get the Humane and Dignified Death Act enacted in all states." "Americans Against Human Suffering: Good Progress," *Hemlock Quarterly* (April 1987), p. 7.

"This political wing of the Hemlock Society has got off to a good start. . . . Hemlock provided the seed money of $50,000. . . ." Derek Humphry, March 20, 1987.

"Our sister organization, Americans Against Human Suffering, is asking Californians to vote for a change in the law. . . ." Letter from Derek Humphry to Ann Landers, printed in the *Hemlock Quarterly* (April 1987), p. 7.

79 Justice Compton's call for medical assistance in bringing about death: Separate concurring opinion in *Bouvia* v. *Superior Court*, 179 Cal. App. 3d. 1127, 225 Cal. Rptr. 297 (1986).

79 "a more striking pronouncement . . .": The pronouncement to which Risley referred was cited six years later in a judge's decision dismissing murder charges against Dr. Jack Kevorkian. (*Michigan* v. *Kevorkian*, Oakland County Circuit Court, 92-115190-FC, 92-DA-5303-AR, July 21, 1992, p. 16. Circuit Court Judge David F. Breck.)

Chapter 5

81 Hemlock's 1986 income: IRS Form 990 for year ending December 31, 1986, filed by Hemlock, May 5, 1987.

83 Description of Debbie's euthanasia death: Editorial, "It's Over, Debbie," *Journal of the American Medical Association*, vol. 259, no. 2 (January 8, 1988), p. 272.

84 Catalyst for the discussion of euthanasia: Lori Oliwenstein, "Ethics: It's Over, Debbie," *Discover* (January 1989), p. 80.

84 "Many of us believe . . . it should . . . be legalized": Marcia Angell, "Euthanasia," *New England Journal of Medicine*, vol. 319, no. 20 (November 17, 1988), p. 1349.

87 Descriptions of the ease with which food and fluids could be provided by gastrostomy tube: Lewis McMurtry, "Modern Gastrostomy for Stricture of the Esophagus, with Report of a Case," and M. F. Coomes, "Gastrostomy, with Report of a Case," *Transactions of the Kentucky Medical Society* (1896), pp. 123–43.

87 Description of insertion of gastrostomy tube: David Major, "The Medical Procedures for Providing Food and Water: Indications and Effects," in *By No Extraordinary Means: The Choice to Forego Life-Sustaining Food and Water*, ed. J. Lynn (1986), p. 26.

88 The case of Mary Hier: In re *Hier*, 18 Mass. App. 200, 464 N.E.2d 959 (1984).

88 Description of the reasons given for denying reinsertion of Mary Hier's feeding tube: "SJC Declines to Review Case of 92-year-old Refusing Surgery," Boston *Globe*, June 10, 1984.

88 "highly intrusive and risky procedure": Ann Bannon, "Rx: Death by Dehydration," *Human Life Review*, vol. 12, no. 3 (1986), p. 74.

88 "minor surgery to correct a nutritional problem": "Rose Kennedy 'Doing Well' After Surgery," Boston *Globe*, July 29, 1984.

90 Discussion of Nancy Ellen Jobes's good health: Brief of Appellant Lincoln Park Nursing and Convalescent Home, pp. 5 and 6, In the Matter of *Nancy Ellen Jobes*, Civil Action on appeal from the Decision of the Superior Court of New Jersey, Chancery Div. No. C-4971-85E. Appeal docketed, No. 26, 117.

90 Settlement of malpractice case: Lawrence Ragonese, "Morris Woman's Kin File Right-to-Die Suit," Newark *Star-Ledger*, October 3, 1985.

90 Testimony of Dr. Fred Plum from In the Matter of *Nancy Ellen Jobes*, Superior Court of New Jersey, Chancery Division—

Morris County, Docket No. C-4971-65E, App. Div. No. A-4087-85T5, Stenographic Transcript of Trial, Morris County Courthouse, Morristown, New Jersey, March 24, 1986, pp. 40 and 74.

90 "monstrosity": Ibid., p. 124.

90 "as in an animal we are working on . . .": Ibid., p. 118.

91 Description of Nancy Ellen Jobes's response to verbal commands: Lawrence Ragonese, "Doctors Testify Morris Woman Isn't Vegetative," Newark *Star-Ledger*, April 2, 1986.

91 Nancy Ellen Jobes's ability to see, hear, and feel pain: In the Matter of *Nancy Ellen Jobes*, Superior Court of New Jersey, Chancery Division—Morris County, Docket No. C-4971-65E, App. Div. No. A-4087-85T5, Stenographic Transcript of Trial, Morris County Courthouse, Morristown, New Jersey, April 1, 1986, pp. 8–14.

91 Possibility that tests performed on Nancy Ellen Jobes may have been invalid: "Doctors Testify Morris Woman Isn't Vegetative," loc. cit.

91 "prolonging the shell . . .": Lawrence Ragonese, "Friends, Family Recount Comatose Woman's Death with Dignity Remarks," Newark *Star-Ledger*, March 27, 1986.

91 "I'd really like to get on with my life . . .": "Comatose Woman's Husband 'Let her rest,'" Bridgewater *Courier News*, March 26, 1986.

91 John Jobes had gone for a year without visiting his wife: Lincoln Park Brief, p. 7.

92 Information about death by dehydration: "A Message to the Community and Staff of Morristown Memorial Hospital," Morristown *Daily Record*, August 2, 1987.

The symptoms listed here were originally described in *Brophy* v. *New England Sinai Hospital*, 398 Mass. 417, 444 n.2, 497 N.E.2d 626,641 n.2, (Mass. 1986). J. Lynch, dissenting.

93 Jeryl Turco's plea for the community to speak out against dehydrating Nancy Ellen Jobes to death: Ibid.

NOTES

93 "like valued cell lines in cancer laboratories": Paul W. Armstrong and B. D. Colen, "From Quinlan to Jobes: The Courts and the PVS Patient," *Hastings Center Report* (February–March 1988), p. 39.

94 Helga Kuhse's advocacy of ending the lives of handicapped newborns: Speaking at a November 1990 ethics symposium at the University of Iowa College of Medicine, Kuhse proposed that newborns be carefully observed for the first month of life and, if serious handicaps are found during that four-week period, the infant either be allowed to die or be killed. Peter Steinfels, "Beliefs," *New York Times*, November 10, 1990.

94 "best interest": Kuhse made this observation during her presentation at the 1984 World Federation of Right to Die Societies' Fifth Biennial Conference in Nice, France.

96 Instructions on committing suicide using a plastic bag: Colin Brewer, "Self-Deliverance with Certainty," *Hemlock Quarterly* (January 1988), p. 3.

97 "as a slobbering wreck": Karen Southwick, "Insider Interview: Colin Brewer," *Health Week* (June 6, 1988), p. 31.

99 "would have made a significant test case . . .": "Suicide Assister Will Not Be Charged," *Hemlock Quarterly* (October 1988), p. 1.

100 "If we're going to murder Ronnie . . .": KING-TV *Evening* program, Seattle, November 1988.

100 Patricia Rosier told that she would die a horrible death: Earl Rinehart, "Defense Says Stepfather Suffocated Ailing Woman," Tampa *Tribune*, November 5, 1988.

100 Description of Patricia Rosier's final evening: Tamar Jacoby with Cheryl Harrison Miller, " 'I Helped Her on Her Way,' " *Newsweek* (November 7, 1988), p. 101.

100 Patricia Rosier's stepfather's role in her death: "Defense Says Stepfather Suffocated Ailing Woman," loc. cit.

267

101 Peter Rosier's intent to have the book published: Earl Rinehart, "Jury Hears Rosier TV Interview," Tampa *Tribune*, November 8, 1988.

101 Peter Rosier's boast about getting rich: Mark Journey, "Ex-friend Tells of Rosier's Alleged Romances," St. Petersburg *Times*, November 23, 1988.

101 Derek's remarks about the verdict: Derek Humphry, "Dr. Rosier's Acquittal Both a Victory and a Warning," *Hemlock Quarterly* (January 1989), p. 1.

102 Proposal of euthanasia for children: "Model Aid-in-Dying Act," *Iowa Law Review*, vol. 75, no. 1 (1989), pp. 163, 165.

102 Right of children to request aid-in-dying: Ibid., p. 170.

102 Definition of aid-in-dying: Ibid., p. 139.

102 Fee and test for those who could administer aid-in-dying: Ibid., p. 204.

102 Cheryl Smith as one of the drafters of Model Aid-in-Dying Act: Ibid., title page.

102 The follow-up on the discussion between Derek and Cheryl Smith: Letter from Cheryl Smith to Derek Humphry, April 5, 1989.

102 "welcome to the team": Memo from Derek Humphry to Cheryl Smith, dated 2/26/89. (Obvious typographical error on a memo of May 26, 1989.)

Chapter 6

103 Hemlock's headquarters moved from California to Eugene, Oregon: Within a year Derek had purchased a small office building, centrally located in Eugene's business district, and leased it to Hemlock for a monthly rate of two thousand dollars. The five-year lease agreement, dated May 1, 1989, was signed by Jean Gillett (for Hemlock in her capacity as director at large) and Derek Humphry (as owner of the property). In 1991 Hemlock paid Derek Humphry $37,529 for the lease of the office.

Annual Periodic Report filed by Hemlock with the office of the California attorney general for the year ending December 31, 1991.

106 Derek's description of their arguments following Ann's diagnosis: Trip Gabriel, "A Fight to the Death," *New York Times Magazine*, December 8, 1991, p. 86.

109 "In these circumstances you do, and I did": *The 5th Estate*, Canadian Broadcasting Company (CBC), February 4, 1992. Segment titled, " 'Final Exits' with Trish Wood," transcript, p. 3.

109 "She was cured of cancer when I left her": *People Are Talking*, WBZ-TV (Boston), October 6, 1992.

109 "utter terror and fear": Letter from Ann Humphry to Derek Humphry, October 17, 1989, p. 1.

109 "an emotional mute": Ibid.

109 "You have been the great love of my life . . .": Ibid.

109 "how much love and loyalty I felt for you . . .": Ibid., p. 4.

110 "somewhat inhumane": Memo from Ann Humphry to National Hemlock Board members, November 2, 1989, p. 1.

111 "crazy . . . insane": Report by Peter D. Moursund, private investigator, of interview of Henry and Barbara Brod, October 14, 1990, pp. 3, 4, 5 and *Humphry* v. *Humphry; The National Hemlock Society; Ralph Mero; Hemlock Society of Washington State*; In the Circuit Court of the State of Oregon for the County of Lane, No. 16-9009223, Fourth Amended Complaint (9/91), pp. 2, 3, 4. Also from discussions with Ann and with Barbara and Henry Brod.

112 Information about Derek's removal of farm equipment: Discussions with Ann and Cal McCrystal, "Love, Death & Loathing on the Road to Windfall Farm," loc. cit.; Moursund Report, p. 6; and *Humphry* v. *Humphry; The National Hemlock Society; Ralph Mero; Hemlock Society of Washington State*; In the Circuit Court of the State of Oregon for the County of Lane, No. 16-9009223, Complaint, filed October 19, 1990, pp. 10, 11; Amended complaint, p. 17.

112 "Derek later acknowledged taking the equipment . . ." McCrystal, "Love, Death & Loathing on the Road to Windfall Farm," loc. cit., p. 10.

112 "in the psychiatric ward . . .": Memorandum from Derek Humphry to All Board Directors, National Hemlock Society, December 14, 1989, p. 2.

112 "directing that all locks at the Hemlock office be changed . . .": Memo from Derek Humphry to Ron Leach, December 7, 1989.

112 "stated that Ann had been giving interviews . . .": Memorandum from Derek Humphry to All Staff, December 7, 1989, p. 1.

113 "I must . . . make the following rules . . .": Ibid.

113 Information about campaign to discredit Ann: Conversations with former Hemlock staff members and Moursund Report, pp. 3, 4, 8.

114 "concern about certain actions and statements made by Ann": Letter from Lee Kersten to Charles Gudger, December 8, 1989, p. 1.

114 "refrain from . . . 'unauthorized contact . . .' ": Ibid.

114 Information that board members did not want Ann to discuss her situation with the staff: Ibid., p. 2.

115 Derek outlined his plans for the time after his scheduled resignation: Memorandum from Derek Humphry to All Staff, December 7, 1989, p. 2.

115 Mero's new annual "consultancy fee": Memo from Derek Humphry to Ron Leach, undated, states, "From January 1, 1990, Ralph Mero's annual consultancy fee will be $46,000." In addition to holding the title of Hemlock's Pacific Northwest Regional

Director, Mero was also President of Hemlock's Washington State Chapter. Letter from Ralph Mero to Cheryl Smith, December 22, 1989.

He also was an ex officio board member of Washington Citizens for Death with Dignity and later was a board member and president of the Washington Hemlock PAC: Letterheads of Initiative 119 Washington Citizens for Death with Dignity and Washington Hemlock PAC.

Mero's compensation for his services as an "educational consultant" increased the following year. In 1991 he was paid $54,861 by the National Hemlock Society. Annual Periodic Report filed by Hemlock with the office of the California attorney general for the year ending December 31, 1991.

Mero's wife, Jane LeCompte, was also being paid a "consultancy fee" by the National Hemlock Society. She was receiving twenty-five hundred dollars a month for her work as office manager and volunteer coordinator for the Washington State Chapter of Hemlock: Letter from Jane LeCompte to Derek Humphry, September 13, 1989; employment agreement between National Hemlock Society and Jane LeCompte, September 19, 1989; and memo to Ron Leach from Derek Humphry of September 19, 1989.

LeCompte also handled the submission of financial data and served on the board of directors of Washington Citizens for Death with Dignity (the officially listed sponsor of Washington State's Initiative 119). Financial data filed with Washington State Public Disclosure Commission, Feburary 8, 1990, and letterhead of Initiative 119 Washington Citizens for Death with Dignity.

115 Private meetings continued until just hours before the January meeting began: Moursund Report, p. 3. Other preparations for dealing with Ann at the board meeting were made by staff and consultants: Letter from Ralph Mero to Cheryl Smith, December 22, 1989.

115 "I no longer loved her": "Why My Marriage to Ann Wickett Failed: A Statement by Derek Humphry," January 6, 1990, p. 2.

116 Derek's rationale for sending memos to the press: Gabriel, "A Fight to the Death," loc. cit. p. 86.

117 Garbesi's reception at the board meeting: Letter from Curt Garbesi to Derek Humphry, January 8, 1990, p. 1.

117 Garbesi referred to his November letter in his letter of January 8, 1990.

117 Derek's reiteration of his previous ruling: Memo from Derek Humphry to Ron Leach, January 9, 1990.

117 Derek's announcement of his new title: Memo from Derek Humphry to All Staff Members, including Seattle and Sarasota branches, January 9, 1990.

118 The transfer of Ann's title of deputy director to someone else: Ibid. In the memo Derek Humphry wrote, "I have appointed Cheryl K. Smith, JD, to be Deputy Executive Director as from today. She is responsible for the running of Hemlock in my absence."

118 Financial irregularities within Hemlock: Moursund Report, p. 2. Henry Brod also pointed to financial irregularities in a January 17, 1990, letter of resignation to the Board of Directors of the Hemlock Society (Oregon) Inc.; in a February 2, 1990, memorandum to all Hemlock chapter leaders and the media; and in a February 8, 1990, news release.

Hemlock's records appear to support Brod's allegations of financial irregularities. In addition to the funds which seemed to have been funneled from Hemlock into political activities, the transfer of funds between the National Hemlock Society and Hemlock of Oregon was somewhat questionable.

The National Hemlock Society made a forty-thousand-dollar "grant" to Hemlock of Oregon on June 25, 1987. Yet according to a November 2, 1989, letter from Derek Humphry to Gregory S. Howard of the California Department of Justice, Hemlock of Oregon was not formed until October 28, 1987—four months after the "grant" was made.

Bylaws for Hemlock of Oregon—which were not adopted until one year later, on October 10, 1988—list Ann and Derek as two of the three original directors of the newly formed corporation.

Financial records of the National Hemlock Society for 1988 contain no information about a "note receivable" from Hemlock of Oregon. Similarly, financial records of Hemlock of Oregon for 1988 make no reference to a "note payable" to the National Hemlock Society. Yet, following scrutiny of the forty-thousand-dollar transaction by the California Department of Justice, Hemlock claimed that the transfer had been a loan, not a grant, and a promissory note for the 1987 fund transfer was signed in January 1990 by Jean Gillett, treasurer of Hemlock of Oregon.

The National Hemlock Society did list a $30,000 note receivable from Hemlock of Oregon in its Annual Periodic Report filed with the office of the California attorney general for the year ending December 31, 1991.

Chapter 7

120 Initial article describing Derek's abandonment of Ann: Reinhold, "Right-to-Die Group Shaken As Leader Leaves Ill Wife," loc. cit.

123 "pscyhologists [*sic*] and a pscyhiatrist [*sic*] have told me . . .": "Why My Marriage to Ann Wickett Failed: A Statement by Derek Humphry," February 13, 1990, p. 3.

123 Derek's admission that he knew of no such diagnosis: *The 5th Estate*, loc. cit., p. 5.

123 "I cared for Jean . . .": "Why My Marriage," p. 4.

123 "frequently signs herself 'Ann Wickett, Ph.D.' ": Ibid.

124 The threatening call was made in February 1990, but Derek later claimed that, after he left Ann in October 1989, his only communication with her had been through his attorneys. After Ann's death he wrote, "I had not spoken to or communicated with her in the two years prior to her death except through lawyers in relation to legal proceedings that she brought against me." See letter to the editor from Derek Humphry, the *Times* (London), November 1, 1991.

127 "pressure on someone to die . . .": Diane Gianelli, "Right-to-Die Leaders' Divorce Dispute Spotlights Rift in National Group," *American Medical News* (February 23, 1990), p. 3.

127 "the ill person owes it to the other person to behave properly . . .": David Grogan and Jeanne Gordon, "The Founder of a 'Right to Die' Group Walks Out on His Wife When Cancer Threatens Her Life," *People* (March 12, 1990), p. 77.

127 "Derek hasn't forbidden Hemlock employees . . .": Letter from Jean Gillett to Landon Y. Jones, Jr., managing editor of *People*, March 12, 1990.

128 "Lightning has hit me twice": *Inside Edition*, March 29, 1990. When the program aired, the word "bitch," which Derek had used to describe Ann, was bleeped.

Chapter 8

136 The Royal Dutch Pharmacists Association booklet has become well known. Articles referring to it include Michael Specter, "Thousands of Dutch Choose Euthanasia's Gentle Ending," *Washington Post*, April 5, 1990.

The pharmacists association guidelines, which were issued in 1987 by a special task force, discuss the criteria for an ideal euthanasia as well as specific advice on carrying out euthanasia. Among the task force members who formulated the guidelines was Dr. Pieter Admiraal. See Koninklijke Nederlandse Maatschappij ter Bevordering der Pharmacie, *Technisch Rapport over Euthantica* (The Hague: K.N.M.P., 1987).

136 Disciplinary action against physician who had refused to perform euthanasia: Bernard Levin, "Under Patient's Orders—to Kill," the *Times* (London), December 11, 1989.

137 "Considering the establishment of Europe 1992": At the time of the Maastricht conference it was expected that 1992 would be the year in which EEC members would take a giant step toward what could eventually become a united Europe.

144 Conclusion that it is morally acceptable for doctors to assist patients to commit suicide: Sidney H. Wanzer, Daniel D. Federman, S. James Adelstein, Christine K. Cassel, Edwin H. Cassem, Ronald E. Cranford, Edward W. Hook, Bernard Lo, Charles G. Moertel, Peter Safar, Alan Stone, and Jan van Eys, "The Physician's Responsibility Toward Hopelessly Ill Patients: A Second Look," *New England Journal of Medicine*, vol. 320, no. 13 (March 30, 1989), p. 848.

144 "strongest public endorsement of doctor-assisted suicide ever published . . .": *MacNeil/Lehrer NewsHour*, PBS, March 30, 1989.

144 "We broke new ground . . .": Ibid.

145 "physician-assisted suicide may not only be permissible . . .": "Dr. Ron Cranford Defines Distinctions Between 'Allowing to Die' and 'Killing,' " *Concern for Dying Newsletter* (Summer 1988), p. 2.

Of the twelve authors, Peter Safar was on the board and Christine Cassel, Bernard Lo, and Sidney Wanzer were on the advisory committee of the Society for the Right to Die. See the letterhead of the Society for the Right to Die.

Wanzer's open advocacy of euthanasia had appeared in print prior to the "report" publication. See Sidney H. Wanzer, "The Euthanasia Debate: The Argument in Favor," *Clinical*

Report on Aging (American Geriatrics Society), vol. 2, no. 5 (1988), p. 1. One year after the report was published, Wanzer called for greater participation by physicians in moving the debate forward and called euthanasia administered by a physician "the final, responsible treatment of helping life to end." See Wanzer, "Maintaining Control in Terminal Illness: Assisted Suicide and Euthanasia," *Humane Medicine*, vol. 6, no. 3 (Summer 1990), pp. 186–88.

In the summer of 1992 Cranford was appointed to the board of directors of Choice in Dying (formerly Concern for Dying/Society for the Right to Die): *Choice in Dying News*, vol. 1, no. 2 (Summer 1992), p. 6.

145 Euthanasia as a possible treatment for nondying patients: Wanzer et al., op. cit., p. 849.

145 Information about Admiraal's attendance at deliberations during which report was formulated: "Second SRD Conference Urges Peaceful Death: Stresses Control of Pain," *Society for the Right to Die Newsletter* (Fall 1989), p. 3.

151 Battin's contention that suicide assistance for the impoverished elderly might be warranted: Joyce Price, "Pro-Suicide Activists Call for Right to Assist," Washington *Times*, March 13, 1987.

151 "the world can be described in terms of facts": Stephen Yarnell and Margaret Battin, "AIDS, Psychiatry and Euthanasia," *Psychiatric Annals*, vol. 18, no. 10 (October 1988), p. 598.

151 "moving away from an absolutist, taboo ethics . . .": Ibid., p. 599.

151 "socially respected way of coming to the end . . .": Ibid., p. 601.

Chapter 9

155 Criteria for practice of euthanasia: Carlos Gomez, *Regulating Death* (New York: Free Press, 1991), p. 32.

156 Of the thousands of annual euthanasia deaths, reported cases from 1987 through 1990 averaged only 273 each year. See I. J. Keown, "The Law and Practice of Euthanasia in the Netherlands," *Law Quarterly Review*, vol. 108 (January 1992), p. 67.

156 "psychic suffering" and "potential disfigurement of personality": Gomez, op. cit., p. 39.

156 Euthanasia administered to people with diabetes, rheumatism, etc.: Mark Shipworth, "Suicide on Prescription," London *Sunday Observer*, April 30, 1989.

156 Reckless practice of euthanasia: Richard Fenigsen, M.D., Willem-Alexander Hospital, 's Hertogenbosch, Netherlands, "A Negative Verdict on Euthanasia," letter to the editor *Medical Economics* (March 7, 1988), p. 18.

157 Official guidelines governing euthanasia in the Netherlands neither enforced nor enforceable: Gomez, op. cit.

157 Underdeveloped pain control and comfort measures in Holland: *Euthanasia: Report of the Working Party to Review the British Medical Association's Guidance on Euthanasia*, British Medical Association, May 5, 1988, p. 49, no. 195.

158 The official government report—*Medische Beslissingen Rond Het Levenseinde*, Sdu Uitgeverij Plantijnstraat (1991), The Hague—was released in two volumes. The 294-page report was the work of the Committee to Investigate the Medical Practice Concerning Euthanasia, appointed on January 17, 1990, by the minister of justice and the state secretary for welfare, public health, and culture. The six-member committee was chaired by Professor J. Remmelink, M.J., the attorney general of the High Council of the Netherlands and professor emeritus of criminal law at the Free University. To assure accurate and complete information, physicians who provided data were granted total anonymity and immunity by the Dutch government.

158 Deaths as a result of doctors killing patients at patients' requests: Ibid., vol. I, p. 13.

159 Deaths resulting from people using medication provided by doctors for that purpose, commonly called assisted suicide: Ibid.

159 Deaths as a result of doctors killing patients without their explicit request that they be killed. According to the Remmelink Report, 0.8 percent of the 130,000 annual deaths in the Netherlands fall within this category: Ibid., p. 15.

159 Death as a result of involuntary euthanasia for competent persons: Ibid., vol. II, p. 49, Table 6.4.

159 Patients who had never given any indication that they would want to be killed by their doctors: Ibid., p. 50, Table 6.6.

159 Deaths occurring after deliberate overdoses of pain medication: Ibid., p. 58, Table 7.2. According to the Remmelink Report, 22,500 (about 17.3 percent) of all deaths in the Netherlands occur after dosages of pain medication that may have shortened life. Of these, 36 percent took place with the physician's deliberate intent to cause death. As a clarification of the intent it may be useful to recognize that in 64 percent of such deaths the intent was to kill the pain; in the remaining 36 percent the intent was to kill the patient.

159 Intentional lethal overdoses of pain medication administered to competent patients without prior discussion: Ibid., p. 61, Table 7.7.

159 Even though the number of annual deaths induced by Dutch physicians number more than 11,000, the vast majority of euthanasia deaths are listed on death certificates as "due to natural causes." See ibid., vol. I, p. 26.

159 Data regarding physician-induced deaths do not include deaths resulting from withholding or withdrawal of medical treatment even when the intent is to cause death: see ibid., vol. II, p. 72, and as stated in personal communication from R. Fenigsen.

159 Involuntary euthanasia on handicapped newborns, children, and psychiatric patients excluded from numbers of patients who die from physician-induced death: Ibid., vol. I, pp. 17–18. Although euthanasia for such groups has been carried out, no specific guidelines have been widely distributed. However, in July 1992 the Dutch Pediatric Association announced that it would soon issue a guide for killing severely handicapped newborns. According to Dr. Zier Versluys, who heads the committee formulating the guidelines, "Both for the parents and the children, an early death is better than life": Abner Katzman, "Dutch Debate Mercy Killing of Babies," Contra Costa *Times*, July 30, 1992. According to an Associated Press story, Versluys "admits to involvement in at least two euthanasia cases": "Pediatric Report Reignites Debate," Calgary *Herald*, July 29, 1992.

160 Refusal by Dutch physicians to take the first step toward euthanasia during World War II: Leo Alexander, "Medical Science Under Dictatorship," *New England Journal of Medicine*, vol. 241 (July 14, 1949), p. 45.

160 Nonparticipation by Dutch physicians in euthanasia during the Nazi occupation: Ibid.

160 "to transform a war crime into an act of compassion": Nancy Gibbs, "Love and Let Die," *Time* (March 19, 1990), p. 67.

Chapter 10
161 "killing machine" and description of parts from which it was assembled: Neal Rubin, "In Royal Oak: The Death Machine," Detroit *Free Press Magazine*, March 18, 1990, p. 4. The previous year Kevorkian had referred to the device as a "self-execution machine" during a radio talk show debate he and I had (WKRC Radio, Cincinnati, Ohio, November 2, 1989). It was not until after the first victim died using his device that more media-friendly labels began to be applied to the gadget.

162 "fine tuning . . .": Ron Rosenbaum, "Angel of Death—The Trial of the Suicide Doctor," *Vanity Fair* (May 1991), p. 208.

163 Kevorkian and Janet Adkins had never spoken to each other until just hours before her death: James Risen, "Doctor Ordered Not to Use Suicide Device," San Francisco *Chronicle*, June 9, 1990.

163 "did not want to be a burden . . .": Stuart Wasserman, "What Drove Woman to Suicide Machine," San Francisco *Chronicle*, June 7, 1990.

163 "an idea whose time has come" and Deale's unwillingness to try to dissuade Adkins from her decision: Bonnie DeSimone, "She Said She Had No Regrets," Detroit *News*, June 7, 1990.

164 "emotionalism over the Nuremberg codes": Rosenbaum, op. cit., p. 211. Kevorkian's reference to what he calls "Nuremberg codes" apparently refers to the charges under which Nazi doctors were tried for war crimes at Nuremberg. Among the crimes against humanity for which physicians stood trial were "inhumane acts," including inhuman medical experiments and the killing of mentally and physically disabled people. For a discussion of these crimes and the Nuremberg trials, see Hugh Gregory Gallagher, *By Trust Betrayed: Patients, Physicians and the License to Kill in the Third Reich* (New York: Henry Holt and Co., 1990) and Robert Jay Lifton, *The Nazi Doctors: Medical Killing and the Psychology of Genocide* (New York: Basic Books, 1986).

164 Kevorkian's speculation about experimentation on prisoners had gone back for years. He acknowledged that it was he, not the inmates on death row, who first brought up the subject. See Rosenbaum, op. cit., pp. 203, 204.

164 Death row medical experiments would include use of condemned prisoners' organs for transplant purposes. Ibid., p. 211.

165 Death as an alternative to a prison sentence of more than three years: Ibid.

165 Kevorkian's plan for making euthanasia beneficial to society: Jack Kevorkian, "A Comprehensive Bioethical Code for Medical Exploitation of Humans Facing Imminent and Unavoidable Death," *Medicine and Law*, vol. 5 (1986), pp. 181–97.

165 "subjects" suitable for Kevorkian's medical experiments and euthanasia: Ibid., p. 195.

165 Description of types of experimentation to be allowed under Kevorkian's plan: Ibid., p. 194.

165 "final biologic death may be induced . . . by an official lay executioner": Ibid., p. 195.

165 Plans for "obitiatry" as a new medical specialty of killing patients: "Death, by Appointment Only," *Health Care Weekly Review*, August 24, 1987. In the article Kevorkian explained that he would not risk charges of first-degree murder but, at first, would practice obitiatry in the area of death management, which could result in charges of abetting a suicide.

165 Kevorkian's claim to a personal friendship with Admiraal and description of Kevorkian's business card: Ibid.

166 "Hemlock would prefer that actions . . .": News release, National Hemlock Society, Eugene, Oregon, June 6, 1990.

166 "uncharted legal territory": "Doctor Defends 'Suicide Device' After It's Used by Alzheimer's Patient," Minneapolis *Star-Tribune*, June 6, 1990.

166 Murder charges against Kevorkian filed for the death of Janet Adkins: Isabel Wilkerson, "Doctor Is Charged with Murder in Suicide Device He Invented," *New York Times*, December 4, 1990.

167 Judge McNally's support for Kevorkian and the portrayal of being killed with a doctor's assistance as a choice similar to deciding what to eat: Maureen Osborne, "Judge Says Suicide

Law Is Tricky Issue to Settle," Clarkston (Mich.) *Reminder*, March 14, 1991.

167 Kevorkian's belief that public health and welfare would improve if disabled people were dead: "Jack Kevorkian, Statement to Oakland County Circuit Court in Response to Complaint for Injunctive Relief and Motion for Temporary Restraining Order," August 17, 1990, p. 11.

167 Hemlock's claim that prohibiting Kevorkian from using his death machine would have a "chilling effect": Silent Intervenor brief filed by Hemlock of Michigan, January 15, 1991, p. 12.

167 "patient self-determination does not encompass self-extermination effectuated by a physician": *Michigan* v. *Kevorkian*, Oakland County Circuit Court, 90-390963-AZ, February 5, 1991. Circuit Court Judge Alice L. Gilbert, p. 33.

168 "his real goal is self-service rather than patient service": Ibid., p. 32.

168 Kevorkian's new and updated death devices credited for the deaths of Wantz and Miller: Isabel Wilkerson, "Rage and Support for Doctor's Role in Suicide," *New York Times*, October 25, 1991.

168 "she felt she was becoming a burden on people": *Michigan* v. *Kevorkian*, Oakland County Circuit Court, 92-115190-FC, 92-DA-5303-AR, Plaintiff's Brief in Support of Answer to Motion to Quash Information and Dismiss Case, April 22, 1992, p. xiv.

168 "an incurable and painful genital tissue disease": Robert Ourlian and Mike Martindale, "She was determined to die," Detroit *News and Free Press*, October 27, 1991.

169 Carbon monoxide death of Sherry Miller: *Michigan* v. *Kevorkian*, loc. cit., pp. ix and xvi.

169 Marjorie Wantz's death occurring prior to Sherry Miller's death: Ibid., pp. xv and xvi.

169 "complexion looks beautiful and pink": "Kevorkian: Doctor Was Almost Discovered by Park Ranger," Detroit *News and Free Press*, October 27, 1991.

169 Kevorkian's lack of information about Wantz's medical condition: *Michigan* v. *Kevorkian*, loc. cit., p. xi.

169 Wantz's disease-free medical condition: James A. McClear, "Murder Charges for Dr. Death?," Detroit *News*, December 19, 1991.

169 Prevalent belief that cancer pain is uncontrollable: Russell Portenoy, "Cancer Pain," *Cancer*, vol. 63, no. 11 (June 1, 1989, Supplement), p. 2298.

169 Examples of articles related to pain management and control: Stefan Ground et al., "Validation of World Health Organization Guidelines for Cancer Pain Relief During the Last Days and Hours of Life," *Journal of Pain and Symptom Management*, vol. 6, no. 7 (October 1991), pp. 411–21. Russell Portenoy, "Cancer Pain," loc. cit., pp. 2298–2307. L. Ohlsson et al., "Cancer Pain Relief by Continuous Administration of Epidural Morphine in a Hospital Setting and at Home," *Pain*, vol. 48 (1992), pp. 349–53. Mitchell Max, "Improving Outcomes of Analgesic Treatment: Is Education Enough?," *Annals of Internal Medicine*, vol. 113, no. 11 (December 1, 1990), pp. 885–89.

170 "cancer pain can be treated satisfactorily until death": Ground et al., "Validation of World Health Organization Guidelines for Cancer Pain Relief During the Last Days and Hours of Life," loc. cit., p. 411.

170 Use of additional medication to alleviate other symptoms as well: Ibid., p. 412.

170 Acknowledgment of need to mitigate fear of pain. Portenoy, "Cancer Pain," loc. cit., p. 2298.

170 "Dr. Kevorkian's motive was purely humanitarian . . .": Press release issued by the National Hemlock Society, October 24, 1991.

171 Homicide as cause in deaths of Wantz and Miller: "Deaths Listed as Homicides," Lansing *State Journal*, December 19, 1991.

171 Kevorkian's modernized plan for death: "A Fail-Safe Model for Justifiable Medically-Assisted Suicide," *American Journal of Forensic Psychiatry*, vol. 13, no. 1 (1992), pp. 7–41.

171 Kevorkian's indictment in deaths of Wantz and Miller: Jerry Dubrowski, "Kevorkian Charged with Murdering 2 Women," San Francisco *Chronicle*, February 6, 1992.

171 Murder charges in deaths of Wantz and Miller were eventually dismissed. See *Michigan* v. *Kevorkian*, Oakland County Circuit Court, 92-115190-FC, 92-DA-5303-AR, July 21, 1992. In his opinion Circuit Court Judge David F. Breck declared that existing Michigan case law prohibits assisted suicide but does not prohibit actions such as those of Kevorkian since he was "acting in the course of a physician-patient relationship" (p. 12). Describing Kevorkian's role in Wantz's and Miller's deaths as that of giving "aid in dying" (p. 2), Breck went on to write a ringing endorsement of physician-induced death, stating that a "person should have the right to insist on treatment which will cause death . . ." (p. 13). "[P]hysician-assisted suicide is not a crime in Michigan, even when the person's condition is not terminal," he wrote (p. 16). After citing American right-to-die cases and reports that describe Dutch euthanasia as laudable social decision making, Breck concluded by addressing Kevorkian directly in language that made his support of Kevorkian unmistakably clear. He wrote: "You have brought to the world's attention the need to give this topic paramount concern. This Judge, however, respectfully requests that you forego any other activities in this field; including counseling, for the time being. To continue I fear hurts your cause, because you may force the Legislature to take hasty, and perhaps improvident, action" (p. 32).

171 "Michigan Doctor at Side of 4th Suicide," *New York Times*, May 16, 1992.

171 "Dear Abby" column giving address for letters supporting Kevorkian's activities was published in newspapers throughout the country, including "Write-In Votes for Kevorkian," San
Francisco *Chronicle*, May 4, 1992.

171 "the loose cannon of the euthanasia movement": Derek
Humphry, "Tactical Errors Defeated Washington Suicide Initiative," Minneapolis *Star-Tribune*, November 15, 1991.

171 "a confused man": Norm Maves, Jr., "A Matter of De-
grees," *The Oregonian*, February 8, 1992.

172 Statement by Kevorkian's attorney that Humphry is an
"absolute liar": "Euthanasia Proponents Lock Horns in Bitter
Dispute over '92 Strategy," Mary Meehan, *National Catholic Regis-
ter*, May 10, 1992.

Chapter 11

175 "to impede and oppress [her] recovery . . . to induce [her]
despair and [her] suicide": *Humphry* v. *Humphry, National Hemlock
Society, Mero, Hemlock of Washington State*, Circuit Court, Lane
County, Oregon, No. 16-90-09223, filed October 19, 1990, pp.
13 and 14, and *Humphry* v. *Humphry; The National Hemlock Society;
Ralph Mero; Hemlock Society of Washington State*; In the Circuit
Court of the State of Oregon for the County of Lane, No. 16-
90-09223, Fourth Amended Complaint (9/91), pp. 19 and 20.
The complaint also alleged that Derek's actions "were maliciously
motivated and wholly intentional, and were timed and calculated
to exploit" Ann's weakened condition.

180 Letter from Ann Humphry to Janet Smith and Susan
Selner, February 10, 1991.

Chapter 12

184 Harper's legal fees paid for in part by the Hemlock Society: "Husband Faces Trial for Aiding Suicide," Wheeling (W.
Va.) *News-Register*, March 3, 1991.

NOTES

184 "an act of love": " 'Act of Love' Defended," Lansing *State Journal*, May 8, 1991.

184 Comparison of plastic bag to wedding veil: *Whose Side Are You On?, with Mike Wallace*, CBS Television, July 19, 1991.

184 Letter written by Virginia Harper: Ibid.

185 No attempt to seek counseling for Virginia Harper after her first suicide attempt: Ibid.

185 The Hemlock pin that Harper wore during his murder trial was but one sign of his membership in the euthanasia organization. Both Harper and his wife had been members of Hemlock, and it was in a Hemlock Society article that they first obtained information that assisted suicide was not illegal in Michigan. "Man Who Aided Suicide Is Cleared," Boston *Globe*, May 11, 1991.

185 Prison sentence for man in death of cat: Tracy Ward, "Cat Killer Gets Up to 4 Years in Jail," Oakland (Mich.) *Press*, May 11, 1991.

185 Humphry has acknowledged that Hemlock was responsible for the Washington State initiative and that plans called for other states to be targeted for legislative change: Humphry, *Final Exit*, loc. cit., p. 180.

185 "an attempt to update the state's decade-old Natural Death Act": Amanda Tipton, "Death Initiative Certified," Seattle *Post-Intelligencer*, January 30, 1991.

185 Definition of aid-in-dying as a "medical service" to end the life of a patient: Initiative 119, Section 2 (9).

186 Among the reports that the "aid" which would be delivered by lethal injection: Diane Gianelli, "Washington Voters Asked if MD's May Offer Active Euthanasia," *American Medical News* (May 18, 1990), p. 1.

186 "Try not to go into methods of aid-in-dying such as lethal injections": "Suggestions for Speakers," distributed at July 1,

1991, meeting of Spokane Friends of Initiative 119. The meeting was chaired by Rob Neils, Spokane County coordinator for Hemlock of Washington State.

186 "protect our rights as patients": "Suggested Format for Speech on Initiative 119," distributed at July 1, 1991, meeting of Spokane Friends of Initiative 119.

186 Description of Initiative 119 as a means to correct flaws in state's living will law: Ibid.

186 "to clarify language in Living Wills": *Newsday*, CNN, July 31, 1990.

186 Quill's account of his role in a patient's suicide: Timothy E. Quill, "Death and Dignity: A Case of Individualized Decision Making," *New England Journal of Medicine*, vol. 324, no. 10 (March 7, 1991), pp. 691–94.

187 "would suffer unspeakably in the process" and "no way I could say any of this would not occur": Ibid., p. 692.

187 Quill's previous involvement with program development supported by the Euthanasia Educational Council: "Medical School Teaches Care of Dying," *Euthanasia News*, vol. 2, no. 4 (November 1976), p. 1.

187 Quill's referral of Diane to Hemlock: Quill, op. cit., p. 693.

187 "was an essential ingredient in a Hemlock Society suicide": Ibid.

187 "uneasy feeling": Ibid.

188 "In our tearful goodbye . . . with dragons swimming in the sunset": Ibid.

188 "deeply moved," "fortunate" to print the "very poignant" story: "Account of Assisted Suicide in Journal Advances Debate," *Medical Ethics Advisor*, vol. 7, no. 4 (April 1991), pp. 45–46.

188 Relman's claim that because Quill's story was signed, it was real: Ibid., p. 45.

188 "I called the medical examiner . . .": Quill, op. cit., p. 694.

189 Medical examiner's office denial that Quill had called: Telephone interview, June 4, 1991.

189 Discovery of Diane's body at a community college: Laura Buterbaugh, "Body Linked to Dr. Quill Discovered," *Rochester (N.Y.) Democrat and Chronicle*, April 27, 1991.

189 Dr. Timothy Johnson's praise for Quill's actions: *Good Morning America*, ABC Television, March 8, 1991.

189 Dr. Louis Weinstein's description of Quill's actions as an "act of love": Telephone interview, May 16, 1991.

190 The full text of Weinstein's oath: Louis Weinstein, M.D., "The Oath of the Healer," letter to the editor, *Journal of the American Medical Association*, vol. 265, no. 19 (May 15, 1991), p. 2484. In the May 16, 1991, telephone interview, Weinstein explained that he had introduced his oath at a presentation he made to members of Alpha Omega Alpha, an honorary society made up of the top 5 to 10 percent of medical students. He said that the future physicians had "thought it was wonderful."

190 *Longevity* is a glossy publication whose readership is primarily made up of upper-middle-class baby boomers interested in physical fitness and self-fulfillment.

190 Results of *Longevity* readers' questionnaire: Carol Mauro, "What You Told Us: Helping Death Along," *Longevity* (June 1991), p. 86.

190 "Such a specialist would be highly respected . . .": Ibid., p. 89.

191 Kevorkian's more detailed description of the death doctor as a medical specialist: Jack Kevorkian, "A Fail-Safe Model for Justifiable Medically-Assisted Suicide," *American Journal of Forensic Psychiatry*, vol. 13, no. 1 (1992), pp. 7–41. In the article Kevorkian explained that "obitiatry," his term for the practice, and "obitiatrist"—"doctor of death"—to denote the practitioner, were derived from a combination of Greek and Latin roots (p. 11). At first, he wrote, obitiatrists would be certified on the basis of a "grandfather clause." Doctors who had been "pioneers" in patient killing would be automatically certified. He envisioned that as the practice developed, there would be postgraduate training programs (residencies) in which the "pioneers" would train others and a board would conduct examinations to certify competence in the field of obitiatry (p. 11.).

191 Kevorkian's *20/20* interview was aired on February 14, 1992. During the interview Kevorkian said that not all doctors should be obitiatrists. "You can't let every doctor do this, because some are outright criminal. You can't allow that, it will be abused," he said. He went on to explain that in addition, some doctors would not want to be obitiatrists, "so you've got to have certain specialists qualified to do this, to whom a doctor can refer a patient like he does everybody."

191 Derek Humphry's description of Washington's Initiative 119 and his statement, "We are within sight of achieving change": *Longevity*, loc. cit., p. 90.

193 Description of Trudi Dallos's morning routine: Heidi Evans, "A Question of Death," New York *Daily News*, July 21, 1991.

195 Bill's desire to set the record straight about his mother: Following the appearance of Cal McCrystal's "Ann Humphry's Final Exit," *Vanity Fair* (January 1992), Bill wrote, in a letter to the editor, that what Derek had done to Ann—calling her mentally ill, discarding her when she became ill, and then taking out an ad, for "damage control," after her death—disgusted him: *Vanity Fair* (March 1992), p. 36.

Interviewed by CBC, Bill said, "I got along with her like I will never get along with anyone else . . . she was a really fascinating person and really—just a really great lady": *The 5th Estate* (February 4, 1992).

Chapter 13

197 "statement of protest . . .": Lawrence K. Altman, "A How to Book on Suicide Surges to Top of Best-Seller List in Week," *New York Times*, August 9, 1991.

197 "poorly written although easy-to-read book": Al Neuharth, "Killer Book Misfires at Life's Happy Game," *USA Today*, August 16, 1991.

198 "media have made this book happen": Dennis L. Breo, "MD-Aided Suicide Voted Down; Both Sides Say Debate to Continue," *JAMA*, vol. 266, no. 20 (November 27, 1991), p. 2899.

198 Humphry's later attempt to claim there had been "no hype" or advertising for *Final Exit*: Derek Humphry, *Dying with Dignity* (New York: Birch Lane Press, 1992), p. 28.

198 Description of Carol Publishing: Roger Cohen, "The Big Sell of 'Final Exit,' " San Francisco *Chronicle*, August 27, 1991. Only two fiction books had been scheduled for Carol's fall 1991 list. One was titled *The Second Greatest Story Ever Told*, a saga about Christ's little sister reincarnated as an American teen.

198 "is interesting or controversial enough to provoke a feature . . .": Cohen, op. cit.

198 Success of Hemlock books as a "personal crusade" for Schragis: Meg Cox, "Suicide Manual for Terminally Ill Stirs Debate," *Wall Street Journal*, July 12, 1991.

198 Description of Schragis's handling of promotion for *Final Exit*: Cohen, op. cit.

199 Prepublication media blitz: Ibid.

199 Review copies of *Final Exit* ignored: Breo, op. cit., p. 2899.

199 Derek's claim that *Final Exit* sold fifteen thousand copies in three months following its publication: Humphry, *Dying with Dignity*, loc. cit., p. 28.

199 Statement that retail sales of *Final Exit* had been fewer than two thousand copies in the first three months of its availability: Press release, Carol Publishing Group, August 19, 1991.

199 Newspaper account that *Final Exit* had sold only one thousand copies in the three months following publication: Cohen, op. cit.

199 "as a match to tinder": Meg Cox as quoted by Roger Cohen, p. 207.

200 "It tells you how, where and when to kill . . .": Chris Mann and Kieran Devaney, "Anger over Wife-Killer's Guide to Perfect Suicide," London *Sunday Express*, July 28, 1991.

200 The four-sentence paragraph that has been described as a warning intended to prevent depressed persons from using the book is titled "Advice": Humphry, *Final Exit*, loc. cit., p. 123.

201 "cannot live on carbon dioxide and nitrogen alone": Ibid., p. 97.

201 Description of practice in use of plastic bag for suffocation: Ibid., pp. 98–99.

201 Section on double suicide refers to death in this manner as an indication of strong love: Ibid., pp. 100–02.

201 Etiquette of suicide: Ibid., pp. 88–89.

201 "Hollywood Style" death: Ibid., pp. 47–50.

202 Dismissal of horrors and implications of German euthanasia: Ibid., p. 43. Incredibly the sole paragraph refering to the killing concludes by calling these heinous actions a "lapse" by medical professionals.

Derek's indication that the German euthanasia practitioners had been brought to justice differs markedly from other accounts. According to Hugh Gregory Gallagher's meticulously researched book *By Trust Betrayed* (New York: Henry Holt, 1990), "Many physicians who had taken part in the euthanasia program went back to their normal professional duties after the war. Post-war efforts to track down and prosecute them met with little success [p. 259]. Even when brought to trial, some were acquitted because they ended the lives of disabled people who were considered to be only the 'husks' of human beings [p. 260]. Yet others rose to new levels of professional respectability. Included among them was Werner Catel who led a commission that ordered the deaths of thousands of infants. Catel became a medical professor and authored textbooks used in the training of health professionals in the late 1970s [p. 261]."

The degree to which culpable physicians were exempted from justice is illustrated by the case of Dr. Georg Renno, one of the chief doctors at the Hartheim Euthanasia Institute, where an estimated thirty thousand deaths took place. Renno was excused from standing trial for health reasons, yet he lived, undisturbed, in the Black Forest for another thirty-five years. See Robert Jay Lifton, *The Nazi Doctors: Medical Killing and the Psychology of Genocide* (New York: Basic Books, 1986), p. 142, and Gerald Posner and John Ware, *Mengele* (New York: Dell, 1986), p. 93.

202 Pros and cons of using cyanide for death: Ibid., pp. 38–46.

202 Inclusion of bizarre types of death to prevent readers from feeling "cheated": Ibid., pp. 51–62.

202 Shooting as a "messy" way to end life: Ibid., p. 54.

202 Death by freezing: Ibid., pp. 56–57.

202 "terminal old age": Ibid., p. 106.

202 Increasing tolerance for induced death after passage of aid-in-dying laws: Ibid., p. 62.

202 Expansion of eligibility for euthanasia to include persons who are not competent: Ibid., p. 107.

202 "long overdue book" for desperate people: Shanna Nix and David Tuller, "Best-seller 'Final Exit' Is Helping People Who Are Considering Suicide," San Francisco *Chronicle*, August 30, 1991.

203 Quindlen's plan to keep book for possible future use: Anna Quindlen, "Death by Suicide Tops the Best-seller List," Seattle *Post-Intelligencer*, August 15, 1991.

203 "Above all, the author is calm, cool . . .": Leon R. Kass, "Suicide Made Easy: The Evil of 'Rational' Humaneness," *Commentary* (December 1991), p. 20.

204 British Columbia deaths: Ann Rees, "Author of 'Final Exit' Blamed for Suicides," Vancouver, B.C., *Province*, November 25, 1991. The article also reported that the province's chief coroner had stated, "It's very clear *Final Exit* was used in all three cases."

204 Derek's statement that it bothers him "not one whit" that his book may have been used in the Buffalo Grove death: Dave McKinney, "Buffalo Grove Suicide Linked to Bestseller, 'Final Exit,' " Buffalo Grove (Ill.) *Daily Herald*, October 3, 1991.

204 Death of woman with chronic fatigue syndrome: Andy Jokelson, "Fatigue Syndrome Disease Sapped Young Life," Contra Costa *Times*, October 8, 1991.

205 Derek's claim that hundreds of people have used his information to kill themselves: Deborah Pinkney, "Humphry Asks Physicians' Help in Suicide Rights Battle," *American Medical News* (April 20, 1992), p. 11. In an interview Derek was asked if there is any protection against a depressed person's using *Final Exit*. He replied that there isn't and said, "I make no apology if someone wishes to kill himself because he's in great anguish living in this world." He said he preferred that such a person use a "calm technique" from his book rather than have someone find him with "his brains scattered all over the kitchen wall": D. C. Denison, "The Interview: Derek Humphry," Boston *Globe Magazine*, July 19, 1992, p. 7.

205 Earnings from *Final Exit* received by the Hemlock Society: Breo, op. cit., p. 2899.

205 "I can do this . . .": Humphry, *Let Me Die Before I Wake* (1986 ed.), loc. cit., p. 52.

205 Strength gained by Mary from killing her mother: Ibid., p. 55.

206 No regrets and "euphoric" feelings: Ibid., pp. 90–91.

Chapter 15

225 "[The officer] discovered 6 empty pill containers . . .": Supplemental Report #1, Deschutes County Sheriff's Department, Case: 91-3151, p. 1.

225 "½ gallon of Chivas Regal. . . . Humphrey's remains were then given to Tabor's Desert Hills Mortuary": Supplemental Report #2, Deschutes County Sheriff's Department, Case: 91-3151, pp. 1 and 2.

225 Thomas Hood, "The Bridge of Sighs," in *F. T. Palgrave's The Golden Treasury of the Best Songs and Lyrical Poems*, ed. Oscar Williams (New York: Mentor Book, 1964), pp. 191–92.

227 "I don't wish to reconcile . . ." McCrystal, "Love, Death & Loathing, on the Road to Windfall Farm," loc. cit., p. 13.

227 "What it comes down to is, he didn't love her": Erica E. Goode, "Defending the Right to Die: Portrait of Derek Humphry," *U.S. News & World Report* (September 30, 1991), p. 40.

227 "I would have liked to have spoken with her": "A Founder of Society for Euthanasia Found Dead," Everett (Wash.) *Herald*, October 8, 1991.

227 "It's not within the philosophy of the Hemlock . . .": "Advocate for Suicide Group Found Dead," *New York Times*, October 10, 1991.

227 "I don't feel accountable . . .": John Hiscock, "Euthanasia Group Founder's Suicide," London *Daily Telegraph*, October 10, 1991. Derek referred to Ann's sisters, although she had only one sister.

227 "It's extremely painful to have lost two wives . . .": Mick Brown, "I Knew Something Would Happen," London *Daily Telegraph*, October 10, 1991.

227 "A year after our marriage I realized . . .": Ibid.

228 "Some of us, when we are terminally ill . . .": Joe Mosley, "Suicide: Society Grapples with Taboo," Eugene (Ore.) *Register-Guard*, October 13, 1991.

231 The large ad was printed in *The New York Times* for the first time on October 14, 1991. It was repeated four days later, correcting typographical errors that had appeared in the original.

231 "Damage control": Gabriel, op. cit., p. 86.

232 McCrystal, "Ann Humphry's Final Exit," loc. cit., p. 80.

Chapter 17

237 "The world is watching . . .": Tony Burton, "A Question of Life and Death," London *Daily Mail*, October 23, 1991.

237 Fund-raising advantage of euthanasia proponents in Washington State campaign: Timothy Egan, "Washington Voters Face Initiative on Mercy Killing," San Francisco *Chronicle*, October 19, 1991.

237 Total expenditures for Initiative 119: Breo, op. cit., p. 2899.

238 A poll of likely voters indicated that Initiative 119 would easily pass. Rob Carson, "Right-to-Die Gets 2–1 Support in Poll," Tacoma *Morning News Tribune*, October 9, 1991.

238 National poll reported in Boston *Globe* two days before Washington State vote: Richard Knox, "Poll: Americans Favor Mercy Killing," Boston *Sunday Globe*, November 3, 1991.

238 Margin of defeat for Initiative 119: Jane Gross, "Voters Turn Down Legal Euthanasia," *New York Times*, November 7, 1991.

238 Attempt to paint euthanasia opponents as religious fanatics: Derek Humphry, "Let Doctors Help Those Who Want to Die," *USA Today*, April 6, 1989.

239 Vast majority of voters opposed Initiative 119 for reasons not associated with religious beliefs: Tracking polls on Initiative

119, conducted by Hebert Research, October 31, 1991, and within one week following the November 5, 1991, vote. Five days before the vote only 9.7 percent of those opposing the measure cited religious reasons for their opposition. Following the measure's defeat, individuals who had previously indicated support for Initiative 119 were again surveyed. Of these previous supporters, 15 percent subsequently opposed the initiative. Religious reasons accounted for only 6.1 percent of this eventual opposition.

239 Acknowledgment that Washington's euthanasia measure had lacked safeguards: Humphry, *Dying with Dignity*, loc. cit., p. 41. Others who favor legalization of euthanasia, including Dr. Timothy Quill, also pointed to the lack of safeguards in both the 1991 Washington and the 1992 California aid-in-dying initiatives. Quill indicated that guidelines should be determined by doctors, "not by legislators or the Hemlock Society": Lynne Friedmann, "Probing the Controversy over Physician-Assisted Suicide," *American College of Physicians Observer* (June 1992), p. 12.

240 Californians Against Human Suffering same organization as Americans Against Human Suffering: In a July 7, 1992, fund appeal letter Robert Risley wrote that the organization had been formed six years earlier. The appeal's reply device identified CAHS as "an operating unit" of AAHS. Although rare, there were reports that CAHS was the same organization that had attempted an aid-in-dying initiative in 1988. Among such reports was Lori Olszewski, "State Prop. 161 Would Legalize Physician-Assisted Suicide," San Francisco *Chronicle*, July 10, 1992.

240 "a medical procedure that will terminate the life . . .": California Death With Dignity Act Petition, official title, p. 1, and definition, Section 2525.2(k), p. 2.

240 "This measure would result in some unknown savings . . .": Communication from the Office of the Attorney General of California, October 7, 1991, File No.: SA 91 RF 0015.

240 Derek's appeal for funds to help place the euthanasia measure on California's 1992 ballot: "Dear Supporter of Death with Dignity" Letter, signed by Derek Humphry, undated. In the appeal Derek referred to his role in bringing about Jean's death and wrote that by doing so, he had broken the law. (The letter stated, "And Washington state is just days away from the first vote anywhere to legalize physician aid-in-dying," thus placing its writing at the end of October 1991.)

241 Advisory board and endorsing organizations: "Campaign News," Californians Against Human Suffering, November 20, 1991, p. 1, and January 1, 1992, p. 2.

241 Assistance of the National Organization for Women's California chapter: "Campaign News," CAHS, January 1, 1992, p. 2.

241 Resolution endorsing aid-in-dying presented to American Bar Association: Submitted to the ABA House of Delegates for consideration in January 1992 by Barry E. Shanley and Michael H. White on behalf of the Beverly Hills Bar Association. Shanley and White are members of the board of directors of Californians Against Human Suffering, and White is also president of the group.

241 "The proposed right to choose aid-in-dying freely and without undue influence is illusory . . .": Memorandum from ABA Commission on Legal Problems of the Elderly to Members of the House of Delegates and Other Interested ABA Entities, January 17, 1992, p. 5.

241 "The lack of access to or the financial burdens of health care . . .": Ibid., p. 2.

241–42 "intentional killing" and "subtle pressures": "Lawyers Say No to Assisted Suicides," Tony Mauro, *USA Today*, February 4, 1992.

242 Defeat of the aid-in-dying resolution was reported by the Associated Press, "ABA Against Doctor Assisted Suicide,"

Steubenville (Ohio) *Herald-Star*, February 4, 1992, and in "Lawyers Say No to Assisted Suicides," loc. cit.

242 Nancy Cruzan's ability to eat by mouth at the time of the insertion of her feeding tube: *Cruzan v. Harmon & Lampkins*, Case No. CV384-9P, in the Circuit Court of Jasper County, Missouri, Probate Division at Carthage, March 9, 1988, to March 11, 1988, Transcript, pp. 283, 423. Although Cruzan was often referred to in news reports as comatose, court records indicate that this was not the case. According to these records, she could hear (T-643) and see (T-754), smiled at amusing stories (T-599), cried at times when visitors left (T-644), sometimes seemed to try to form words (T-653), and experienced pain from menstrual cramps (T-618). She was not on any type of life support equipment such as a ventilator, and she required no skilled nursing (T-614). She could have been cared for in a home setting (T-615), and she required no care except food, fluids, personal hygiene, and repositioning to prevent bedsores (T-316).

242 U.S. Supreme Court ruling in case of Nancy Beth Cruzan: *Cruzan v. Director, Missouri Department of Health*, 110 S.Ct. 2841 (1990).

243 Continuing coverage of the entire case by PBS *Frontline*: While many have claimed that information about Nancy Beth Cruzan became public only after outsiders intruded, her case was first made public by her family. PBS *Frontline* was present to record the case for national television viewing from the time that the Cruzans first met with the families of other patients at the Missouri Rehabilitation Center to announce that they had decided to remove Nancy's food and water. The Cruzans' initial meeting with their attorney was also televised, as were seemingly private moments over the course of the next three and one-half years. This chronicle was first shown on national television on PBS *Frontline*'s "Let My Daughter Die" (March 1, 1988).

243 "about how to set aside the role of healer . . .": Guy I. Benrubi, "Euthanasia—the Need for Procedural Safeguards," *New England Journal of Medicine*, vol. 326, no. 3 (January 16, 1992), p. 198.

243 Benrubi's description of role of specialists in euthanasia: Ibid.

244 Pridonoff as new Hemlock director: Gordon Smith, "Hemlock Society Has Reverent New Leader," San Diego *Union-Tribune*, August 28, 1992. Previously Pridonoff had been the administrator of the Counseling Center in San Diego and had served as editor of the *Forum*, the national newsletter of the Association for Death Education and Counseling: *Hemlock Quarterly* (October 1992), p. 1.

244 Announcement of Derek Humphry's retirement: Press release from the National Hemlock Society, February 13, 1992.

244 Derek Humphry's work for passage of Proposition 161: During the California campaign, Derek Humphry again tried to frame the issue as one which had only religious implications, saying, "What this election boils down to is a vote on how you see God. . . . The opposition to the law is religious. We are trying to overturn 2000 years of Christian tradition." Lori Olszewski, "Right-to-Die Advocate in S.F.," San Francisco *Chronicle*, August 28, 1992. Churches did vehemently oppose the measure; however, Proposition 161 had many other powerful opponents as well, including the American Cancer Society's California Division, American Lung Association of California, California Association of Hospitals and Health Systems, California Commission on Aging, California Medical Association, California Nurses Association, the California Psychiatric Association, and the California State Hospice Association. In addition, major newspapers throughout the state, including the Los Angeles *Times*, the San Francisco *Chronicle*, and the San Diego

Union Tribune, as well as *USA Today*, took editorial positions opposing the measure.

244 Plans to continue efforts to legalize euthanasia were described in several articles, including Vlae Kershner, "California Voters Reject 9 of 13 Ballot Measures," San Francisco *Chronicle*, November 5, 1992.

244 "Hemlock movement will try an initiative again. . . .": Derek Humphry, "Death with Dignity Effort May Be Tried Here Again," San Francisco *Chronicle*, November 13, 1992.

245 "emotional and social effects are largely unknown": Timothy E. Quill, Christine K. Cassel, Diane E. Meier, "Care of the Hopelessly Ill: Proposed Clinical Criteria for Physician-Assisted Suicide," *New England Journal of Medicine*, vol. 327, no. 19 (November 5, 1992), p. 1383. For those unable to swallow or move sufficiently for self-infliction of death, the authors suggest what they call a solution that is "less than ideal": death by starvation and dehydration. Ibid., p. 1381.

245 Kevorkian case before the Michigan Court of Appeals: *Michigan* v. *Kevorkian*, Court of Appeals No. 154740, Circuit Court Case No. 92-115190-FC. Kevorkian announced in an October speech at the National Press Club in Washington, D.C., that he had additional patients waiting for his services. "Suicide Doctor Says 5 More Want to Die," San Francisco *Chronicle*, October 28, 1992. Although his license to practice medicine in Michigan was suspended following the deaths of Marjorie Wantz and Sherry Miller, he holds a valid California medical license.

Afterword

247 The greeting card for a person faced with a life-threatening illness was from "Grief Songs" Greeting Cards. It was described on the program and purchased at "Reforming the Law: The 5th National Conference on Voluntary Euthanasia," sponsored by the National Hemlock Society and the Metro Denver Hemlock Society, November 15 and 16, 1991, Denver, Colorado.

248 High-profile cases about disabled people: The first four people to receive Jack Kevorkian's "services" were disabled women: Janet Adkins had early Alzheimer's disease, Marjorie Wantz had no physical disease detectable at autopsy. Both Sherry Miller and Susan Williams had multiple sclerosis. (A fifth woman, fifty-two-year-old Lois Hawes, who died on September 29, 1992, after using a mask attached to a canister of carbon monoxide provided by Kevorkian, was said to have had lung cancer. "Kevorkian Aids in 5th Suicide," San Francisco *Examiner*, September 27, 1992.)

248 Aid-in-dying laws would affect severely disabled people: Carol Gill, who is president of the Chicago Institute of Disability Research, wrote, "If 161 passes, I could receive a lethal treatment more readily than a prisoner on Death Row. I would have fewer legal protections for my life than a prison inmate." Carol Gill, "Deciding Whose Life Has Value," Los Angeles *Times*, October 21, 1992.

249 "credibility only when asking to die!": Carol Gill, "Suicide Intervention for People with Disabilities: A Lesson in Inequality," *Issues in Law and Medicine*, vol. 8, no. 1 (Summer 1992), p. 52.

249 The manner in which suicide requests from disabled persons are treated differently than such requests from members of other minority groups has been described by historian Paul Longmore:

> If a non-handicapped person expressed a desire to commit suicide, that person immediately would get crisis intervention therapy. Let a disabled person express such despair, and he or she is assumed to be "rational."
>
> If a poor black woman asked for help to end her life

because she found poverty and prejudice unendurable, society would at least make some gesture of offering her a job and decent housing.

Paul Longmore, "The Shameful Treatment of Larry McAfee," Atlanta *Journal-Constitution*, September 10, 1989.

INDEX

■ ■ ■

Love Isn't Quite Enough
The Psychology of Male–Female Relationships

Maryon Tysoe

Finding out that love isn't quite enough is something most men and women do the hard way.

The traditional Western myth of romantic love has much to answer for. Both sexes can be devastated when they discover that, far from having the power of a psychological superglue, love is only one of many elements needed to sustain a relationship. Even those who are aware of – or reluctantly suspect – this are left floundering as to what other mysterious processes might be involved.

In *Love Isn't Quite Enough*, Dr Maryon Tysoe, widely admired social psychologist and journalist, has written an indispensable book for those seeking a better understanding of how relationships really work, why they fail and what we need to know to make them succeed. With characteristic wit and insight, she draws on a great deal of untapped psychological research to explore the route towards more realistic, and hence potentially more successful, relationships between the sexes.

'A wise, witty and highly readable book'   Dr Anthony Clare

The Successful Self
Freeing our Hidden Inner Strengths

Dorothy Rowe

Is it possible to be truly successful as a person? Or must we, as most of us do, continue to live our lives feeling in some way trapped and oppressed, frustrated, irritable, haunted by worries and regrets, creating misery for ourselves and others?

In *The Successful Self* leading psychologist Dorothy Rowe, author of *Beyond Fear*, shows us how to live more comfortably and creatively within ourselves by achieving a fuller understanding of how we experience our existence and how we perceive the threat of its annihilation.

She demonstrates how to develop the social and personal skills we lack, retaining the uniqueness of our individuality while becoming an integral part of the life around us and learning how to value and accept ourselves.

With characteristic originality, clarity and unfailing wisdom, Dorothy Rowe enables us to revolutionise our own lives and the lives of others in the process of becoming a Successful Self.

'Dorothy Rowe stands out amongst psychologists for her clear insight into human experience: her writing is refreshingly free from the dubious theoretical constructs and jargon ideas which plague this subject.'   Oliver Gillie, *Independent*

'A very brightly written book that intriguingly makes you question something most of us discuss: do we really like ourselves? Then it goes on to help us do so.'   Mavis Nicholson

The Origins of Unhappiness
A New Understanding of Personal Distress

David Smail

The normal interpretation of emotional distress – more usually labelled as 'neurosis' or 'mental illness' – is that it originates from within the individual.

Unlike others who have looked at the outside world as a cause of fear, pain and unhappiness, David Smail offers a radical account of what this view means for a therapeutic practice that still, for the most part, 'treats' people. Through his examination of how visible and invisible social power – institutions, politics, the Establishment – wields an influence over our lives often beyond our immediate control, he leads us to an understanding of distress which has never been clearer.

Taking as case studies the experience of people who suffered from the 1980s 'business culture', when failure to meet impossible demands was considered the fault of the individual, Smail illustrates the sometimes devastating effects of the interplay between personal and political power. Finally, he analyses the failings of psychiatry and psychotherapy in Britain, and offers a vision of psychology which recognizes that it is the society we live in rather than the individual that needs to be treated.

ISBN 0 00 637797 1

What Do Women Want?

Luise Eichenbaum and Susie Orbach

Many women today feel that they pour love, commitment and understanding into their relationships, but that it is not returned in kind. He seems secure and independent, she feels insecure and clingy.

The truth is that men and women are *both* dependent. But his needs are catered to so well – first by his mother, then by his girlfriend or wife – that he doesn't know he has them, while her needs – for closeness and tenderness – are constantly rebuffed as he retreats from intimacy.

Susie Orbach and Luise Eichenbaum set out to explore this crisis in the relationships of men and women. They explain how men have learned to 'manage' their dependency needs very differently from women, and *why* women feel dependent and hungry for love. Finally they show why dependency on both sides is the essential core of any successful relationship.

ISBN 0 00 638252 5

☐	UNLAWFUL CARNAL KNOWLEDGE Wendy Holden	0-00-638258-4	£5.99
☐	DEADLIER THAN THE MALE Alix Kirsta	0-00-637849-8	£5.99
☐	LIFE'S DOMINION Ronald Dworkin	0-00-686309-4	£7.99
☐	SEXING THE MILLENNIUM Linda Grant	0-00-637768-8	£7.99

All these books are available from your local bookseller or can be ordered direct from the publishers.

To order direct just tick the titles you want and fill in the form below:

Name:

Address:

Postcode:

Send to: HarperCollins Mail Order, Dept 8, HarperCollins *Publishers*, Westerhill Road, Bishopbriggs, Glasgow G64 2QT.

Please enclose a cheque or postal order or your authority to debit your Visa/Access account –

Credit card no:

Expiry date:

Signature:

– to the value of the cover price plus:

UK & BFPO: Add £1.00 for the first and 25p for each additional book ordered.

Overseas orders including Eire, please add £2.95 service charge.

Books will be sent by surface mail but quotes for airmail despatches will be given on request.

24 HOUR TELEPHONE ORDERING SERVICE FOR ACCESS/VISA CARDHOLDERS –

TEL: GLASGOW 041-772 2281 or LONDON 081-307 4052